Lack and Transcendence

Lack and Transcendence

The Problem of Death and Life in Psychotherapy, Existentialism, and Buddhism

David Loy

Humanity Books

an imprint of Prometheus Books
59 John Glenn Drive, Amherst, New York 14228-2197

Published by Humanity Books, an imprint of Prometheus Books

Inquiries should be addressed to
Humanity Books
59 John Glenn Drive
Amherst, New York 14228–2197
VOICE: 716–691–0133, ext. 207
FAX: 716–564–2711
WWW.PROMETHEUSBOOKS.COM

08 07 06   10 9

Library of Congress Cataloging-in-Publication Data

Loy, David
    Lack and transcendence : the problem of death and life in psychotherapy,
existentialism, and Buddhism / David Loy.
        p. cm.
    Originally published in paperback: Atlantic Highlands, N.J.: Humanities
Press, 1996.
    Includes bibliographical references and index.
    ISBN 1–57392–720–1 (paper : alk. paper) — ISBN 1–57392–492–X (cloth)
    1. Existential psychotherapy. 2. Buddhism—Doctrines. 3. Existentialism.
4. Death—Pyschological aspects. 5. Death—Religious aspects—Buddhism. I. Title.

RC489.E93 L69 2000
616.89'14—dc21   00-059760

Printed in the United States of America on acid-free paper

to Linda Goodhew
  who wants it to have a happy ending
and Brigitte D'Ortschy
  who showed us it can

Acknowledgments

Material from earlier drafts of this book has been incorporated into the following papers. Permission from the following journals and publishers to reprint this material is gratefully acknowledged.

"The Nonduality of Life and Death: A Buddhist View of Repression," in *Philosophy East and West* 40, no. 2 (April 1990).

"What's Wrong with Heidegger's *Being and Time*: A Buddhist Critique," in *Time and Society* 1, no. 2 (May 1992).

"The Deconstruction of Buddhism," in *Derrida and Negative Theology*, ed. Harold Coward and Toby Foshay (Albany, N.Y.: State University of New York Press, 1992). "Avoiding the Void: The Lack of Self in Psychotherapy and Buddhism," in *Journal of Transpersonal Psychology* 24, no. 2 (1992).

"Indra's Postmodern Net," in *Philosophy East and West*, 43, no. 3 (July 1993).

"Trying to Become Real: A Buddhist Critique of Some Secular Heresies," in *International Philosophical Quarterly* 32, no. 4 (December 1992)

"Transcendence East and West," in *Man and World* 26, no. 4 (1993).

Introduction

This book grew out of the cross-fertilization of two basic ideas. One is the Freudian concept of repression, including the return of the repressed in symbolic form as a symptom. The other is the Buddhist doctrine of *anātman*, "no-self." If our sense of self as something autonomous and self-grounded is a fiction, if the ego is in fact mentally constructed and socially internalized, then perhaps our primal repression is not sexual wishes (as Freud thought) nor fear of death (as many existential psychologists think) but the quite valid suspicion that *"I" am not real.* This shift in emphasis from libido-instinct to the way we understand our situation in the world opens up possibilities that classical psychoanalysis did not allow—many of which existentialism and Buddhism have explored, as we shall see.

When those possibilities are taken seriously, a web of relationships begins to spin among fields of inquiry usually understood to be distinct.

It is a sad comment on our balkanized intellectual world that this book must begin with an *apologia* for hitching together three supposedly different horses. The defense is straightforward: Whatever the differences in their methods and goals, psychotherapy, existentialism, and Buddhism are concerned with many of the same fundamental issues, and therefore we can benefit from comparing what they think they have learned. In addition to an historical affinity between psychoanalysis and existentialism (see below) and more recent links between Buddhism and Western psychology (such as transpersonal psychology), there have been many studies of Buddhism and existentialism: Nietzsche and Buddhism, Heidegger and Buddhism, and so on. Then, why not bring all three traditions together, in a study receptive to the insights of each? Important figures in each tradition have arrived at many of the same conclusions about the problems of life and death and life-in-death: for example, that what passes for normalcy today is a low grade of psychopathology, usually unnoticed because so common; that the denial of death poisons life; that the supposedly autonomous ego-self is conditioned in ways it is normally unaware of; and that it is possible to become more free by becoming more aware of our mental processes—a transformation that all three traditions encourage. Noticing these and other similarities made me wonder about the relationships among them. How do such agreements constellate? In spite of the differences one would expect, might an interdisciplinary study nevertheless adumbrate some shared understanding about the human condition—perhaps even some basic reasons for our notorious inability to be happy?

Much has happened to psychoanalysis in a century, and Freud today would have difficulty recognizing many of his progeny. Among those descendants, Jungian analysis and more recently transpersonal psychology have attracted most of the attention of students of religion. This book focuses on existential psychoanalysis, which originated from an early cross-fertilization between Freudianism and phenomenology, especially Heidegger's *Being and Time*. The most innovative figure was the Swiss psychiatrist Ludwig Binswanger, who is also distinguished by the fact that he was able to disagree with Freud without that leading to a break between them. For reasons that become apparent in chapter 2, I think this original movement made a mistake in allying itself with the early Heidegger, and what follows is more influenced by the second- and third-generation of existential psychologists in the United States: among the analysts, Rollo May and Irvin Yalom; of the scholars, Norman O. Brown and most of all Ernest Becker, whose influential books *The Denial of Death* and *Escape from Evil* (the second unfinished at his own death) are used in chapter 1 to summarize the existential approach to psychoanalysis.

These figures are more pragmatic than the first generation. For them, the "existential" in existential psychology means not so much existentialism as being rooted in the fundamental issues of life and death, freedom and responsibility, groundlessness and meaninglessness. Despite this—or is it because of this?—their findings display a remarkable agreement with the best of the existentialist tradition. Becker refers often to Pascal and Kierkegaard, and he could have found as much in Nietzsche and Sartre to buttress his conclusions. This confluence is important because it is one of the fertile places where science and philosophy meet today. Psychoanalysis/psychotherapy is many things: a religion (with founder, dogma, and schisms), a philosophy (Freud and many since him couldn't resist metaphysical extrapolations), but also perhaps the rudimentary, groping beginnings of something that is capable of learning from its mistakes. One important example of such self-correction: In place of the doctrinal disputes which preoccupied early psychoanalysis, contemporary therapists are more aware of the relativity of their theoretical constructs. Yet this hardly a recent discovery, as we shall see.

The most important existentialist thinkers also stress that philosophizing should lead to a personal transformation in the way we live, an emphasis which makes their philosophies therapeutic as well as conceptual. Nietzsche discovered our *ressentiment* and how we project a higher "spiritual" world to compensate for our inability to be comfortable in this one. The modern disappearance of that other world has left us nihilistic and with the difficult task of revaluing this world. Heidegger's *Being and Time* argues that awareness of death can open up the possibility of authentic life, and emphasizes the intimate connection between such authenticity and the way we experience time. Sartre is more pessimistic: Human consciousness is always a lack because our nothingness cannot help craving the supposed self-grounded being of objective things. Kierkegaard's solution to the anxiety that bedevils our lives is to become thoroughly anxious: to let anxiety dredge up and devour all our "finite ends," those psychological securities we have hedged around us and then "forgotten" in order to hide in a safe but constricted world.

In this book the above issues will be contemplated and integrated into a framework which is predominantly Buddhist, because sympathetic to what Buddhism says about the relationship between *duḥkha* (our human disease) and the delusive sense-of-self. Like Nietzsche, Buddhism denies both God and any "higher world," for the difference between *saṃsāra* and *nirvāṇa* is found in the ways we experience this world. Like *Being and Time*, Buddhism notices a relationship between authenticity and another way of experiencing time, yet its understanding of that relation implies a critique of the temporality Heidegger recommends. Buddhism agrees with Sartre that our ego-consciousness is a lack, but its deconstruction of the duality between consciousness and object allows for a solution that Sartre does not envision. Like Kierkegaard's attitude toward anxiety, the Buddhist solution to the problem of *duḥkha* is not to evade it but to become it and see what that does to us.

Śākyamuni Buddha declared that he taught only the fact of our *duḥkha* and how to end it. The path that ends *duḥkha* requires developing our awareness, since, as in psychotherapy, transformation occurs through insight. And the most important insight is realizing how the self does not exist: For Buddhism, the root cause of our suffering is the delusion of self. In response to existential-psychological emphasis on death-repression, Buddhism views the problem of life-fearing-death as merely one version of our more general problem with bipolar thinking. We distinguish one pole (e.g., success) from its opposite (failure) in order to attain the first and reject the other, but that bifurcation does not work because the two terms are interdependent. Since the meaning of each depends on negating the other, we can have both or neither, the two sides of a single coin. So, our hope for success is shadowed by an equal fear of failure, and in the same manner *our repression of death represses life*. For those who deny death, the interdependence of life and death implies a death-in-life.

That is the issue in the first chapter, "The Nonduality of Life and Death." Insofar as we repress our fear of death, the repressed returns as our compulsion to secure and if possible immortalize ourselves symbolically. Our yearning for fame is a good example, for "how can he be dead, who lives immortal in the hearts of men?" Unfortunately, no amount of fame can satisfy me if it's not really fame I want. The Buddhist approach to this issue is presented mainly by explicating what the twelfth-century Japanese Zen master Dōgen wrote about the dualism of life-and-death. However, from the Buddhist perspective, our primary repression is not death-terror but another fear even more fundamental: the suspicion that *"I" am not real*. Rather than being autonomous in some

Cartesian fashion, our sense of self is mentally and socially conditioned, therefore ungrounded and (as the mentally ill remind us) fragile.

In many ways the difference between this approach and death-repression is slight, and much of Becker's argument remains valid with some adjustments. The main distinction is that death-repression allows us to project our problem into the future, as we dread losing what we think we have now, whereas the repression of our groundlessness is a way to avoid facing what we are (or are not) right now. Freud and many others have noticed the peculiarity of fearing one's own death: There's nothing to fear if I will not be here to notice that I'm missing. Epicurus concluded that "the most horrible of ends, death, is nothing to us," and the early Freud supposed that death-fear must disguise other repressions, notably castration. Yet that fear is all too understandable if it is the closest we usually come to glimpsing our own groundlessness. The difference becomes crucial because of the different possibilities they allow.

The Buddhist emphasis on the groundlessness of the ego-self implies that our most troublesome dualism is not life-versus-death but *being versus nothingness* (or *no-thing-ness*): the anxious self intuiting and dreading its own lack of being (or thing-ness). As a result, our sense-of-self is shadowed by a sense of *lack* that it perpetually yet vainly tries to resolve. The interdependence of bipolar dualisms still holds: To the extent I come to feel autonomous, my consciousness is also infected with a gnawing sense of unreality, usually experienced as the vague feeling that "there is something wrong with me." Since we do not know how to cope with such an intimate sense of *lack*, it is repressed, only to return in projected form as the compulsive ways we attempt to make ourselves real in the world—which implies, among other things, a time orientation focused on the future.

In *Being and Time*, Heidegger claims that consciousness of my finitude cuts through the chance possibilities which normally distract me by making me consider what I really want to do during my short time on this earth. That unifies the scattered "nows" of the inauthentic present into the care-full and thus future-oriented concern of the authentic present. Chapter 2 "The Moving Image of Eternity" argues that this approach is insightful but upside-down. *Being and Time* presents essentially the same relations among death, self, guilt, and time as chapter 1 does, yet draws the opposite conclusions because it absolutizes temporality. From a psychotherapeutic standpoint, Heidegger misses the return of the repressed in symbolic form, which makes future-oriented time into a schema for the expiation of guilt, as Norman O. Brown put it. In more Buddhist terms, the sense of time as something objective that we are *in* derives from our sense of *lack* and our projects to fill up that *lack*. Both of Heidegger's alternatives, inauthentic and authentic, are preoccupied with the future because they are our two main ways of reacting to the inevitable possibility of death. In order to glimpse how time might be experienced without the shadow of death, the last part of chapter 2 offers a Buddhist deconstruction of time.

Chapter 3 "The Pain of Being Human" evaluates in more detail the claim that a dissatisfaction with life is intrinsic to the ego-self as it usually functions. . The first part surveys the psychoanalytic understanding of ontological guilt and basic anxiety, both now recognized as ineliminable even from a "well-adjusted" ego. The two most important Western philosophies of *lack* are quite pessimistic, and their challenge to wishful thinking is addressed in the second part. Yet Schopenhauer's monism of unsatisfiable will may be criticized for projecting our sense of *lack* onto the cosmos, and Sartre's ontological dualism between the for-itself and the in-itself is also questionable. The last part of this chapter (and the crux of this book) discusses how the Buddhist deconstruction of the ego-self can end its *duḥkha*. The Mahāyāna critique of self-existence is explained by considering Nāgārjuna's arguments about interdependence and the Hua-yen analogy of Indra's Net.

The Buddhist solution to bipolar dualisms usually involves accepting the term that has been denied. If our worst fear is death, the answer is to die now. To study Buddhism is to study yourself, says Dōgen, and to study yourself is to forget yourself. The ego-self's attempt to make itself real is a self-reflexive effort to grasp itself, an impossibility that leads to self-paralysis; Buddhist meditation, in which I become absorbed into my practice, is thus an exercise in de-reflection. To yield to my groundlessness is to realize that I have always been grounded: not as a sense-of-self, but insofar as I have never been separate from the world, never been other than the world.

Chapter 4, "The Meaning of It All," considers what the previous chapters imply about our understanding of morality, the search for truth, and the meaning of our lives. These implications are developed by engaging in a dialogue with Nietzsche, perhaps the first Western thinker to realize that they are not discovered but constructed: internalized games we learn from each other and play with ourselves. Nietzsche sees how moral codes gain their psychological compulsion because they provide a symbolic way for us to gain some grip on our fate. His solution is to reverse valency and replace slave morality with master morality, yet he does not see how much the heroic ego of his Overman is a fantasy project for overcoming our *lack*. In contrast, Buddhism undercuts the ethical problem by emphasizing an interdependence so great that I *am* you. Nietzsche sees that our search for truth also tends to be a sublimated attempt to secure ourselves: We want to grasp the symbols that enable us to grasp reality, because they reflect it. Stripped of its will-to-power, Nietzschean perspectivism, which liberates all truths from the supervision of a dominant one, turns out to be similar to Nāgārjuna's realization that "no truth has been taught by a Buddha to anyone, anywhere."

Eternal recurrence is Nietzsche's attempt to resolve nihilism by revaluing this world, yet it is not a good enough myth because it still seeks being: it attempts to make the here-and-now *real* by making it recur (or by acting as if it recurs) eternally. For Buddhism, however, nihilism is not the meaningless-ness of life but our fear of that meaninglessness and the ways we evade it—ways which include myths about eternal recurrence. To accept meaninglessness, as part of the process of yielding to the no-thing-ness we dread, is to realize what might be called *meaningfreeness*. As a result, life becomes more playful. Yet, the question is not whether we play but how. Do we suffer our various games because they are sublimated life-or-death struggles, or do we dance with the light feet that Nietzsche called the first attribute of divinity? The problem is that anyone who *must* play—because he or she needs to get something *from* their play—cannot *play*.

Chapter 5, "Trying to Become Real," discusses some of our more compul-sive games, four of the most popular ways we symbolically try to fill up our sense of *lack*: the craving for fame, the love of love, the money complex, and our collective Oedipal project of technological development. Although now so widespread we take them for granted, these pursuits are not "natural" (i.e., not needing to be explained) but historically conditioned. All four began to become important just before or during the Renaissance, when the Western individual sense of self—and therefore its shadow sense of *lack* as well—became hypertrophied. Each of the four can be viewed as a demonic secular religion: *secular* because by pursuing it we seek a salvation for the self in *this* world; *religious* because in that pursuit a basically spiritual urge for *reality* manifests in distorted form; and tending to become *demonic* because the inability to overcome our sense of unreality through these pursuits is usually experienced as "I do not yet have enough. . . ."

If the concept of *lack* can illuminate such aspects of Western culture, might it also shed light on other cultures? In place of a more conventional summary, the conclusion speculates about the differences among Indian, Sino-Japanese, and Western cultures and about the possible role of *lack* in those differences: some key distinguishing features may be understood as different ways of re-sponding to our sense-of-*lack*. The distinction between this world and another transcendental dimension is fundamental to India but much less important in China and Japan, which emphasize this phenomenal world. In terms of *lack*, Indian culture traditionally orients itself to another reality that can fill up the sense of *lack* we feel here, while China and Japan try to resolve human ground-lessness by grounding their members more tightly into a hierarchical social system. In the West, an early transcendental dimension was gradually internal-ized to become the supposedly autonomous and self-directed individual ad-dressed above.

The argument in this book provides another version of the often-made claim that today, as usual, our deepest problem is a *spiritual* one. Since that word is not respectable in some circles and too respectable in some others, let me emphasize the special sense of the word as it is employed in the interpretation of Buddhism that follows. Our problem is spiritual insofar as the sense-of-self's lack of being compels it to seek being one way or another, consciously or unconsciously. The solution is spiritual insofar as what is necessary is a *metanoia*, a turning-around or rather a letting-go, at our "empty" core. It should not be assumed that this puts us in touch with some other transcendental dimension; according to Mahāyāna Buddhism what it reveals is the actual nature of the world we have understood ourselves to be in yet always felt ourselves to be separate from. That sense of separation from the world is what motivates me to try to secure myself within it, but according to Buddhism the only satisfactory resolution is to realize I am not other than it.

In contrast to the various types of reductionism that have been predominant in the twentieth century—Marxist, Freudian, behaviorist, materialist, etc.—the chapters that follow argue for what might be called a transcendental reduction, or a "transcendentalization." The reduction goes the other way, up instead of down, by noticing how our ultimate concern, the need to ground the groundless sense-of-self, cannot be denied. When we attempt to ignore it, by devoting ourselves to secular pursuits, we end up sacralizing them— and therefore demonize them, as chapter 5 argues. According to Nāgārjuna's famous dictum, the limit (*koti*) of *nirvāṇa* is the limit of the everyday world; there is not even the subtlest difference between them (*Mūlamadhyamikakārikā* XXV.20). Then, the sacred/secular distinction too needs to be conflated, by demonstrating how each term is complicit in the other. Nietzsche attempted such a deconstruction with his critique of all "higher worlds," only to become impaled on the other horn by celebrating the will-to-power of a heroic ego. His brave new world eliminated the sacred without doing the same to its opposite, which we perceive as the secular. In sum, the concept of repression can help us see ultimate concerns functioning in so-called secular pursuits, although in a distorted, unconscious, and compulsive fashion.

If there is no difference between *nirvāṇa* and the everyday world, the sacred can be nothing other than the true nature of the secular. To realize this is to experience our phenomenal world as holy: not because it is God's creation or *śūnyatā*'s form, not because it recurs again and again, not as symbolic or symptomatic of something else, but as what it is. The question, finally, is not whether the world can be resacralized but whether we will sacralize it fetishistically, because unconsciously, or wholeheartedly, because awake.

Prologue

Why was I born, if it wasn't forever?

—Ionesco

Every fear is fear of death.

—Stekel

Is there any meaning in my life that the inevitable death awaiting me does not destroy?

—Tolstoy

The thought that really crushes us is the thought of the futility of life of which death is the visible manifestation.

—Leopardi

The meaning of life is that it stops.

—Kafka

The nature of finite things is to have the seed of their passing-away as their essential being: the hour of their birth is the hour of their death.

—Hegel

The major sin is the sin of being born.

—Beckett

The terrible thing about death is that it transforms life into destiny.

—Malraux

Yaksha: What is the greatest wonder in the world?
Yudhishthira: Every day men see others called to their death, yet those who remain live as if they were immortal.

—*The Mahābhārata*

The king is surrounded by persons whose only thought is to divert the king, and to prevent his thinking of self. For he is unhappy, king though he be, if he thinks of himself.

This is all that men have been able to discover to make themselves happy. And those who philosophize on the matter, and who think men unreasonable for spending a whole day in chasing a hare which they would not have bought, scarce know our nature. The hare in itself would not screen us from the sight of death and calamities; but the chase which turns away our attention from these, does screen us.

—Pascal

One can no more look steadily at death than at the sun.

—La Rochefoucauld

xix

We do not fear death, but the thought of death.

—Seneca

Death is easier to bear without thinking of it, than is the thought of death without peril.

—Pascal

All our knowledge merely helps us to die a more painful death than the animals who know nothing.

—Maeterlinck

He who most resembles the dead is the most reluctant to die.

—La Fontaine

The irony of man's condition is that the deepest need is to be free of the anxiety of death and annihilation; but it is life itself which awakens it, and so we must shrink from being fully alive.

—Roy Waldman

"I had to die to keep from dying."

—Common schizophrenic remark

History is what man does with death.

—Hegel

The self-assertion of technological objectification is the constant negation of death.

—Heidegger

If what we call the problem of life, the problem of bread, were once solved, the earth would be turned into a hell by the emergence in a more violent form of the struggle for survival.

—Unamuno

The struggle for success becomes such a powerful force because it is the equivalent of self-preservation and self-esteem.

—Kardiner

Immortality means being loved by many anonymous people.

—Freud

One must pay dearly for immortality: one has to die several times while still alive.

—Nietzsche

The most horrible of all evils, death, is nothing to us, for when we exist, death is not present; but when death is present, then we are not.

—Epicurus

For life in the present there is no death. Death is not an event in life. It is not a fact in the world. Our life is endless, in just the same way that our field of vision has no boundaries.

—Wittgenstein

By avoiding death, men pursue it.

—Democritus

Striving for life, I seek death; seeking death, I find life.

—Shakespeare

Man has forgotten how to die because he does not know how to live.

—Rousseau

How could those who never live at the right time die at the right time?

—Nietzsche

While you do not know life, how can you know about death?

—Confucius

It is true: we love life not because we are used to living but because we are used to loving.

—Nietzsche

Whoever rightly understands and celebrates death, at the same time magnifies life.

—Rilke

The artist carries death in him like a good priest his breviary.

—Böll

Art has two constants, two unending concerns: it always meditates on death and thus always creates life.

—Pasternak

Only the man who no longer fears death has ceased to be a slave.

—Montaigne

A free man thinks of nothing less than of death, and his wisdom is a meditation not on death but on life.

—Spinoza

To live in the face of death is to die unto death.

—Kierkegaard

The Kingdom of God is for none but the thoroughly dead.

—Eckhart

Since anxiety is the ego's incapacity to accept death, the sexual organizations were perhaps constructed by the ego in its flight from death, and could be abolished by an ego strong enough to die.

—Norman Brown

As long as you do not know how to die and come to life again, you are but a poor guest on this dark earth.

—Goethe

Who knows if what we call death is life, and what we call life is death?

—Euripides

We live in a world of generation and death, and this world we must cast off.

—Blake

Q: Do not one's actions affect the person in after-births?
A: Are you born now? Why do you think of other births? The fact is that there is neither birth nor death. Let him who is born think of death and palliatives therefor.

—Ramana Maharshi

Just understand that birth-and-death is itself nirvana. There is nothing such as birth and death to be avoided; there is nothing such as nirvana to be sought. Only when you realize this are you free from birth and death.

—Dōgen

1

The Nonduality of
Life and Death

All of life is but keeping away the thoughts of death.
— Samuel Johnson

The concern of this chapter is not death but death-in-life: how and why we
make the easiest thing of all into the most difficult, and the effects of that
denial upon our lives. Today any serious discussion of this issue must take
account of psychoanalysis, and that means beginning with Freud. Freud's life
and work demonstrate how inevitably the two dimensions of this issue are
linked. We seek to understand, as clearly and objectively as possible, the psychological impact of human mortality on human vitality, yet this concern is
inescapably colored by the need that each of us has to come to terms with our
own personal fate. A psychotherapeutic understanding can help us cope with
our own mortality, but Freud's life demonstrates the reverse as well: that the
problem of accepting one's own death cannot help affecting one's scientific
inquiries in this direction. Along with his contributions to our understanding
of the mind, Freud's difficulties in this regard reverberate through the subsequent history of psychoanalysis. We set the stage by recounting Freud's own
struggles with our heaviest demon.

Freud. Freud's writings still have the power to shock, and none more than his
theoretical discussions of death, which employ some of his more hasty gener-
alizations and dubious arguments. Freud was rightly suspicious of his attraction to philosophy, yet no attempt to explain the structure of the mind can
avoid the ultimate questions, which is why the most important problems raised
by psychology inevitably become philosophical and religious as well. A science
of the mind that attempts to avoid these issues will have them sneaking in the
back door, by remaining oblivious to its own metaphysical presuppositions.
Freud was not afraid to explore the philosophical implications of his discoveries, but in doing so he was not able to escape his own time. Even the most

1

revolutionary thinkers cannot stand on their own shoulders:

> The attempt to understand Freud's theoretical system, or that of any creative systematic thinker, cannot be successful unless we recognize that, and why, every system as it is developed and presented by its author is *necessarily* erroneous. . . . the creative thinker must think in the terms of the logic, the thought patterns, the expressible concepts of his culture. That means he has not yet the proper words to express the creative, the new, the liberating idea. He is forced to solve an insoluble problem: to express the new thought in concepts and words that do not yet exist in his language. . . . The consequence is that the new thought as he formulated it is a blend of what is truly new and the conventional thought which it transcends. The thinker, however, is not conscious of this contradiction.[1]

Otto Rank, originally a member of Freud's inner circle, came to a similar conclusion: "Freud, without knowing it, interpreted the analytic situation in terms of his world-view and did not, as he thought, analyze the individual's unconscious objectively."[2] A century later we have more perspective on that world-view molded in nineteenth-century Vienna, with its bourgeois character-structure of self-discipline and sexual inhibition, in which scientific positivism contended with a pessimistic Schopenhauerian voluntarism. Both are found in the two aspects of Freud's character. On the one side there is the mechanistic, deterministic Neo-Kantianism of Helmholtz ("one of my idols"), encountered mainly through his stern psychology professor, Brucke ("the greatest authority who affected me more than any other in my whole life"), and evident in Freud's never-abandoned hope to ground his theories in physiology. On the other side are the tragic conclusions about human nature that his instinct theories finally brought him to, for Freud's concept of *libido* bears more than a passing resemblance to Schopenhauer's will which can resolve its predicament only by negating itself.

Freud's life and character have been scrutinized as carefully as anyone's. One feature which stands out is that he admitted to being haunted by death anxiety, to the point of thinking about death every day.

> As far back as we know anything of his life he seems to have been prepossessed by thoughts about death, more so than any other man I can think of except perhaps Sir Thomas Browne and Montaigne. Even in the early years of our acquaintance he had the disconcerting habit of parting with the words, "Goodbye; you may never see me again." There were the repeated attacks of what he called *Todesangst* (dread of death). He hated growing old, even as early as his forties, and as he did so the thoughts of death became increasingly clamorous.[3]

This characteristic has been analyzed by Ernest Becker and Irvin Yalom, among many others.[4] Yalom points to Freud's compensatory need to be famous, and Becker shows how the psychoanalytic movement became Freud's own "immortality project," his unconscious way of surmounting death symbolically. The problem with such immortality projects (a phrase coined by Otto Rank) is the problem with unconscious motivation generally: When our conscious concerns only re-present what really drives us, they become symptoms and we become compulsive. This supports Fromm's conclusion that Freud's self-analysis was in important respects a failure—something that has serious ramifications for psychoanalysis, especially for those analysts who trace their lineage and credentials back to those analyzed by him. But once fear of death has been uncovered, what can be done with it except sublimate it in some way, as Freud did?

One can reveal the role that death-anxiety and death-denial play in life. The problem with Freud, finally, is that he did not discover that, in his theory or in his life. Death always occupied an awkward place in the development of his ideas, contorted one way and then another, in an attempt to fit it in which never quite worked and never could work as long as there was something Freud did not want to see. In *Studies in Hysteria*, his first book, "death so pervades the clinical histories of these patients that only by a supreme effort of inattention could Freud have omitted it from his discussion of precipitating traumas."[5] But the fear of death as an explanatory factor was hardly new—it can be traced back at least as far as the epic of Gilgamesh—whereas the theory of sexual libido repression might be a pathway to fame. So Freud had both personal and theoretical reasons for denying death in his early works, and there it languishes without an independent representation in the mind: "The unconscious seems to contain nothing that could give any content to our concept of the annihilation of life." Instead, he inclined to view the fear of death "as analogous to the fear of castration and that the situation to which the ego is reacting is one of being abandoned by the protecting super-ego."[6] These supposedly deeper fears are rooted in the conflicts of Oedipal and pre-Oedipal stages of development, according to the hydraulics of id, ego, and superego that direct the cathexis of libido. Not for the last time, "postulated strivings must take theoretical precedence over observed phenomena."[7] Having severed any direct connection between anxiety and death, Freud never rejoined them. Although he soon reversed himself and concluded that repression does not produce anxiety but vice versa, even his later death-drive had no theoretical connection with anxiety; the farthest he went was to state, vaguely, that what the ego fears in anxiety "is in the nature of an overthrow or an extinction."[8]

Most of Freud's followers followed him on this. Otto Fenichel, summarizing the conclusions of psychoanalytic literature before World War I, echoed Freud in doubting whether there is such a thing as a normal fear of death: The idea of one's own death is subjectively inconceivable, and therefore it must cover other unconscious ideas. The outbreak of hostilities turned Freud's mind more to the problem of human destructiveness. He could see motivations beyond those accounted for in his earlier theories—"I can no longer

understand how we could have overlooked the universality of non-erotic aggression and destruction"—and he concluded that "the tendency to aggression
is an innate, independent, instinctual disposition in man," one which he was
later to describe as "the derivative and main representative of the death-instinct."[9]
   In "Timely Thoughts on War and Death" (1915), Freud noticed that a
bottom "nobody believes in his own death. Or, and this is the same. In his
unconscious, every one of us is convinced of his immortality." On this matter,
at least, Jung agreed:

> On the whole, I was astonished to see how little ado the unconscious psyche
> makes of death. It would seem as though death were something relatively
> unimportant, or perhaps our psyche does not bother about what happens to
> the individual. But it does seem that the unconscious is all the more inter-
> ested in *how* one does it; that is, whether the attitude of consciousness is
> adjusted to dying or not.[10]

From this lack of concern, however, one can draw opposite conclusions, by
regarding it either as a revelation about the immortality of the collective unconscious or as a costly delusion. In another short essay at the end of the war,
Freud recommended more consciousness of death. "Would it not be better to
give death the place in actuality and in our thoughts which is its due, and to
yield a little more prominence to that unconscious attitude towards death which
we have hitherto so carefully suppressed?. . . *Si vis vitam, para mortem.* If you
would endure life, be prepared for death."[11]
   Soon after this, however, Freud found another role for death in attempting
to patch up his instinct theory. *Beyond the Pleasure Principle* (1920) contrasts
the pleasure principle, which naturally seeks repetition, with the more perplex-
ing repetition compulsion found in fixations on traumatic experiences, which
bring repeated suffering upon oneself. Freud put this fixation in the same category as a homeostatic tendency ("the Nirvana-principle") to recede to an earlier state of things, and concluded that life necessarily seeks death. "If we are
to take it as a truth that knows no exception that everything dies for *internal*
reasons—becomes inorganic once again—then we shall be compelled to say
that '*the aim of all life is death.*'"[12] In accordance with a dualistic predisposi-
tion, perhaps inherited from Brucke (who reduced all forces to attraction and
repulsion), Freud postulated two antagonistic instincts: the anabolic, which
contributes to growth and development, and the catabolic, which expends energy. *The Ego and the Id* (1923) adds aggression, which may be projected outward (sadism) or harnessed by the superego and turned inward (masochism) in
order to pacify one's own guilt. Putting these three phenomena together in his
last major work, *An Outline of Psychoanalysis* (1938), Freud ended up with a
basic and admittedly speculative dichotomy between two cosmic tendencies,
the life-drive that tends toward greater unities and the death-drive that tends
to undo these unities and destroy. Eros and Thanatos are doomed to perpetual

conflict or, at best, uneasy and temporary compromise.

One need not be a philosopher to marvel at the breathtaking leap from these three psychological patterns to such a metaphysical conclusion. The logic is hard to follow, unless one is already committed to an instinctual libido theory which must be patched up if it is one's claim to immortality. The rest of us may harbor doubts, as did many of Freud's own followers.

Jung, no longer one of them, criticized this cosmological duality, which he believed to reflect the attitude of the conscious mind more than the dynamics of the unconscious. For Jung, the logical opposite of love/eros is hate, but the psychological opposite of love is a will-to-power, for when one predominates the other will be lacking. From his understanding of the collective unconscious (a monism which Freud's dualism was a self-conscious attempt to avoid), Jung viewed Freud's theory as a psychological prejudice: Eros is not the same as life, but someone who thinks so will naturally oppose Eros to death, confronting the highest principle of good with the evil of destruction.

From that perspective, Freud's final, Manichaean dualism amounts to another version of our oldest psychological tendency, here extrapolated into humankind's most basic psychic forces. If aggression in particular is grounded in a biological drive, the result can only be his tragic attitude toward the human condition: a pessimistic view of therapeutic possibilities leading to grim conclusions about the future of humanity. Is this an objective view of our situation, or a projection of Freud's own death fears? Freud jumped from one extreme to the other. First death was not an important element in mental functioning, then it became one of our two primordial instincts. Despite Freud's awareness of his own death-anxiety, *neither approach allows an independent role for death-fear*. Making death a drive reduces death-*anxiety* almost to an epiphenomenon, an effect rather than a significant determinant of human behavior. As Robert Jay Lifton concluded about Freud's libido theory, this "de-deathifies death." So Freud courageously endured his own death anxiety without analyzing its effects on his life and his work. His blindness here is too remarkable to be anything other than a willful inattention, a *not wanting to see*, which is of course the definition of repression.

Life and death do require each other insofar as awareness of one implies awareness of the other. We can fear death (which is not the same as resisting dying) only if we know—or believe—ourselves to be alive. There cannot be life without death, whether they are antagonistic instincts or, more humbly, a dualistic way of thinking. This raises another therapeutic possibility. Rather than antagonistic forces that batter the ego, might Eros and Thanatos be the two tendencies of the ego itself, which is mentally constituted only to find itself in the tragic situation of contemplating its inevitable demise? For Freud, the death-instinct never reveals itself directly but insinuates itself inside the manifestations of Eros. Then perhaps the death-instinct is really the equal-but-opposite force of Eros: tails to its head, but one coin not two. That would mean, on one side, the life-fear that existentialists and psychoanalysts have described so well, and, on the other side, a death-wish which intuits the meaninglessness of the whole struggle and wearies of it. If, however, this situation is not a war of instincts but a way of thinking—a life-versus-death game that one unwittingly plays with oneself—there may be an alternative. If the ego is constituted by that game, what happens if that game ends?

This chapter will explore that possibility, which is suggested by Buddhism. It is not a perspective that Freud would have been sympathetic to. Rather than *seeing through* the dualism, he exhorts us to fight on the side of life. In spite of his reference to a Nirvana principle, Freud's few references to Buddhism are hostile and uncomprehending. His last works repeat his contemptuous rejection of the consolations of religion. We should fight the good fight as long as we can. There is no place in Freud's thought for coming to terms with the death principle by finding a meaning for death.

Repression. However unsatisfactory Freud's final understanding of death may finally be, that does not reduce the importance of what he discovered, and that is first and foremost repression, which for him is the foundation-stone of psychoanalysis: "The essence of repression lies simply in the function of rejecting and keeping something out of consciousness." Something (a mental wish, according to Freud) makes me uncomfortable, and since I do not want to cope with it consciously I ignore or "forget" it. This clears the way for me to concentrate on something else more agreeable, but at a price: what has been repressed retains "a strong upward-striving force, an impulsion to get through to consciousness." Therefore the process of repression demands a continuous expenditure of effort. Freud compared the repressed mental wish to a guest who is not allowed into the drawing room. An ever-present guardian censor is necessary to guard the door, for the impetuous guest might otherwise force his way in.[13] We experience the effect of this as a persistent psychic tension.

Yet a repressed phenomenon tends to make it back into the drawing room of consciousness anyway, by adopting a disguise which allows it to pass the censor. For a neurotic, this disguise is the symptom. What is not admitted into awareness irrupts in obsessive ways that affect consciousness with precisely those qualities it strives to exclude. Since the symptom re-presents the repressed phenomenon in distorted form, symptoms are symbolic. Freud described this tendency to symptom-formation as *the return of the repressed.* The phrase suggests that this process is not just negative. The tendency to return to consciousness is also a blind impulse to resolve the problem, to heal the psychic wound caused by this alienation between consciousness and some of its contents. "The dialectic of neurosis contains its own 'attempts at explanation and cure,' energized by the ceaseless upward pressure of the repressed unconscious and producing the return of the repressed to consciousness, although in an increasingly distorted form, as long as the basic repression (denial) is maintained and the neurosis endures" (Brown).[14] The therapeutic process can assist this natural impulse toward a resolution by helping to translate the symbolized symptom (which has become fixated) back into its original form. This book may be viewed as an attempt to understand more of the implications of this process: implications which extend beyond what Freud envisioned and which may also go beyond what contemporary psychotherapists theorize.

Freud traced the hysterias and phobias of his middle-class Viennese patients back to repressed sexual wishes, to conclude that sexual repression is the primal human repression—although, as occurs with many of us, his attention gradually shifted from sex to death as he aged. Today psychoanalytic attention has joined him there, although having taken a different route which concludes that consciousness of death is our main repression.[15]

In focusing on the psychological effects of death-denial, Ernest Becker's last two books, *The Denial of Death* and *Escape from Evil*, synthesize the work of many predecessors, especially Otto Rank and Norman O. Brown. Becker builds on an insight of William James: "Mankind's common instinct for reality . . . has always held the world to be essentially a theater for heroism." Why do we want to be heroes? Our natural narcissism and need for self-esteem mean that each of us yearns to feel of special value, first in the universe. Heroism (in the broad sense: e.g., Freud as an intellectual hero) is how we justify that need to count more than anyone or anything else. Human society can be understood as a codified hero system, a symbolic-action structure whose roles and rules function as a vehicle for heroism. For Becker, this is the common denominator behind the cultural relativity that anthropology discovers, which is nothing other than the relativity of hero-systems.[16] Primitive peoples often believed that their rituals were responsible for keeping the universe going, and much of the problem with contemporary society is that technological man, increasingly reduced to a consumer, has difficulty attributing any such a role to himself.

But, to carry the analysis a step further, why do we need to be special? This reaches one of the wellsprings of human motivation: that desire is first of all and most of all a reflex of the terror of death. We need to be heroes because heroism is what can qualify us for a special destiny. And we need that special destiny because the alternative is literally too much to contemplate. The irony of our unique ability to symbolize—language—is that it serves to reveal our fate more clearly. Man is the animal that knows it will die. This fear of death is useful in keeping our organism armed toward self-preservation, but it must also be repressed for us to function with any modicum of psychological comfort. The result is us: hyperanxious animals who even invent reasons for anxiety when there are none. This is also the conclusion of Otto Rank, Melanie Klein, Norman O. Brown, and more recently Irvin Yalom, who argues that a considerable part of our life energy is consumed in the denial of death.[17] Most

animals have fears programmed into them as instincts, but we humans fashion
our fears out of the ways we perceive the world—which unlocks a door that
Becker himself does not open, since it suggests that if we can come to experience the world differently we might fashion our fears differently too. Or is it
the other way around: Do our fears cause us to perceive the world in the way
we do, and might someone come to experience the world differently who was
brave enough to confront the thing we most avoid?

The reason man's essence was never found, says Becker, "was that there was
no essence, that the essence of man is really his *paradoxical* nature, the fact
that he is half animal and half symbolic."[18] But this moves too easily from an
existentialist view that man has no essence to the familiar claim that our essence is dualistic: in Becker's terms, a god with an anus and all the other
accoutrements of mortality. Does such a modernized mind-body dualism grasp
our immutable human condition, or is it another historically determined understanding, one of many possible? The question is important because this
duality lies at the heart of Becker's argument. The mind looks down at the
body, realizes what flesh implies, and panics. As a consequence, "everything
that man does in his symbolic world is an attempt to deny and overcome his
grotesque fate. He literally drives himself into a blind obliviousness with social
games, psychological tricks, personal preoccupations so far removed from the
reality of his situation that they are forms of madness." Even our character
traits are examples of this. Ferenczi called them secret psychoses, not much
different from a repetition compulsion, because they mechanize a particular
way of reacting. These sedimented habits are a necessary protection, for without them we become overtly psychotic. To see the world as it really is is not
only terrifying but devastating, because "it *makes routine, automatic, secure,
self-confident activity impossible.* . . . It places a trembling animal at the mercy
of the entire cosmos and the problem of the meaning of it." Thus the bite in
Pascal's aphorism: "Men are so necessarily mad that not to be mad would
amount to another form of madness." For Becker, this is literally true: Normality is our collective, protective madness, in which we repress the truth of
the human condition, and those who have difficulty playing this game are the
ones we call mentally ill. Rank describes neurosis as nothing but the individual
coming to feel the metaphysical problem of human existence. If schizophrenics
are suffering from the whole truth, because they feel that metaphysical problem more deeply, then William Burroughs is right: a paranoid is someone who
knows a little of what's going on. Psychoanalysis reveals the high price of
denying this truth about man's condition, what might be called "the costs of
pretending not to be mad."[19]
This gives a more existential slant to such key Freudian concepts as guilt
and the Oedipal complex. In spite of all that Freud discovered about childhood

development, his libido-instinct theory kept him from grasping the main point. According to Becker, the early experience of children is their attempt to deny the anxiety of their emergence, their fear of losing support and having to stand alone, helpless within an awesome world. This leads to what he calls the great scientific simplification of psychoanalysis:

> This despair he avoids by building defenses; and these defenses allow him to feel a basic sense of self-worth, of meaningfulness, of power. They allow him to feel that he *controls* his life and his death, that he really does live and act as a willful and free individual, that he has a unique and self-fashioned identity, that he is *somebody*. . . .[20]

Freud traced guilt back to early ambivalent feelings of the child, particularly hate and death wishes toward parents alternating with fears of losing them. But there is a simpler explanation: "Guilt, as the existentialists put it, is the guilt of being itself. It reflects the self-conscious animal's bafflement at having emerged from nature, at sticking out too much without knowing what for, at not being able to securely place himself in an eternal meaning system."[21] Such "pure" guilt has nothing to do with infringements or punishment for secret wishes; the major sin is the sin of being born, as Beckett put it. For existential psychologists, it is the worm in the heart of the human condition, apparently an inescapable consequence of self-consciousness itself. Schizophrenics sometimes say they feel guilty just for existing. Perhaps here too they suffer from the truth, whereas the rules of our collective, protective madness require us to find a more specific fault to feel guilty about.

Becker sees the origin of this guilt in the child's reaction to bodily processes and their urges. "Guilt as inhibition, as determinism, as smallness and boundedness" is implied by the constraints that our basic animal condition imposes upon us symbol-using gods. But this may beg the question. Is such mind-body dualism the cause of our anxiety or its effect? Do we panic because we discover ourselves to be consciousnesses with bodies, or is our panic what motivates us to dualize ego-consciousness from body?

The most detailed historical study of death in Western culture is Philippe Aries' *The Hour of Our Death*, a monumental—indeed, interminable—survey of the last millennium. Although Aries' approach is not psychoanalytic, his conclusions are all the more relevant, since his evidence comes from a different perspective. At the moment the most interesting for us are the first two stages of death-awareness he distinguishes. In striking contrast to what came later, death in the Middle Ages was "tame." While recognized as "evil," it was nonetheless accepted because inseparable from life. Contrary to the universalist implications of Becker's thesis about death-repression, there do not seem to have been the extremes of terror and denial that we now associate with death; it was a repose, a peaceful sleep from which one might or might not reawaken with the eventual resurrection of the body.

But this changed. "The strong individual of the later Middle Ages could not be satisfied with the peaceful but passive conception of *requies*. . . . He split into two parts: a body that experienced pleasure or pain and an immortal soul that was released by death."[22] Evidently it was this dualism that later attained philosophical reification in the *Meditations* of Descartes, whose legacy we still struggle with.

Aries' argument supplements what Johan Huizinga wrote in *The Waning of the Middle Ages*, Chapter 2 of which begins: "At the close of the Middle Ages, a sombre melancholy weighs on people's souls. Whether we read a chronicle, a poem, a sermon, a legal document even, the same impression of immense sadness is produced by them all." Huizinga does not seek the cause of this melancholy, but Chapter 11 begins: "No other epoch has laid so much stress as the expiring Middle Ages on the thought of death. An everlasting call of *memento mori* resounds through life."[23] Is it a coincidence that this new awareness of death spread just before the acceleration of Western civilization which began with the Renaissance? If history is what man does with death, as Hegel put it, then a more death-conscious society will create more history.

> The Renaissance humanists themselves evidently needed a fantasy of misery and catastrophe in order to contain the renascent energy they were riding. Ficino never ceased complaining of pain and melancholy, yet this "bitter desperation" was the source of his psychological philosophy. Petrarch kept before his mind the "great overarching reality of man's life: his death." Yet the more occupied with death, the more these humanists thought, built, wrote, painted, and sang.[24]

Burckhardt pointed out that although the Renaissance brought an increased feeling of strength and freedom, this was accompanied by "an increased isolation, doubt, skepticism and—resulting from all these—anxiety."[25] He also noticed the most outstanding symptom, now so common we take it for granted and scarcely notice it: a morbid craving for fame. The desire to be famous (which will be discussed in chapter 5) is a good example of how something repressed (such as death-terror) reappears in consciousness in distorted form (the passion for *symbolic* immortality), which is therefore a symptom of our problem (if what I really want is personal immortality, no fame will ever be enough—but that is usually experienced as "I am not yet famous enough"). This craving and the other traits Burckhardt mentions are associated with greater self-consciousness. Increased consciousness is increased awareness of the end, and therefore increased need to resolve the anxiety such awareness brings with it, whether by becoming an immaterial soul or by attaining some symbolic immortality through one's reputation.

All this suggests that the Platonic, Cartesian, and now commonsense mind-body dualism that Becker too presupposes might not be the unvarying essence of our human nature but another example of nurture being taken for nature:

an historically determined conception now so deeply ingrained that its meta-physical origin has been forgotten. And if this dualistic conception is a result of our death-anxiety, it falls under the definition of repression, something which can afflict whole civilizations as well as individuals.

This can be made clearer by relating it to the existential-psychological per-spective on the Oedipal complex. Contemporary psychoanalytic theory under-stands the Oedipal complex as a shorthand term for the early conditioning of the child. An existentialist perspective understands this early conditioning as what Norman O. Brown has renamed the Oedipal *project*. Here too a Freud-ian interpretation approaches yet does not quite grasp the main point: The Oedipal desire is not to reunite with one's mother by becoming the father, but to resolve that separation from mother by becoming one's own father. Why? To become one's own father would be to become the creator and sustainer of one's own life, so "the essence of the Oedipal project is the project of becom-ing God—in Spinoza's formula, *causa sui*, self-caused; in Sartre's, *être-en-soi-pour-soi*."[26] To be one's own father is to be one's own origin. Becker calls this a flight from contingency, and this flight is precisely what Buddhism finds problematic. From the Buddhist viewpoint, the Oedipal project is the attempt of the developing ego-self to attain closure on itself, to foreclose its depen-dence on others by becoming a self-sufficient Cartesian-like ego. It is the wish to become what the Mahāyāna philosopher Nāgārjuna described as *svabhāva*, "self-existing"—something that is not possible. Yet that does not stop us from trying, for this is the way the burgeoning sense-of-self strives to compensate for its burgeoning sense of unreality. Rather than just a way to conquer death, however, this is more immediately the quest to deny one's groundlessness by becoming one's own ground: the socially conditioned (but nonetheless illu-sory) ground that we know as being an individual, autonomous person.

Then what Freud called the Oedipal complex is due to the child's discovery that he is not part of mother, after all. The problem is not so much that Dad has first claim on Mom, as what that contributes to the child's dawning reali-zation of separateness: "But if I'm not part of Mom, what am I part of?" This generates the need to discover one's own ground, or rather (since there is none to be found) the need to create it. This is an Oedipal *project* because it never succeeds, except insofar as I create some security for myself by identifying with certain social groups and their values, goals, etc. Then growing up is not a matter of discovering who or what one really is, but joining the general amne-sia whereby each of us pretends to be an autonomous person and learns how to play the social game of constantly reassuring each other that, yes, you are a person, just like me, and I'm okay, you're okay.

If this is what happens, the Oedipal project is problematic for a different reason than Freud offers or even Becker suspects. The basic difficulty is a sense of *lack*, which originates from the fact that our self-consciousness is not something self-existing but a mental construct. Rather than being self-sufficient, the sense-of-self is more like the surface of the sea: dependent on depths it cannot grasp because it is a manifestation of them. Buddhism makes this point by deconstructing the sense-of-self into sets of interrelating physical and mental phenomena; consciousness is only one factor, an effect of certain conditions and a cause of others. Problems arise when such a conditioned consciousness seeks to ground itself, that is, wants to become unconditioned and autonomous, which is to say *real.* If consciousness is ungrounded it can try to realize itself only by trying to objectify itself. I strive to become real by becoming some*thing.* Then the Oedipal project can never be completed because there is a contradiction in the very attempt: the ego-self is the effort of awareness to objectify itself in order to grasp itself—which it can no more do than a hand can shake itself or an eye see itself. The sense-of-self that arises is a fiction, a mental construct which is delusive insofar as, in grasping at it out of the need to ground ourselves, what-is-grasped is confused with what grasps.[27]

*The consequence is that the sense-of-self always has, as its inescapable shadow, a sense-of-*lack*, which it always tries to escape.* It is here that the theory of repression becomes so valuable, for Freud's concept of the return of the repressed— that what-has-been-repressed returns to consciousness distorted into a symptom—shows us how to link this fundamental yet hopeless situation with the symbolic ways we try to overcome our sense of *lack* by making ourselves real *in* the world. We experience this deep sense of *lack* as the feeling that "there is something wrong with me." To the extent that we have a sense of autonomous self, we also have this sense of *lack*, but it manifests itself in many different forms and we respond to it in many different ways. In its "purer" forms *lack* appears as ontological guilt or, even more basic, an ontological anxiety at the very core of one's being, which becomes almost unbearable because it gnaws on that core. For that reason, all anxiety wants to become objectified into fear *of* something (as Spinoza might say, fear is anxiety associated with an object), because then we know what to do: we have ways to defend ourselves against particular feared things.

The tragedy of these objectifications, however, is that nothing objective can ever be enough if it is not really something objective we want. When we do not understand what is actually motivating us—because what we *think* we need is only a symptom of something else—we end up compulsive. Then is the guilt that seems to bedevil humankind not the cause of our unhappiness but its effect? "The ultimate problem is not guilt but the incapacity to live. The illusion of guilt is necessary for an animal that cannot enjoy life, in order to organize a life of nonenjoyment" (Brown).[28] In Buddhist terms, if the autonomy of *self*-consciousness is a delusion which can never quite shake off the feeling that "something is wrong with me," that sense of inadequacy will need to be rationalized away. Such an approach implies that no satisfactory mental health can be gained except by resolving the sense-of-*lack* that shadows the sense-of-self, by somehow resolving—ending? transforming in some yet-to-be-understood way?—the sense-of-self's Oedipal project of self-grounding.

Transference. The insightful things that existential psychology has discovered about transference are illuminated further by the Buddhist idea of a groundless *lack* that needs to find security and meaning somewhere.

Transference in the narrow sense is our unconscious tendency to take emotions and behavior felt toward one person (e.g., a parent) and project them onto another (e.g., psychoanalyst). But if transference in the wider sense is distortion of encounter, as Rollo May defined it, then we all do it most of the time, which is what Freud concluded: It is a "universal phenomenon of the human mind" that "dominates the whole of each person's relation to his human environment." It is our earliest and our most natural way of trying to fill up our sense-of-*lack*: by identifying with someone who, we think, *is* real. Transference reveals that we never grow up, remaining children who distort the world in order to relieve our sense of helplessness, who perceive things as we wish them to be for our own safety. The need to find security by subjecting ourselves to others persists, transferred from parents to teachers, supervisors, and rulers. This is not simply an emotional mistake but a matter of experiencing the other as one's *whole world*, just as the family is for the child. In this way, we tame the terror of life, by focusing the power and horror of the universe in one place. "*Mirabile!* The transference object, being endowed with the transcendent powers of the universe, now has in himself the power to control, order, and combat them." This natural fetishization of man's highest yearnings and strivings explains our urge to deify the other: "The more they have, the more rubs off on us. We participate in their immortality, and so we create immortals." Rank said that we need to erect a god-ideal outside ourselves in order to live at all, and the transference-object fits the bill.[29]

The problem is that this process is unconscious and uncritical, a regression to wishful thinking which is not fully in one's control, and therefore dangerous. We children of the twentieth century do not need to think very hard to come up with examples of this phenomenon, but examples have never been lacking. Humans have always been hypnotized by those who represent life or *being*, and eager to submit to charismatic personalities who legitimize their power with a little symbolic mystification. "Each society elevates and rewards leaders who are talented at giving the masses heroic victory, expiation for guilt, relief of personal conflicts." Alas, these leaders are usually the grandest, most mindless patriots, "who embrace the ongoing system of death denial with the heartiest hug, the hottest tears, the least critical distance."[30] Government is the organization of idolatry, as Shaw put it. The source of privilege is prestige, and the etymology of prestige reveals its roots in deception and enchantment.[31]

If we contemplate the phenomenon of transference on the broadest possible scale, what does it reveal? From the Buddhist perspective, the functions that psychoanalysis identifies as transference exemplify a psychic tendency which is almost universal. Since transference includes ego-models, we can do it with someone we have never met. Figures like Socrates and Wittgenstein tend to become models—*heroes*—for philosophers, even as sports champions and film stars are for many others. The person not fascinated by one model is fascinated by another, because *this is how we choose the cosmology for our own heroics*, even if those heroics must be vicarious; at least we can identify our universe with the one that our hero lived, thought, and acted within. And that brings us closer to the heart of the matter, for transference applies to more than people: We admire not only outstanding sportsmen, but their teams; we identify not only with national leaders, but with nations; not only are we impressed by Freud or the Buddha, we are converted to psychoanalysis and Buddhism.

The Buddhist term for all this is attachment, yet that is such a vague, indiscriminate concept that this is an area where Buddhism has much to learn from psychotherapy, which has been investigating more methodically how delusion functions. What ties all these together into a nearly universal phenomenon of the human mind is more than our desire to tame the terror of death: it is our need to organize the chaos of life by finding a unifying meaning-system that gives us knowledge about the world and a life-program for living in it, informing us both what is and what we should do. A meaning-system teaches us what our *lack* really is and how we can overcome it. Children absorb this from their parents as part of what it means to be a person; we locate ourselves in the universe by internalizing the meaning-system of someone we identify with. Then we wake up to find ourselves comfortably inside such a meaning-system. "All of us are driven to be supported in a self-forgetful way, ignorant of what energies we really draw on, of the kind of lie we have fashioned in order to live securely and serenely."[32]

Also essential to that lie is *negative* transference, for our antipathies are as important to our meaning-system as our sympathies: history is the story of how we work out our problems on others. If transference is distortion of encounter, what transferences are more powerful than hatred and resentment? Negativity is the best example of a karmic projection that rebounds to haunt us. It is our usual way of dealing with what Jung so aptly called *the shadow*: those aspects of ourselves that we cannot cope with because they threaten the particular identifications by which we try to overcome our sense of *lack*. If that sense-of-*lack* manifests in consciousness as an obsession with certain symbols, the shadow is a constellation of those symbols that represent failure to us, which we cannot accept or integrate.

This guilt-feeling based on the existence of the shadow is discharged from the system in the same way both by the individual and the collective—that is to say, by the phenomenon of the *projection of the shadow*. The shadow, which is in conflict with the acknowledged values, cannot be accepted as a negative part of one's own psyche and is therefore projected—that is, it is transferred to the outside world and experienced as an outside object. It is combated, punished, and exterminated as "the alien out there" instead of being dealt with as one's own inner problem. (Neumann)[33]

Freud's view of aggression was pessimistic. The sad truth "is that men are not gentle, friendly creatures, wishing for love, who simply defend themselves if they are attacked, but that a powerful measure of desire for aggression has to be reckoned as a part of their instinctual endowment." Again, the bedrock of libido-instinct, which allows only a dim prognosis for the future. But if history is what man does with death, there is a reason why we try to work out our problems through others. "The death fear of the ego is lessened by the killing, the sacrifice, of the other; through the death of the other, one buys oneself free from the penalty of dying, of being killed" (Rank). We feel that we are the masters of life and death when we control the fate of others. This allows us to project death/*lack* outside us, personified in the enemy who is perceived as trying to kill us. No wonder, then, that people tend to rejoice when war finally breaks out, as even Freud and Rilke did at the beginning of the Great War. Projecting death/*lack* over there liberates the space for life here. We feel newly bonded to our fellows in a joint life-against-death project which no longer festers unconsciously because it is no longer individual but has become collective, is no longer unwinnable but something we have some measure of conscious control over. Our private "immortality accounts" become merged: we mourn our dead, but not too much if the number of enemy dead is greater.[34]

Thus war is sacred. It seems to give us the most purchase on our amorphous sense-of-*lack*, which we otherwise struggle with in a far more abstracted and symbolic form. "War is a ritual for the emergence of heroes, and so for the transmutation of common, selfish values. In war men live their own ennoblement. But what we are reluctant to admit is that the admiration of the hero is a vicarious catharsis of our own fears."[35] A catharsis of our own fears about our own death, and about our own sense of *lack*. In this ritual, the enemy has an important role to play, for only through Judas can evil be redeemed. "War is a blessing for the world and for all nations," the Ayatollah Khomeini proclaimed in 1984: "Through war God purifies the Earth." War is an attempt at moral cloture. "The irony is that men are always dissatisfied and guilty in small and large ways, and this is what drives them to a search for purity where all dissatisfaction can come to a head and be wiped away." The irony may be greater than that. Rank declared that all our human problems and their sufferings are due to man's attempt to perfect the world. As Becker put it, evil arises from our urge to heroic victory over evil.[36]

Paradoxically, the amount of evil humans bring into the world has increased at the same time that we have ceased believing in evil. Look at our agonies over Nazi crematoriums. We cannot understand how such a thing could have happened in the supposedly civilized West. On the last page of *The Hour of our Death*, Aries is struck by what he calls a contradiction: "The belief in evil was necessary to the taming of death; the disappearance of the belief has restored death to its savage state." As a consequence, today "neither the individual nor the community is strong enough to recognize the existence of death." But Aries' contradiction is not so puzzling. A belief in evil is necessary for a belief in goodness, and, however painful their struggle may be, it is a reassuring game. We know where we are, we expect to cash in our chips. But if there are no chips and no place to cash them in, *no sacred redemption of the secular*, then the only alternative is a secular redemption—and the pressure that exerts on the secular becomes demonic if redemption is not possible in that form. When wars and revolutions do not bring the absolution we need, we will need repeated wars and continuing revolutions. "The Devil is the one who prevents the heroic victory of immortality [victory over *lack*] in each culture—even the atheistic, scientific ones."[37] If so, when religions decline we will have to find a secular satan. How could either capitalist or communist countries have justified their own horrors without the other! Since we can never attain cloture on the security we crave, never fill up our *lack* and make ourselves really real, we always need a devil to rationalize our failure and to fight against. But as long as we do so, the chief cause of our problems will continue to be our attempted solutions.

"The striving for perfection reflects man's effort to get some human grip on his eligibility for immortality."[38] Then we can never be perfect enough—and that, in a nutshell, is the problem with all these distorted, because heavily symbolized, immortality/becoming-real projects. When we play the game according to these rules we cannot win. The best we can do is hide the fact from ourselves by projecting our victory sometime into the future. As Hazlitt realized, it is essential to the triumph of reform that it should never succeed. But we cannot afford to play that game anymore. Today civilization is not likely to survive a heroism that redeems evil by eliminating the enemy, which is why that form of struggle has for the most developed countries been largely sublimated into economic competition. Yet, neither can our biosphere support the delusion of victory through sustained economic growth, the cult of an ever-increasing Gross National Product.

Death-in-life. A century of theory and practice has brought psychoanalysis to one of the great insights of existentialism: Anxiety is not adventitous but essential to the self, not something we have but something we are. Many have concluded that it is not possible to eliminate our anxiety, yet that conclusion does not necessarily follow. What is implied, rather, is that such an end would also end the ego-self as usually experienced. Norman O. Brown is sympathetic to such a possibility: "Since anxiety is the ego's incapacity to accept death, the sexual organizations were perhaps constructed by the ego in its flight from death, and could be abolished by an ego strong enough to die."[39] But for Rank and Becker, as for Freud, anxiety cannot all be overcome therapeutically, because it is impossible to stand up to the terrible truth of one's condition without it.|Rollo May and Irvin Yalom view anxiety more positively, as a guide that can point the way to a more authentic life; the aim of therapy, therefore, is to reduce it to a more manageable level.[40]|

Evidently we must choose between anxiety and repression. If we cannot face the truth of our condition, which is mortality (or groundlessness, according to my Buddhist interpretation), we must forget that truth, which is to repress it. The difference between neurosis and normality—that undramatic, unnoticed psychopathology of the average, according to Maslow—is how successful that repression is. The neurotic has a better memory than most of us, so anxiety keeps breaking through into consciousness and must be dealt with more harshly in order to preserve some purchase on one's fate, some circumscribed sphere of action. All of us react to our anxiety by "partializing" our world, by restricting our consciousness within narrow bounds, to areas that we can more or less control which provide us a sense of self-confidence. The neurotic, who is inhabited by meanings that she cannot cope with, has more difficulty sustaining the illusion of self-confidence and so must confine herself even more narrowly. The psychotic can do this hardly at all, and in self-protection de-animates himself, often referring to himself as a toy, a puppet, or a machine. The literature on schizophrenia is full of expressions like "I had to die to keep from dying."[41] Lucretius mentions those who commit suicide because of their intense fear of death. Better an end with terror than a terror without end; best of all to die without actual death, by de-animating.

The difference between these three is a matter of degree. When you grow up unable to give yourself freely to the cultural roles available to you, your life becomes a problem. Tillich called neurosis the way of avoiding nonbeing by avoiding being. Rank said the constant restriction of the neurotic's life is because "he refuses the loan (life) in order thus to avoid paying the debt (death)." Then the anguish and despair that the neurotic complains of are not the result of symptoms but their cause; those symptoms are what shield one from the tragic contradictions at the heart of the human situation: death, guilt, meaninglessness, groundlessness." *The irony of man's condition is that the deepest need is to be free of the anxiety of death and annihilation; but it is life itself which awakens it, and so we must shrink from being fully alive.*"[42] Thus we bind ourselves without a rope, to use the Zen expression, by selling our birthright of freedom for a pottage of petty securities, to use a biblical one. In order to avoid pain we choose not to look at something, but that something is so crucial to life that we end up restricting our consciousness within very narrow limits. We become the diner in a restaurant who complains that the food is inedible and moreover the portions are too small. This supports Jung: Life and death may be logical opposites but they are not psychological opposites. Buddhist teachings contain many admonitions against such dualistic thinking. We differentiate between good and evil, success and failure, life and death, because we want one and not the other. This does not work, however, because the two terms are interdependent: each gains its meaning only by negating the other, so affirming one half also maintains its opposite, the pole we strive to avoid. In order to live a self-consciously "pure" life, I must be preoccupied with impurity; my hope for success is proportional to my dread of failure; and my clinging to life will equal my fear of death.

The problem is that true life is negated by clinging to it. If the difference between normality and psychosis is a matter of degree, the restriction of the psychotic life-sphere merely aggravates our usual partial paralysis into a complete death-in-life. Since fear of death rebounds as fear of life, they become two sides of the same coin. Then genuine life cannot be opposed to death but must embrace both life and death. Rightly understanding and celebrating death also magnifies life, declared Rilke. Anticipating her death in a German concentration camp, Etty Hillesum experienced this paradox:

> By "coming to terms with life" I mean: the reality of death has become a definite part of my life; my life has, so to speak, been extended by death, by my looking death in the eye and accepting it, by accepting destruction as part of life and no longer wasting my energies on fear of death or the refusal to acknowledge its inevitability. It sounds paradoxical: by excluding death from our life we cannot live a full life, and by admitting death into our life we enlarge and enrich it.[43]

So the great irony is that as long as we crave immortality we are dead. This gives a different slant to the famous antiphon of Notker Balbulus: *media vita in morte sumus*, in the middle of life we are in death. La Fontaine noticed that those who already resemble the dead are the most reluctant to die. Aries is struck by the fact that in the late Middle Ages the idea of death was replaced by the concept of mortality in general: "The sense of death henceforth diluted and distributed over the whole of life, and thus lost its intensity." Yet life too lost its intensity at the same time, as he notices elsewhere: "It is a curious and seemingly paradoxical fact that life ceased to be so desirable at the same time that death ceased to seem so punctual or so powerful."[44] In the seventeenth and eighteenth centuries, the living corpse became a common literary theme; what better image could there be of our situation today? Aries' study supports the conclusion that the subdued neurosis of death-in-life which now passes for normality does not reflect man's unchanging nature, but characterizes only one particular, historically conditioned nature: ours. The issue becomes whether such a conditioned nature can be reconditioned or deconditioned.

An End to Transference? Becker is dubious. Transference is necessary for the "safe heroism" which is all that most of us can manage. Such projections are necessary to endure our life and our death, for "life is possible only with illusions." The problem is that even the most individuated and creative people can manage only a limited amount of autonomy. None of us can endure being our own sun. We must erect a god-ideal outside ourselves in order to live at all, and to avoid this being perceived as our own creation we must forget we have erected it. For this reason, Becker believes the promises of non-Western traditions such as Buddhism are deluded: "There is no way of standing on one's own center without outside support, only now this support is made to seem to come from the inside. The person is conditioned to function under his own control from his own center, from the spiritual powers that well up within him. Actually, of course, the support comes from the transference certification by the guru that what the disciple is doing is true and good."[45]

Freud and Ferenczi saw a more positive side to transference, for it also indicates a natural attempt to heal oneself through creating the larger reality one needs to discover oneself, as part of the patient's effort to cure himself. Thus Rank concluded that "projection is a *necessary unburdening* of the individual; man cannot live closed in upon himself and for himself." Then the question becomes how to choose between transference-objects: What is *creative* projection? What is *life-enhancing* illusion?[46] As Jung put it: What myth shall we live by? How can we ensure that our illusions are capable of correction, that they will not deteriorate into more dangerous delusions? This allows a more sympathetic view of religious faith than Freud had. Hegel pointed out that God is the perfect spiritual object precisely because he is the most abstract. If the problem with transference is that it fetishizes our highest yearnings into the narrow compass of particular objects, one solution is to expand those strivings and feelings of awe to the greatest possible extent: into the cosmos as a whole. "It also takes the problem of self-justification and removes it from the objects near at hand. We no longer have to please those around us, but the very source of creation".[47]

For existential psychologists such as Becker and Yalom, however, this can only be a lesser evil. Since transference involves projection, repression, and thus self-deception, all transference heroics are demeaning because they are unconscious and not fully in one's control. Man cowering before any god, even God, is not a satisfactory solution if transference always involves sheltering oneself in alien—because alienated—powers. "Transference, even after we admit its necessary and ideal dimensions, reflects some universal betrayal of man's own powers, which is why he is always submerged by the larger structures of society." So Becker too cannot help hoping. His exposition of Kierkegaard lets pass without criticism Kierkegaard's idea that, once the self has demolished all its unconscious power linkages and supports—the energies we usually draw on while unaware of their true source, the lie we have fashioned to live securely— "the self can begin to relate to powers beyond itself." He is even sympathetic to Tillich's version of this, the hope that man may become "truly centered" on his own energies.[48]

That brings us to the crux of the matter: If we consciously destroy our unconscious power linkages, those securities big and small that compose our character structure and stabilize our world, what will happen?

> Take stock of those around you and you will . . . hear them talk in precise terms about themselves and their surroundings, which would seem to point to them having ideas on the matter. But start to analyse those ideas and you will find that they hardly reflect in any way the reality to which they appear to refer, and if you go deeper you will discover that there is not even an attempt to adjust the ideas to this reality. Quite the contrary: through these notions the individual is trying to cut off any personal vision of reality, of his own very life. For life is at the start a chaos in which one is lost. The individual suspects this, but he is frightened at finding himself face to face with this terrible reality, and tries to cover it over with a curtain of fantasy, where everything is clear. It does not worry him that his "ideas" are not true, he uses them as trenches for the defense of his existence, as scarecrows to frighten away reality. . . . The man with the clear head is the man who frees himself from those fantastic "ideas" and looks life in the face, realizes that everything in it is problematic, and feels himself lost. And this is the simple truth—that to live is to feel oneself lost—he who accepts it has already begun to find himself, to be on firm ground. Instinctively, as do the shipwrecked, he will look round for something to which to cling, and that tragic, ruthless glance, absolutely sincere, because it is a question of his salvation, will cause him to bring order into the chaos of his life. These are the only genuine ideas; the ideas of the shipwrecked. All the rest is rhetoric, posturing, farce. He who does not really feel himself lost, is without remission; that is to say, he never finds himself, never comes up against his own reality. (Ortega y Gasset, *The Revolt of the Masses*[49]

This passage is so much to the point that I hesitate to quibble, but there is a difficulty: Its conclusion does not resolve the problem raised at the beginning. The individual should free himself from those fantastic "ideas," yet to what end? Feeling himself lost, shipwrecked, he looks around ruthlessly for something to cling to and ends up grasping at "genuine ideas." Are these genuine ideas any the less trenches for the defense of his existence? Or, to continue the analogy, can't a piece of driftwood sometimes work as well as a boat, and therefore, in Ortega's own terms, be as problematic? If ideas are what serve to shore up the self and shield us from anxiety, those of the shipwrecked may be as reassuring and therefore as dangerous as any other. Is there another alternative? Ortega's assumption here seems to be the same as Becker's: Once we realize that the human condition is chaotic and terrifying, we must cling to whatever we can in order to make sense of it. But what if, instead of finding oneself in such a fashion, one were truly to *lose* oneself—that is, let go, sink, drown? What might happen then? Do we really know? Madness is one possibility; is there another? R. D. Laing opined that the mystic swims in the same sea the psychotic drowns in. Are there different ways to die, with different consequences? Can one die *to oneself*? Then what is it that remains to live? And if we do not know the answers to these questions, how may we find them?

We have seen that existential psychology replaces Freud's sexual reductionism with the fear of death and (a hope within every fear) the desire for immortality. As different as these monologies are, they both imply tragic conclusions about the human condition. The most that the early Freud could offer was sublimation or rational control of the libido by the ego, which tries to make the best of a bad thing. There are times when psychoanalysis can only "transform your hysterical misery into common unhappiness."[50] His later view was more pessimistic, postulating a struggle between the life and death drives that death will always win. Becker can hardly be called more optimistic: If our deepest, most repressed fear is of death, we are stuck with various transference-projections or psychotically acknowledging the terror of our situation; for each of us is indeed going to die. Again, death always wins—in this case even before we die, in the psychic paralysis of death-in-life.

> Since there is no secular way to resolve the primal mystery of life and death, all secular societies are lies. And since there is no sure human answer to such a mystery, all religious integrations are mystifications. . . . *Each society is a hero system which promises victory over evil and death.* But . . . it is not within man's means to triumph over evil and death.[51]

The difference between Freud and Becker is that Eros and Thanatos are instinctual drives, while anxiety about death is a reaction of the animal who is conscious enough to have become aware of itself and its inevitable fate; so it is something we have *learned*. But what have we learned? Is the dilemma of life-confronting-death an objective fact we just come to see, or is this another dualistic way of thinking that has been mentally constructed and projected, that is, *a deeply repressed game which each of us is playing with oneself?* More precisely, the Buddhist critique of ego-self suggests that life-versus-death is not a game the ego plays, but that game whose play is the ego.

Then death/nonbeing-terror is not something the ego has, it is what the ego is. Anxiety is generated by this fictional self-reflection for the simple reason that I do not know and cannot know what this thing I supposedly am *is*. Hence the sense-of-*self* will inevitably be "shadowed" by a sense-of-*lack*. The irony is that this death/nonbeing-terror that is ego defends only itself. Fear becomes the only thing inside, which makes everything else the outside: that which one is afraid of. The tragicomic aspect is that the self-protection this generates is self-defeating, for the barriers the ego erects reinforce the suspicion that there is indeed something lacking in the innermost sanctum which needs protection. And if what is innermost is so weak because it is *nothing*, then no amount of protection will ever seem enough.

"Central to human experience is the struggle to evoke and preserve the sense of self as alive, and avoid the sense of the self as dead" (Lifton).[52] This gets at the dualism of life-versus-death, how each term feeds off the other; but is this struggle inevitable, as Lifton supposes, or is there an alternative which resolves that struggle? Any threat to our particular symbolic life-versus-death game becomes a danger to be taken with the utmost seriousness. But if the ego *is* that game, then ending that game should end the ego—which implies that the reflexive sense-of-self can die. What makes this more than idle speculation is that there is such abundant testimony to the possibility and perhaps the necessity of ego-death:

> No one gets so much of God as the man who is completely dead. (St. Gregory)

> The Kingdom of God is for none but the thoroughly dead. (Eckhart)

> Your glory lies where you cease to exist. (Ramana Maharshi)

> We are in a world of generation and death, and this world we must cast off. (William Blake)

A moving example of death and resurrection is one of the primary sources of Western culture, but examples are found in many religious traditions. The problem is demythologizing these myths, in order for their truth to spring to life again within our myth—in this instance, within the technical, more objectified language of modern psychology. Blake's quotation (from *The Vision of the Last Judgment*) points the way by implying that we are not seeing clearly but projecting when we perceive the world in terms of the dualistic categories of generation and death.

Buddhism. Blake's claim is central to the Buddhist tradition. "Why was I born if it wasn't forever?" cried Ionesco. The answer is in the *anātman*, "no self," doctrine: We cannot die because we were never born. Anātman is thus a middle way between the extremes of eternalism (the self survives death) and annihilationism (the self is destroyed at death). Buddhism resolves the problem of life and death by deconstructing it. The evaporation of this dualistic way of thinking reveals what is prior to it. There are many names for this prior, but it is significant that one of the most common is *the unborn*.

In the oldest Buddhist scriptures, the sutras of the Pali Canon, there are many references to *nirvāṇa*, the state of liberation, but few descriptions of it. The two best known accounts both refer to "the unborn," where "neither this world nor the other, nor coming, going or standing, neither death nor birth, nor sense-objects are to be found."

There is, O monks, an unborn, an unbecome, an unmade, an unconditioned; if, O monks, there were not here this unborn, unbecome, unmade,
unconditioned, there would not here be an escape from the born, the become,
the made, the conditioned. But because there is an unborn. . . . therefore
there is an escape from the born. . . .[53]

In another sutra, the Buddha declares: "The sage who is at peace is not born,
does not age, does not die, does not tremble, does not yearn. For him there
does not exist that on account of which he might be reborn. Not being born,
how can he age? Not aging, how can he die?" Escaping from the born suggests
soul-body dualism, yet other texts make it clear that this is precisely what is
being denied. In one curious passage such immortality is said to be attained
"by physical means," for the sage "touches the deathless element with his body."[54]

Similar claims are common in the later Mahāyāna scriptures and commentaries.
The most important term in Mahāyāna philosophy is *śūnyatā*, and the adjectives
commonly used to explain *śūnyatā* are unborn, uncreated, and unproduced.
The best-known Mahāyāna text, the laconic *Heart Sutra*, explains that all things
are *śūnya* because they are "not created, not annihilated, not impure and not
pure, not increasing and not decreasing." Nāgārjuna echoes this in the prefatory
verse to his *Mūlamadhyamikakārikās*, the most important work of Mahayana
philosophy, which uses eight negations to describe the true nature of things:
they do not die and they are not born, they do not cease to be and they are
not eternal, they are not the same and they are not different, they do not come
and they do not go.

In Chinese Buddhism, the *Cheng-tao Kê* of Yung-chia, a disciple of the sixth
Ch'an (Zen) patriarch, proclaims: "Since I abruptly realized the unborn, I have
had no reason for joy or sorrow at any honor or disgrace."[55] The seventeenth-
century master Bankei, one of the most creative and beloved figures in Japanese
Zen, believed he was at the point of death from tuberculosis when the following
experience transformed him:

> Then I felt a strange sensation in my throat. I spat against a wall. A mass of
> black phlegm large as a soapberry rolled down the side. It seemed to relieve
> the discomfort in my chest. Suddenly, just at that moment it came to me. I
> realized what it was that had escaped me until now: All things are perfectly
> resolved in the Unborn. I realized too that what I had been doing all this
> time had been mistaken. I knew all my efforts had been in vain.[56]

The Unborn became his central teaching. "When you dwell in the Unborn
itself, you're dwelling at the very wellhead of Buddhas and patriarchs." The Unborn
is the Buddha-mind, and this Buddha-mind is beyond living and dying.[57]

These passages (and many more could be cited) are important because, although it may not be clear to us what the unborn refers to, they are not just
philosophical statements but refer to some transformative experience. For a
case that combines such personal experience with a profound philosophical

acumen, we shall turn shortly to Japan's foremost Zen master and philosopher, Dōgen (A.D. 1200–1253).

We have seen that for Buddhism the dualism between life and death is only one instance of our more general problem with dualistic thinking. The paradox of such dualism is that the opposites are so dependent on each other that each might be said to contain the other. This paradox is more than an intellectual game. If it is important for me to live a pure life, I must be preoccupied with impurity: I must discriminate all situations and my responses to them into pure and impure. To bifurcate in this way is also to bifurcate myself from the situation; being *pure* in a situation becomes more important than *living* that situation. That is why "the only true purity is to live in a way which transcends purity and impurity," as Ch'an master Hui-hai put it.

Replacing the concepts purity and impurity with life and death yields a proposition by now familiar: The only true life is to live in a way which transcends life and death. The same problem applies to the dualism between life and death. We discriminate between life and death in order to affirm one and deny the other, and our tragedy lies in the paradox that these two opposites are also interdependent: There is no life without death and—what we are more likely to overlook—there is no death without life. This means our problem is not death but life-and-death.

> At issue are the boundaries of the self as a symbolized entity, and for that issue the end and the beginning are of a piece. There is a clear sense of the relationship between awareness of death and a delineated self. The second is impossible without the first. Even prior to the disturbing syllogism, "If death exists, then I will die," there is an earlier one: "Since 'I' was born and will die, 'I' must exist." (Lifton)[58]

There is an implication here Lifton does not consider: If we can realize that there is no delineated ego-self which is alive *now*, the *problem* of life and death is solved. Such is the Buddhist goal: to experience that which cannot die because it was never born. This is not a clever intellectual argument which claims to solve the problem logically while leaving our anguish as deep as before. The examples above refer to some experience more transformative than our usual conceptual understanding. It is no coincidence that the *prajñāpāramitā* scriptures of Mahāyāna also emphasize that *there are no sentient beings.*

> [The Buddha:] "Subhūti, what do you think? Let no one say the Tathāgata cherishes the idea: 'I must liberate living beings.' Allow no such thought, Subhūti. Wherefore? Because in reality there are no living beings to be liberated by the Tathāgata. If there were living beings for the Tathāgata to liberate, he would partake in the idea of selfhood, personality, ego entity and separate individuality."[59]

Such a claim is possible only if the dualism of life and death is not something in the objective world but a way of thinking projected onto the world, one of the conceptual structures with which we organize it. And if our minds have created this dualism, they should be able to un-create or deconstruct it.

This provides the context we need to understand the cryptic remarks of Dōgen, for whom the clarification of life and death is the most important issue in Buddhism. Dōgen's most pointed comments on life and death—his preferred terms are "birth and death"—are found in three fascicles of his major work, the *Shōbōgenzō*. First, from *Shōji*, "Birth and Death":

> If you search for a Buddha outside birth and death, it will be like trying to go to the southern country of Yue with your spear heading towards the north, or like trying to see the Big Dipper while you are facing south; you will cause yourself to remain all the more in birth and death and lose the way of emancipation.
>
> Just understand that birth-and-death is itself nirvana. There is nothing such as birth and death to be avoided; there is nothing such as nirvana to be sought. Only when you realize this are you free from birth and death.
>
> It is a mistake to suppose that birth turns into death. Birth is a phase that is an entire period of itself, with its own past and future. For this reason, in buddha-dharma birth is understood as no-birth. Death is a phase that is an entire period of itself, with its own past and future. For this reason, death is understood as no-death.
>
> In birth there is nothing but birth and in death there is nothing but death. Accordingly, when birth comes, face and actualize birth, and when death comes, face and actualize death. Do not avoid them or desire them.

From *Shinjin-gakudō*, "Body-and-Mind Study of the Way":

> Not abandoning birth, you see death. Not abandoning death, you see birth. Birth does not hinder death. Death does not hinder birth.
>
> Death is not the opposite of birth; birth is not the opposite of death.

The following passage, from the most important fascicle, *Genjō-kōan*, relates birth-and-death to time:

> Firewood becomes ash, and it does not become firewood again. Yet, do not suppose that the ash is future and the firewood past. You should understand that firewood abides in the phenomenal expression of firewood, which fully includes past and future and is independent of past and future. Ash abides in the phenomenal expression of ash, which fully includes future and past. Just as firewood does not become firewood again after it is ash, you do not return to birth after death.
>
> This being so, it is an established way in buddha-dharma to deny that birth turns into death. Accordingly, birth is understood as no-birth. It is an unshakeable teaching in Buddha's discourse that death does not turn into birth. Accordingly, death is understood as no-death.
>
> Birth is an expression complete this moment. Death is an expression complete this moment. They are like winter and spring. You do not call winter the beginning of spring, nor summer the end of spring.[60]

What is Dōgen saying in these passages?

Enlightenment is not other than birth-and-death: Dōgen does not offer the consolation of some heavenly pure realm or anywhere else transcendental, nor even the usual Buddhist expectation of rebirth (although he does not deny that possibility). We cannot escape birth and death, yet there is liberation in or rather *as* birth-and-death if we realize something about them.

Birth and death are not opposites: Birth is nothing but birth, death is nothing but death. Face and actualize them, says Dōgen: "Do not avoid them or desire them." Do not grasp at one and try to push the other away. Instead of repressing the problem of life and death, Dōgen's solution is a complete affirmation of both terms that is very different from our usual way of resigning ourselves to them. This does not contradict what was said earlier about the interdependence of life and death. To deny that life and death are opposites is another way to point out the problem with dualistic thinking. The mutual dependence of those supposed opposites means I live my life paralyzed by dread of death, and I resist my death clinging to the scraps of life that are being torn from my grasp. When life and death are not experienced as opposites they will not "hinder" each other in this way.

Then birth is no-birth, death is no-death: When at the time for dying there is nothing but death—with no repulsion from it nor seeking after it—then death is experienced as no-death. Elsewhere Dōgen correlates this with an alternative way of experiencing time, a present "which fully includes future and past" and so is independent of future and past. Chapter 2 will discuss how our flight from death takes the form of trying to make ourselves real *in* time, as something that persists *through* time; and how I must accept my death in order to experience the *now* which is outside time. (In) that *now*, birth is no-birth because no ego-self is ever born. But *if no "I" is ever born*, then there is only the act of birth, and if there is only the *act* of birth *then there is really no birth*. Instead, the act of birth-in-itself and (in exactly the same way) the act of death-in-itself become *lack*ing-nothing events, each of which may be realized to be complete and whole in itself when not experienced in relation to something else. As an earlier Ch'an master expressed it, when Buddha is in life and death there is no life and no death.

Yet, something does come to an end: the attempt at self-reflexivity which constitutes the Oedipal project which *is* the ego. If the ego-self is not some self-grounded consciousness but the process whereby consciousness tries to grasp itself—only to end up self-paralyzed—unmediated experience "of" the unborn is the final shipwreck of that project. The problem is resolved at its source. The ego-self, which has been preoccupied with making itself real, collapses and becomes no-thing. In terms of life-versus-death, the ego-self forecloses on its greatest anxiety by letting-go and dying right now. Die before you die, so that when you come to die you will not have to die, as the Sufi saying puts it. Of course, if the sense-of-self is a construct—composed of automatized, mutually reinforcing ways of thinking, feeling and acting—it cannot really die, it can only evaporate in the sense that those cease to recur. Insofar as these constitute our basic psychological defenses against the world, however, this letting-go will not be easy. It means giving up my most cherished thoughts and feelings about myself (notice the reflexivity), *which are what I think I am*, to stand naked and exposed. Hence, Buddhism calls it the Great Death. If there is no greater psychological suffering, perhaps there is also none more therapeutic, for this burns away the dross of life, all the symbolized money and power and prestige games that usually obsess us because they seem to offer us the hope of finally securing ourselves in the world.[61]

Earlier it was suggested that, if a sense-of-*lack* shadows the sense-of-self, the "purest" form of that lack is unprojected anxiety. Without any object to defend itself against, such anxiety can only gnaw on the sense-of-self. Chapter 3 will develop this by considering what Kierkegaard writes in *The Concept of Anxiety*, where he defines the paradox that the way to resolve anxiety is to become completely anxious: to let anxiety dredge up and devour all our "finite ends," those psychological securities we have hedged around us and then forgotten, in order to feel secure in a safe yet constricted world.

Needless to say, no such collapse of the ego-self can save the physical body from aging and rotting. Then, how does it solve our problem? Because the Buddhist critique of the "empty" ego-self implies that, contrary to existential psychology, death is not our deepest fear and (a hope inside every fear) immortality is not our deepest wish. They too are symptoms that represent something else: the desire of the sense-of-self to become a real self, to transform its anguished *lack* of being into genuine being. Even the terror of death represses something, for that terror is preferable to facing one's lack of being now: death-fear at least allows us to project the problem into the future. In that way we avoid facing what we are (or are *not*) right now.

One way to approach this is to reflect on whether immortality—the actuality of an existence that never ended—could really satisfy us. As much as we may fear death, would ceaseless life be the solution to our problems? Perhaps the only thing worse than not living forever would be living forever. Many have suspected that, like "the immortal" in Borges' story of the same title, our existence would sooner or later become a burden unless we discovered an eternal meaning-system to place it in, a cosmology wherein we have home and role. As the interminable succession of centuries undermined all my reality-projects, what anguish would accumulate! Mere immortality would become unbearable as soon as I no longer craved it. As with other symbolized (because repressed) games, victory in this form cannot satisfy me if it is really something else I want.

In this fashion, even our hope of immortality is reduced to a symptom, the most common symbolic way that what is actually an unrecognized spiritual craving to become *real* surfaces into consciousness. Conversely, death for us has become a complex symbol representing the feared failure of this reality-project, as well as a catch-all for all the ugly, negative, tragic aspects of existence that we cannot cope with and so project as the Shadow of Life which cannot be shaken off.

Then, Freud's death-drive may be as genuine as our desire for immortality: not an instinct, but a distorted, because still symbolized, way in which the desire to "let go" of ourselves manifests consciously or unconsciously. If the sense-of-self is a perpetual yet futile attempt to grasp and ground ourselves, the effort involved must sometimes become wearisome. Then there is no need to postulate two distinct drives. "Death and existence may exclude each other in rational philosophy, but they are not psychologically contrary. Death can be experienced as a state of being, an existential condition. The impulse to death may not be conceived as an anti-life movement; it may be a demand for an encounter with absolute reality, a demand for a fuller life through the death experience" (James Hillman).[62] If the sense-of-self implies death-terror, the possibility of genuine life may seem to require death. The danger, of course, is that one might confuse psychological death of the sense-of-self with physical death of the body-mind.

Why do we need to keep projecting ourselves indefinitely into the future, unless something is felt to be lacking *now?* The obvious answer is that we are afraid of losing something then that we have now, yet, many besides Freud and Ferenczi have found this unpersuasive. The standard reply is that if life is not something we have but something we are, there is nothing to fear because we shall not be around to notice (what) we are missing. As Epicurus stoically claimed, "The most horrible of all evils, death, is nothing to us, for when we exist, death is not present; but when death is present, then we are not." Montaigne too believed that we should fear death less than nothing: "Neither can it in any way concern you, whether you are living or dead: living by reason that you are still in being, dead because you are no more."[63] For life in the present there is no death, agreed Wittgenstein: Death is not an event in life, one does not experience death. Our life is endless in the same way that our field of vision is boundless.[64]

Their point is well taken, for it gets at the heart of what is wrong with making death-fear our primal repression—unless that death-fear is itself symbolic of a yet deeper fear, that right here and now I am not real. The Buddhist approach implies that, if nothing is lacking now, the issue of immortality loses its compulsion as the way to resolve our *lack*, and whether or not we survive physical death in some form is no longer the main point.

Such reflections inevitably bring us to the issue of time, which will be taken up in the next chapter. This is not a shift from psychology to metaphysics, but from one metaphysical conception to another, for a metaphysics of time is inescapable. Our choice is between a repressed metaphysics disguised as the objective, commonsense temporal system that we normally find ourselves within, or a more explicit and deconstructive approach which brings the repressed back into consciousness by revealing how we ourselves have constructed the time schema that now constricts us. Time does not really exist without unrest, wrote Kierkegaard; it does not exist for dumb animals, who are absolutely without anxiety. The basic problem is that our grasping at the future rejects the present; we reach for what could be because we feel something lacking in what is. Brown summarizes the matter brilliantly: Time is "a schema for the expiation of guilt,"[65] which in Buddhist terms becomes, Time originates from our sense of *lack* and our projects to fill in that *lack*. Pascal put it most bluntly: We are not; we hope to be. This tends to develop into a vicious circle. Uncomfortable with our sense-of-*lack* today, we look forward to that day in the future when we will feel truly alive; we use that hope to rationalize the way we have to live now, a sacrifice which then increases our demands of the future.

In this century the most influential philosophical examination of death and time has been Martin Heidegger's *Being and Time*. It had a significant impact on the first generation of existential psychoanalysts. For example, Ludwig Binswanger's influential paper "The Case of Ellen West" criticizes the lack of a temporal standard in the insane and contrasts their "inauthentically momentary mode of temporalization," such as occurs in "enjoying" (*sic!*), with "the authentic temporalization of ripening" that Heidegger considers to be the mark of authentic existence.[66] In the next chapter we shall see what is wrong with this understanding of temporality because we are now in a position to see what is wrong with Heidegger's understanding of death and time in *Being and Time*.

2

The Moving Image
of Eternity

The distraction of human life to the war against death . . . results in death's
dominion over life. The war against death takes the form of a preoccupation
with the past and with the future, and the present tense, the tense of life,
is lost.

Norman Brown[1]

Clor: Do you believe in the life to come?
Hamm: Mine was always that.

Samuel Beckett, *Endgame*

Being and Time

It can hardly be coincidental that Martin Heidegger's *Being and Time* develops
essentially the same relations among death, self, guilt, and time that have been
outlined in chapter 1—but inverts them. Heidegger's unfinished magnum opus
presents a mirror-image of that perspective, and so it is not surprising that he
draws the opposite conclusions.

The primary concern of *Being and Time* seems to be very different from the
psychological issues that were addressed in the previous chapter: not repression,
not even the nature of the human mind, but "Being." Heidegger regrets that
the recent eclipse of metaphysics means Being has been forgotten in our
preoccupation with beings *in* the world. He does not discuss the unconscious,
yet references to "forgetfulness of Being" soon make it clear that Heidegger
too is concerned with something much like repression. Again, the key repression
is death, and awareness of our own finitude is what can open the door to
authentic existence. For Heidegger the philosopher, however, understanding
death is even more important as a means to disclose the nature of Being,
whose "horizon" turns out to be *temporality*. The first part of this chapter will
summarize the double route—inauthentic and authentic—that *Being and Time*
travels from death to the self constituted by care, itself grounded in time, to
show that Heidegger's authenticity is not authentic enough. Both of his alternatives

30

are preoccupied with the future because they are our two ways of reacting to the inevitable possibility of death. In order to see how time might be experienced without the shadow of death, the second part of this chapter presents a Buddhist deconstruction of time, which discloses another alternative: deconstructing the dualism between the sense-of-self and time.[2]

Authenticity. *Being and Time* begins not with death but with a phenomenology of *everydayness*, the way we usually experience things in everyday life. Skeptical of metaphysical approaches seeking some eternal Being outside of time, Heidegger follows Husserl's dictum—to the things themselves!—and purports to ground his study with a look at the way we actually live. This will yield an understanding of the Being of humankind, and from that understanding we should be able to extrapolate to the nature of Being generally. In this way Heidegger hopes to escape the traditional difficulty for systematic metaphysics insofar as it tries, in Oedipal fashion, to ground itself by deriving everything from axiomatic self-evident principles. Although we can sympathize with the problem of a starting-point and Heidegger's attempt to find a new one, this one may be subject to another pitfall that Nietzsche warned of: "All philosophers have the common failing of starting out from man as he is now and thinking they can reach their goal through an analysis of him. . . . Everything the philosopher has declared about man is, however, at bottom no more than a testimony as to the man of a *very limited* period of time."[3] Does Heidegger's phenomenology allow him to explicate our true Being, or does his methodology too generalize a particular historical understanding of humans and their destiny? The latter seems to have happened to Freud in nineteenth-century Vienna, where sexual repression was evidently a major cause of neurosis; today classical neuroses with a sexual etiology, of the sort Freud built his theories upon, have become hard to find in the United States. This raises the more general philosophical question whether we can ever escape metaphysical categories. Does beginning with the structure of everydayness avoid metaphysics, or is there a metaphysics already embedded in our commonsense understanding of existence? For example, Buddhism criticizes our everyday way of living as *saṁsāra*: We experience life as frustrating because our usual understanding of it is deluded. Buddhism holds out the possibility of an alternative to this, a liberation from delusion, but such liberation is not common and so cannot be derived from an analysis of everyday life. The danger with Heidegger's approach is that it may conclude by reinstating and formalizing those historically and metaphysically conditioned intuitions which are implicit in our daily lives but are nonetheless wrong.

Heidegger distinguishes authentic (*eigentlich*) existence from our usual inauthentic existence, yet that raises the same problem in another form. How can we know whether his two possibilities are truly exhaustive, that there are not other perspectives from which both of Heidegger's possibilities look inauthentic? Life changes, our understanding of it changes too, and as we mature (or age) what once appeared authentic may come to seem inauthentic. Heidegger grounds his alternatives in the nature of temporality, but the range of his notions of temporality is just what can be questioned, as we shall see.

Heidegger's analysis of everydayness concludes that human Being is Care (*Sorge*).[4] If we avoid the usual metaphysical temptation to postulate some permanent essence in persons—a psyche or soul or Cartesian *cogito*—we can see that we are always concerned about deciding who and what we are becoming. In that sense we are forever ahead of ourselves, never complete but always in the process of planning and projecting future possibilities. Then how can we ever be whole? The emphasis on care seems to imply we are forever scattered by our daily concerns, dispersed into many unfinished affairs. It also seems to frustrate the philosophical and psychoanalytic quests for self-knowledge, for, if we are always ahead of ourselves how can any attempt at self-understanding ever be complete—and if not complete, how can any such self-understanding be accepted as certain, as irrevocably genuine?

Only if we can exist in a way that unifies our past, present, and future, says Heidegger. Such a "self-gathering" occurs in the resolute anticipation of my own death. Since my death is precisely the one event that I can never gather, the meaning of death is found not in its actuality but in its possibility: not in *being-at-an-end* but in *being-toward-the-end*. The usual inauthentic or "fallen" understanding perverts death into a public event that "one" encounters. Just as we gossip about what "they say," so it is "they" who die. Death is levelled off into an occurrence which eventually will reach me too, but which belongs to no one in particular—and as for me, not yet. This understands death only as actuality and overlooks its implications as always impending, irrevocable possibility. Freud also pointed out that at bottom nobody believes in his own death; we are all eager to demote death from a necessity to mere accident.[5] For Heidegger, this evasion in the face of death is an inauthentic Being-*toward*-death. More authentic openness to death reveals my uttermost possibility, which individuates me: Knowing that I must *be* my own death, that even the longest life is brief, can have the effect of pulling me together out of my dispersal in the idle talk and chance possibilities promoted by the anonymous "they." Such resolute anticipation of my death frees me to be myself.

> When, by anticipation, one becomes free *for* one's own death, one is liberated from one's lostness in those possibilities which may accidentally thrust themselves upon one ... for the first time one can authentically understand and choose among the factical possibilities lying ahead of that possibility which is not to be outstripped.

For this to happen death must be grasped, cultivated, and endured "*as possibility*." Heidegger summarizes his characterization of authentic Being-towards-death:

> Anticipation reveals to Dasein [literally "being-here," Heidegger's neologism for human life] its lostness in the they-self, and brings it face-to-face with

the possibility of being itself, primarily unsupported by concernful solicitude, but of being itself, rather, in an impassioned *freedom towards death*—a freedom which has been released from the illusions of the "they," and which is factical, certain of itself, and anxious.[6]

"Being-toward-death is essentially anxiety" because anxiety is the state of mind that keeps this constant threat before such an individualized person. This contrasts with the tranquillization of the everyday inauthentic attitude, which "does not permit us the courage for anxiety in the face of death." In anxiety "Dasein finds itself *face to face* with the 'nothing' of the possible impossibility of its existence."[7] Yet, this formulation also reduces my nothing to a possibility: Like death, such nothingness is something threatening me in the future, rather than characterizing my situation right now.

In *Being and Nothingness*, Sartre challenges Heidegger's view of death. It is true that dying is something nobody can do for another, but that does not distinguish death: It is just as true to say that nobody can breathe for me or sleep for me. There is no personalizing virtue peculiar to *my* death. The inescapable element of chance always infecting my projects is not my possibility but the "nihilation" of all my possibilities. From this Sartre draws the opposite conclusions: Death is never that which gives life its meaning, but on the contrary that which in principle removes all meaning from life.[8]

There is something wrong with this argument, yet something right about its conclusion. Sartre misses or chooses to ignore Heidegger's main point, which is the individuating effect that awareness of my death can have on my life. In psychoanalytic terms, it is the repression of death-awareness that paralyzes one's life, not the automatization of breathing or sleeping, which is why there may be a unique personalizing virtue in bringing that repression back into consciousness. But Sartre nonetheless points to the other truth about death: Awareness of my mortality not only may inspire me to seek the meaning of my life, it may also undermine those attempts by emphasizing their ephemerality. Tolstoy asked whether there was any meaning to his life which his inevitable death would not destroy, and that is not an easy question to answer as long as we remain within the duality of life-versus-death.

The key terms in the first part of *Being and Time* are resoluteness and authenticity. The relationship between them is clearer in German. The latter term, *Eigentlichkeit*, is more literally "ownedness" or "self-possessedness."[9] For Heidegger, what is important is to possess oneself: to bind one's inclinations into a whole, so one is not at the mercy of chance possibilities and casual distractions. This approach has unacknowledged predecessors—particularly Kierkegaard and Tolstoy's *The Death of Ivan Illich*—but Heidegger's formulation is nonetheless impressive, especially if read at the right age, in late adolescence or early adulthood, when one needs to decide what to do with one's life. I too have been moved by these words, yet more thought-provoking now is the question why they appeal so deeply and what they appeal to.

Perhaps the key metaphor in *Being and Time* is this need to "pull oneself together" out of the dispersion and disconnectedness of everyday, inauthentic existence, in which we are liable to be distracted by whatever the moment brings. This voluntaristic metaphor persists into the later analysis of temporality, where we read that resoluteness pulls the present out of dispersal on objects of immediate concern and holds it firmly in the future and past. But this image needs to be complemented by another one: the person so driven by his life-project that he never is where he is because he is always hurrying somewhere else—usually clawing his way up the ladder of social or economic success. Today, at least, such people are as familiar to us as the dispersed people Heidegger finds inauthentic, and as a solution to the problem of life this attitude may be just as inadequate. Heidegger is careful not to dilute his ontological analysis with ethical recommendations, so he leaves open the question of where to direct one's resoluteness. One is free to choose one's own life-project, for Heidegger's Being does not have any specific guidelines to offer.

This is where Heidegger needs to be supplemented by a psychoanalytic approach, for the theory of repression adds something that Heidegger misses: the return of the repressed in symbolic form. Both approaches see the need to become more conscious of death, to accept and integrate the anxiety that fear of death arouses, in order to liberate life. Becker perceives limits on how much death anxiety we can cope with, so our choices are stark: either the psychosis of those unable to forget their fate, or the repression that translates our death-anxiety into transferences and other more socially acceptable symptoms. Such repression often manifests itself as a deep need for security, as part of the low-grade neurosis called normality, but it can also appear as the compulsiveness of the person who *must* become wealthy or famous or powerful. Chapter 3 will consider Irvin Yalom's dual paradigm of death-denial: fusion and individuation. *Fusion* is hiding in the crowd and hoping to be taken care of; *individuation* seeks the specialness of heroism that tries to qualify for a better fate by becoming better than others.[10] How authentic will the resoluteness that Heidegger recommends be when it involves attempting to escape death through an immortality project? If it tries to fill up one's sense-of-*lack* by attaining some symbolic reality such as fame? Chapter 1 concluded that even preoccupation with the future can be a reflex of death-terror and *lack*-anxiety, an unconscious and therefore compulsive attempt to transcend death and groundlessness symbolically. That is the trap Heidegger fails to guard against and may himself have fallen into. Becker and Yalom, among others, have argued convincingly that Freud never analyzed his own fear of death, and therefore the psychoanalytic movement became his own immortality project, which is one reason why he reacted so strongly against any perceived threat to his patriarchy. Recent biographies of Heidegger provide considerable evidence to support similar conclusions: for example, his predilection to belittle other philosophers, especially contemporaries; a deep reluctance to admit he was ever wrong, either philosophically or politically; and, the most revealing, his obvious need to qualify as "a world-historical thinker."[11]

If there is something inauthentic about Heidegger's authenticity, is there yet another possibility more authentic? In Brown's *Life against Death* there is a striking passage that begins by agreeing with Heidegger, but only to draw opposite conclusions:

> If death gives life individuality and if man is the organism which represses death, then man is the organism which represses his own individuality. Then our proud views of humanity as a species endowed with individuality denied to lower animals turns out to be wrong. The lilies of the field have it because they take no thought of the morrow, and we do not. Lower organisms live the life proper to their species; their individuality consists in their being concrete embodiments of the essence of their species in a particular life which ends in death.[12]

If Brown and Becker are right, fear of death remains a problem whether it is repressed or not. Conscious or unconscious, it casts a shadow over our life. But what if death is not an event in life, as Wittgenstein says, nor a never-outstripped possibility, as Heidegger says, but one of the terms in a dualistic game we are playing with ourselves? Chapter 1 has argued that life-versus-death is a pre-eminent example of the dualistic way of thinking that deludes us, an important part of the conceptual structure we superimpose upon our world. Nāgārjuna's critique of *svabhāva*, "self-existence," implies that when we experience the world as a collection of things which are born and die, we are thinking as much as seeing. Jung said that some people are able to take their transference-projections back into themselves, and Buddhism recommends we do the same with these mental superimpositions. Then someone who does not project such dualisms, who dies to the devices that we use to flee the present, should experience time differently: not because one pulls oneself together but because without these superimpositions one is able to *let-go* of oneself.

> Not any self-control or self-limitation for the sake of specific ends, but rather a carefree letting go of oneself: not caution, but rather a wise blindness;
>
> not working to acquire silent, slowly increasing possessions, but rather a continuous squandering of all perishable values. This way of being has something naive and instinctive about it, and resembles that period of the unconscious best characterized by a joyous confidence, namely the period of childhood. (Rilke)[13]

Heidegger's own discussion of guilt can be turned around and used to invoke such a critique. For Heidegger, the call of conscience is what testifies that authentic resoluteness is in fact realizable. Conscience is an appeal to our innermost potential for being. This summons is silent, without any particular content.

Who calls? "The call comes *from* me and yet *from beyond me and over me.*" It is the voice of Being itself, he says, a summons to acknowledge that in the depths of our existence we are guilty, *schuldig.* Heidegger understands this guilt ontologically. It does not refer to any offense we have made or might make, for all moral blame presupposes this primordial guilt which is intrinsic to our being and which we must realize and accept in order to live authentically. He defines this guilt as "being the ground of a being determined by a 'not.'" The *not* refers to our finitude. We are finite because we do not choose when and where to be born but find ourselves thrown into existence, with limited options. Each choice limits us further by closing the doors on other possibilities. "By disclosing our finitude, conscience calls on us to decide in favor of our own possibilities and to abandon our delusions about a dead past and an impossible future."[14]

Our thrownness means, among other things, that we are not self-grounded. For Heidegger too, each of us is a nullity whose never-ending project is trying to become our own ground. "The Self, which as such has to lay the ground for itself, can *never* get that ground into its power; and yet, as existing, it must take over Being-a-ground. To be its own thrown ground is that potentiality-for-Being which is the issue for care."[15] This project of becoming-one's-own-ground is the origin of care. That is why only in anticipatory resoluteness is our potentiality-for-Being-guilty understood authentically and wholly: Clearly realizing my groundlessness implies shouldering the perpetual task of trying to become (but never becoming) my own ground.

This crucial issue of groundedness/groundlessness will be addressed in chapter 3, but here we see the connection between groundlessness and ontological guilt. An etymological point which Heidegger would appreciate is that the *schuld* of *schuldig* also means "lack." Chapter 1 has argued that the sense-of-self is always accompanied by a discomforting sense-of-*lack*, which it vainly tries to fill up. Heidegger, Sartre, and Buddhism agree in locating this *lack* at the very core of our being, for it refers to our essential groundlessness which is unable to ground itself. But they respond to this situation differently. Heidegger's account is abstract and dispassionate, although there is some philosophical bravado in his call for resoluteness and in his eagerness to contend "violently" against our tendency to let the meaning of Being be covered up. One senses that he, at least, hoped to fill up his own sense of *lack* by becoming a "world-historical thinker" who finally reveals the true nature of Being to a grateful posterity. The urbane Sartre is more pessimistic: Man is a futile passion and we are condemned to freedom. The insatiable for-itself, running after itself in an eternal and useless pursuit, is the source of time. Both thinkers accept our *lack* as fixed and try to make the best of it, but there remains a tragic undertone, more audible in Sartre, obscured yet also present in the early Heidegger.[16] We shall see that Buddhism is more optimistic that we can end our sense of a *lack* and our flight from it into the future, by realizing that from the beginning nothing has ever been lacking.

Temporality. Both death and guilt are implicit in care, and so is the self. For Heidegger the ground of them all is finally discovered in time. Authentic temporality is future-oriented. Anticipatory resoluteness, cultivating death as not-to-be-forgotten possibility and activated by the call of conscience that reveals the "lack" of my groundlessness, pulls me together out of my dispersion in chance possibilities and illumines my being as care. This implies a sense of the self which cannot be understood simply as a rational ego-subject *in* time. "The ego cannot be conceived as temporal, i.e., as intra-temporal precisely because *the self* originally and in its innermost essence *is* time *itself*."[17] More basic than the personal ego is the temporality that generates itself, determining the categories of the subject and enabling the subject to be self-conscious. The abiding nature of the self is grounded in the self-unifying nature of temporality.[18] We shall see that Buddhist thinkers like Nāgārjuna and Dōgen also claim the self *is* time rather than *in* time, but from that they draw different conclusions: To end the self is to end time.

In such fashion all the issues discussed above boil down to the nature of time, which is revealed as the "horizon" of the Being that Heidegger seeks, as close to it as we get in this unfinished work. In *Being and Time*, to be means to appear according to the temporal "ecstasies" of past, present, and especially the future. In *Kant and the Problem of Metaphysics*, Heidegger criticizes Kant for recoiling from a similar realization, in the first edition of *The Critique of Pure Reason*, that temporality is the source not only of pure intuition but of the categories of the understanding. Yet, we may make a similar critique of Heidegger, for he never asks *whether anything generates time*. Well, one must stop somewhere, but the irony is that Heidegger's own analysis provides the answer: It merely needs to be read backward in order to realize that "time is a schema necessary for the expiation of guilt."

It comes as no surprise that Heidegger's treatment of temporality also distinguishes two ways of experiencing time, inauthentic and authentic. The question, again, is whether these alternatives exhaust the possibilities.

With inauthentic life, scattered by the distractions of everyday concerns, we experience and understand time as an interminable sequence of "nows" that consecutively arise and pass away. These nows have been levelled off, each shorn of its intrinsic relations with the others so that they simply line up one after the other to make a uniform succession. One's attention is caught, now by this, then by that, because in this dispersal there is nothing to hold the nows together—which means there is nothing to hold one's life together. Such a levelling-off is inauthentic because it is "a fleeing which covers up," "a fleeing in the face of death."[19] In psychoanalytic terms, awareness of death, which threatens us in the future, is repressed by living only for the now, for it makes that now a sequence of scattered distractions.

In terms of these diminished, de-structured nows, Heidegger believes it is not possible to clarify the true nature of time. Authentic temporality, which "temporalizes itself primarily in terms of the future," is revealed only in resoluteness. "*Temporality gets experienced in a phenomenally primordial way in Dasein's authentic Being-a-whole, in the phenomenon of anticipatory resoluteness.*" Such resoluteness pulls the present out of its dispersal on objects of immediate concern and holds it firmly in the future and the past; this gives us the authentic present, which Heidegger terms *Augenblick*, "the Moment." In this way Heidegger understands our usual now-moment only in terms of something else he considers even more basic: the stretching-along of future-oriented temporality. "The 'now' is not pregnant with the 'not-yet-now,' but the Present arises from the future in the primordial ecstatical unity of the temporalizing of temporality."[20]

Yet, what if there is a now that *is* pregnant with the not-yet-now? Which cannot be understood as a mere sequence of levelled-off moments? The *nunc stans* or "standing now" of medieval philosophy (and the *philosophia perennis* generally) has traditionally been offered as such an alternative, yet Heidegger brusquely rejects this possibility in a footnote: Eternity conceived as a *nunc stans* has been derived from the ordinary (i.e., inauthentic) way of understanding time and as such does not need to be discussed in detail.[21]   From a Buddhist perspective, however, this dismissal overlooks something about the now-as-*now*.

The problem with both of Heidegger's alternatives, authentic and inauthentic, is that they are preoccupied with the future because in different ways they are both reactions to the ever-threatening possibility of death; thus they are two different ways of running away from the present. Inauthentic existence scattered into a series of disconnected nows is a fleeing in the face of death; authentic life pulled out of this dispersal by the inevitable possibility of death is more aware of its impending death yet still driven by it. Neither experiences the present for what it is in itself, but only through a shadow that the inescapable future casts over it.

> [W]hen man *denies death*, he refuses to live without a future, and therefore he refuses to live timelessly. In denying death he denies the condition of no-future, and thus he denies eternity. In short, to deny death is to demand a future—in order to avoid death, man pictures his separate self going forward in time. He wants to meet himself tomorrow. . . . Time is a substitute for eternity, for it allows one the illusion of continuing and continuing and continuing.[22]

What the present might be without the shadow of death remains undisclosed by Heidegger's analysis. A life scattered by chance distractions, insofar as it is in unconscious flight from death, is determined by that fear: perhaps paralyzed by it, perhaps propelled into a frantic quest for pleasure or reassurance. This does not imply that the only alternative is a future-oriented preoccupation with one's projects—which, as we have seen, may be a scarcely more conscious flight from death. "The 'purposive' man is always trying to secure a spurious and delusive immortality for his acts by pushing his interest in them forward into time" (John Maynard Keynes). Why? "We do not rest satisfied with the present," answers Pascal, "for the present is generally painful to us."[23] This contradicts Heidegger's conception of vulgar temporality, which for him is "lost" in the present, but ten minutes' meditation (e.g., *zazen*) confirms it. If our root problem is not fear of death, which looms in the future, but an always gnawing sense of *lack* right now, the reason becomes obvious: Dwelling (in) the present is uncomfortable because it discloses our nothingness, our groundlessness, and time is the schema we construct to escape that sense of inadequacy. Foucault points out that the mentally ill invoke the past only as a substitute for the present, as a need to defend against the present, and that the past is realized only to the extent that it involves a de-realization of the present.[24] In contrast, those usually considered well-adjusted use the future to defend against the present. Time allows us to flee into the future (when, we believe, our sense of *lack* will finally be resolved) or the past (when, as we recollect, there was little or no *lack*). As Dr. Johnson put it, complete felicity is discoverable only in our recollections or in our expectations. Each tends to feed on the other. Individually and collectively, we dream of the Golden Age to come, which will restore the dimly remembered Golden Age of the past (our childhood, Periclean Greece, the 1960s).[25]

In sum, time is the canvas we erect before us to hide the sneering skull, the bottomless void. On that canvas we paint the dreams that fascinate us, because they distract us from our immediate situation and offer the hope of filling up our sense-of-*lack*. But if our experience of time is conditioned by our fear of death and our denial of groundlessness, true acceptance of them should reveal something hitherto unrealized about the nature of time and the things "in" time.

Being-Time

He to whom time is the same as eternity
And eternity the same as time
Is free from all contention. (Boehme)

Eternity. If time is a schema for the expiation of guilt, a mentally constructed field-of-play wherein we labor to absolve our sense of *lack*, then to end that sense of *lack* would be to end time. That raises the issue of eternity.

In the Western tradition, eternity has usually been understood in one of two ways. The more familiar is the endlessness of time, duration without cessation. This is the commonsense notion embodied in popular religious images of immortality—for example, unending survival of the soul after death—although there are more sophisticated versions such as Nietzsche's doctrine of eternal recurrence, which will be discussed in chapter 4. However much we may want to live on indefinitely, there are serious problems with such a conception.

If the future is opened indefinitely, the pressure is taken off the present. There is nothing that cannot wait. . . . Like opening a sealed vessel to an infinite vacuum, the elements of life would blow out in all directions. What does it matter how the first several acts of the drama develop when there is an endless number to come? How can it be a drama at all? Life would have no risk, nothing would be at stake. There could be no curiosity about a future in which anything could happen that one wishes to happen. History would have no fascination or importance. It is even quite likely that the personality itself would vanish into the vacuum, since its temporal structures would have become meaningless. A person's character is shaped by tragedy, suspense, hope, regret, an occasional victory over improbable odds, and an occasional irreversible defeat—but in an indefinite existence all this would be meaningless. (Carse)[26]

The second conception of eternity, more favored by philosophers, understands eternity as outside time. The paradigm case for this is Plato's Ideas, mental forms subsisting in a timeless realm distinguished from the visible world of ever-changing sensory phenomena. This seems to have been an attempt to reconcile the unborn, immovable, and imperishable Being of Parmenides with the ceaseless flux of Heraclitus, although Heidegger and others have argued that there is no contradiction between them. Most of Western philosophy is a series of footnotes to Plato because it can be understood as various efforts to resolve the tension established by Plato's dualism between eternal forms and temporal phenomena: the medieval God and his creation, Descartes' mental and physical realms, Spinoza's substance and its modes, Kant's noumena and phenomena, and so forth. In each of these, the first term has explicit or implicit priority over the second, and Nietzsche was able to predict the nihilism of twentieth-century Western civilization because he realized that disappearance of that first term—God, substance, etc.—leaves us with the difficult task of revaluing the devalued second term. Even those who saw the problem with this dualism were not able to escape it: Hegel's dialectic finally subsumes the historical into the eternal, and Kierkegaard still understands the moment (*Augenblick*) as an intersection between the temporal and the eternal—a conjunction which presupposes their difference.

Boehme's little verse above, which he liked to write as an autograph, offers a third understanding of eternity: that it is *identical* with time. The only way to approach such a paradox is to view temporal relations and eternity as different perspectives on the same experience. Where can these two perspectives intersect?

In contrast to Heidegger's future-oriented temporality in *Being and Time*, this implies the pre-eminence of the present, that there is something about the nature of the *now* that we do not usually realize. According to my interpretation of Buddhism, this is due to our preoccupation with trying to make ourselves real *in* time, for the *now* does not offer security to the sense-of-self but requires us to confront the very insecurity we flee from because it threatens our sense-of-self. Perhaps that is why this third conception of eternity, despite its persistence within the *philosophia perennis* (see next paragraph), has remained a subterranean current in Western thought: because it does not grant us eternity in either of the two ways we want it, by perpetuating ourselves forever or by coming into relation with a reality that is impervious to the ravages of time. The attraction of both these conceptions is that they promise to ground us. The first denies our finitude by projecting us interminably ahead of ourselves, the second puts us in touch with a Ground that subsists outside time. If we can no longer believe in either of these eternities we must seek elsewhere, for a solution which does not involve gaining anything but uncovering something obscured by the way we have tried to fill up our *lack*. In existential terms, we need a *finite* eternity.

When we look for them, there are many versions of Boehme's identity between time and eternity in the now. Before Abraham was I *am*, said Christ, a paradox echoed seven centuries later by Ch'an master Chao-chou: "Even before the world was, this reality *is*." Plotinus: "There is all one day, series has no place; no yesterday and no tomorrow." Nicolas of Cusa: "All temporal succession coincides in one and the same Eternal Now. So there is nothing past or future." Ch'an master Huang-po: "Beginningless time and the present moment are the same. . . . You have only to understand that time has no real existence." According to Rumi, a true Sufi is called a "son of the Moment; he is not of time , . . the past and the future and time without beginning and time without end do not exist".[27]

It is easy to expose the elementary logical errors in such claims. Bertrand Russell's modern refutation of Parmenides' "block universe" rehashes Aristotle's classical objection: "If the before and after are both in one and the same Now, then what happened ten thousand years ago would be simultaneous with what is happening today, and nothing would be before or after anything else." The problem with this criticism is that it attempts to cram all temporal relations into the present as we usually understand it—one of a series of falling-away now-moments—whereas the above quotations are pointing at a different way of experiencing the present, however inadequate we may find their description of that experience. In order to gain some understanding what that different way involves, let us turn to the deconstruction of time found in the Buddhist tradition.

42   LACK AND TRANSCENDENCE

Nunc stans. The Greek debate between Heraclitean flux and Parmenidean Being has a striking parallel in the classical Indian controversy between the impermanence of early Buddhism and the immutable Brahman of Advaita Vedānta.[28] But when we look for a dialectical synthesis of the two alternatives, comparable perhaps to Plato's, we find a very different view of time/eternity presented in the "middle way" of Mādhyamika Buddhism. Rather than combining them in a hierarchical fashion which tacitly accepts the reality of both, Nāgārjuna refutes both permanence and impermanence by demonstrating their interdependence, leaving us with a paradox that denies the dualism between them: "All things are impermanent, which means there is neither permanence nor impermanence."[29] One way to express this paradox is to affirm that there is indeed that which does not change, and this is nothing other than the flux of change itself. Rather than contradicting the other, each alternative actually implies the other, for to make time absolute and to negate it altogether amount to the same thing. We can realize this if we stop thinking of ourselves as things *in* time.

As a thought-experiment, consider a solitary rock protruding above an ocean current. Whether one is on the rock or floating past it, it is the relation between the two that creates both movement and rest. The current will be measured by the rate of movement past the rock, but the rock is said to be at rest only because something else is defined as moving in relation to it. In the same way, our concept of impermanence—time changing—also requires some fixed standard against which time is measured. Conversely, the concept of permanence is dependent upon impermanence because permanence means persisting unchanged through time—that is, while other things are changing. As our lives change, what provides this standard of constancy for us?

For both Vedānta and early, pre-Madhyamika Buddhism, the self is that which does not change. They disagree about whether this concept actually corresponds to anything existent: for Vedānta, the true Self is immutable Brahman, for Buddhism the self is a delusion. But more important than this quarrel is that they both deny any dualism between self and world—in terms of the analogy, between rock and current. They negate this dualism in opposite ways. Early Buddhism denies there is any rock, for there is only a flux of interdependent conditions. The rock is a thought-construction, and the sense-of-self rather like a bubble which flows because it is part of the water, or a function of the water. In contrast, Vedānta denies that anything really flows, because there is in effect *only* rock. Change is not ignored but ultimately it is subsumed as illusory by the realization of immutable Brahman. However, this does not affirm the rock in relation to the current. Like Buddhism, Vedānta denies the self-existence of the rock as an ego-self counterposed to something objective. Vedānta avoids this by making the rock absolute: The rock negates the flux by expanding to incorporate it. For Vedānta, all phenomena are only transient name-and-form manifestations of Brahman; yet this can be done to the rock only by divesting it of all its rocklike characteristics—of *all* characteristics. According to Vedānta, Brahman in itself is *nirguṇa*, without any qualities of its own, which is why it can manifest as anything. Buddhism makes the same point about qualitylessness by saying everything is *śūnya*, "empty."

In terms of the analogy, then, Advaita Vedānta and Buddhism end up taking much the same position. Whether the rock disappears, as in Buddhism, or expands to encompass everything by becoming no-thing, as in Vedānta, what is experienciable is *the water flowing*. But now the dialectic reverses. If there is no rock at rest relative to the water, *there is no longer a perspective from which to be aware of any current*. Since everything is carried along together in the current, it means that the experience will be of *no current at all*. In short, if there is no permanent self (and no sense-of-self that thinks of itself as nontemporal) apart from the current, then there can be no sense of change. Or, to put it more precisely, change will be experienced as no-change, as will be explained below.

This becomes clearer when we realize that the Buddhist emphasis on impermanence does not involve accepting time and change as we usually understand them. *Saṁsāra*, literally, "going round and round," is the temporal cycle of birth-and-death that is somehow negated in nirvāṇa. For both Buddhism and Vedānta, time is a problem, not an abstract one but a very personal and immediate one in which our desire for eternity clashes with our increasing awareness of aging and death. Yet, time does not really exist without unrest, as Kierkegaard realized. What Hannah Arendt says about Plotinus makes the Buddhist point as well: "Time is generated by the mind's restlessness, its stretching out to the future, its projects, and its negation of 'the present state.'"[30] Since there is no future without a past, both Buddhism and Vedānta emphasize the role of "memory wrongly interpreted" (this phrase is used in the *Lankāvatāra Sutra*) in creating the illusory sense of a continuity *in* time which reifies into the sense-of-self. In contrast to Heidegger, however, they view this pulling-oneself-together as the problem rather than the solution. Such memories and expectations act as a mental superimposition obscuring the present, usually so much that we can hardly be said to experience it—which is ironic, of course, since from another perspective all experience can only be "in" the present. As Schopenhauer put it, no man has lived in the past and none will ever live in the future. But the ceaseless stream of our intention-al, purposeful activity tends to devalue the present moment into one of a falling-away series of causal relations, the means whereby we strive to actualize our ends.

The consequence of this is the same kind of karmic reversal that occurs with all repressed projections. Having projected these temporal/causal sequences to objectify time as something out there, I then discover that objectified time is something I am *in*. Instead of the past being experienced as a function of memories and the future as a function of expectations, the present is reduced to a single falling-away moment in a time-stream understood to exist objectively—a container, as it were, like space, *within which* things exist and events occur. In this way a delusive bifurcation occurs between time and the things in time, because time cannot be a container unless there is something for it to contain: objects. And in order for objects to be in time, they must in themselves be non-temporal: that is, self-existing . As a result of this objectification, we experience time and things as separate from each other, and each gains a spurious reality of its own—spurious, because the supposed self-existence of each is actually dependent on the other.

The first object to be reified in this way, the most important thing to be hypostatized as nontemporal (because it is the condition of all the others), is me: the sense-of-self as something permanent and self-existing. So the objectification of time is also the subjectification of a self, which arises only to discover itself in the anxious situation of being an apparently nontemporal entity nonetheless trapped within time and subject to it. This entity seems to have an autonomous reality, but the nature of its supposed existence is necessarily opaque to itself, since really it is nothing, or no-thing. As a mental construction, the sense-of-self has no ground that it could call its own. Chapter 1 argued that this illusory sense-of-self is shadowed by a sense-of-*lack*, because the feeling "something is wrong with me" is how we become aware of our nonbeing or no-thing-ness. It is not surprising that life becomes for us the futile project of trying to make ourselves real in one way or another.

This gives us a different perspective on Heidegger's grounding the self in temporality. The important point is not whether the self is grounded in time or vice versa, but that the spurious reality of each is dependent on the spurious reality of the other, since the apparent self-existence of both arises from their bifurcation. That points to the Buddhist solution, which eliminates this dualism dialectically by realizing that I am not *in* time because I am time; and if I *am* time I cannot be trapped by time. To be time is to be free from time.

To explain this we may turn a spatial analogy—usually dangerous, because spatial metaphors objectify time—to our advantage. We normally think of objects such as cups to be *in* space, which implies that in themselves such objects have a self-existence that is distinct from space. But of course a cup is irremediably spatial: without the spatial relations among its bottom, sides and handle, the cup could not be a cup. One way to express this is that the cup is not *in* space but *is* a particular kind of space, or is what space is doing in that place. The same is true for the temporality of the cup. The cup is not a nontemporal, self-existing object that just happens to be *in* time, for its being is also irremediably temporal.

This deconstructs the duality we have thought-constructed between things and time. As soon as we try to express this nonduality, however, we find ourselves limited by the dualism inherent in language, which bifurcates the subject of a sentence from its temporal predicates. To overcome this, Dōgen takes the liberty of poets to contort language, and conflates this duality by reducing one of the two opposing terms to the other: by saying that *objects are time* (objects have no self-existence because they are necessarily temporal, in which case they are not objects as usually understood); and, conversely, that *time is objects* (time manifests itself not in but as the ephemera we call objects, in which case time is different than usually understood). "The time we call spring blossoms directly as an existence called flowers. The flowers, in turn, express the time called spring. This is not existence within time; existence itself is time."[31] In the *Shōbōgenzō*, Dōgen combines subject and predicate in his term *uji*, "being-time." This illuminates some of his most cryptic statements:

"Being-time" here means that time itself is being . . . and all being is time. Each moment is all being, is the entire world. Reflect now whether any being or any world is left out of the present moment.

Time is not separate from you, and as you are present, time does not go away.

Do not think that time merely flies away. Do not see flying away as the only function of time. If time merely flies away, you would be separated from time. The reason you do not clearly understand being-time is that you think of time as only passing.

You may suppose that time is only passing-away, and do not understand that time never arrives. . . . People only see time's coming and going, and do not thoroughly understand that being-time abides in each moment.

Being-time has the quality of flowing. . . . Because flowing is a quality of time, moments of past and present do not overlap or line up side by side.

Do not think flowing is like wind and rain moving from east to west. The entire world is not unchangeable, is not immovable. It flows. Flowing is like spring. Spring with all its numerous aspects is called flowing. When spring flows there is nothing outside of spring. . . . Thus, flowing is completed at just this moment of spring.[32]

According to Dōgen, time never arrives or passes away, yet it does flow. This apparent inconsistency gets at the heart of the matter, but in order to resolve it we must also notice the second prong of the dialectic. It is not enough to use the interdependence of objects and time to demonstrate that objects are unreal, for their relativity also implies the unreality of time. As we saw with the ocean current analogy, if there is only time then there is no time, because there can be no container without a contained. If there are no nouns, there are no referents for temporal predicates. When there are no things that have an existence apart from time, then it makes no sense to speak of things as being young or old. "So the young man does not grow old nor does the old man grow old" (Nāgārjuna).[33] Dōgen makes the same point using the image of firewood and ashes, in a passage I have quoted in chapter 1:

Firewood becomes ash, and it does not become firewood again. Yet, do

not suppose that the ash is future and the firewood past. You should understand that firewood abides in the phenomenal expression of firewood, which
fully includes past and future and is independent of past and future. Ash
abides in the phenomenal expression of ash, which fully includes future and
past. Just as firewood does not become firewood again after it is ash, you do
not return to birth after death.

This being so, it is an established way in buddha-dharma to deny that
birth turns into death. Accordingly, birth is understood as no-birth. It is an
unshakeable teaching in Buddha's discourse that death does not turn into
birth. Accordingly, death is understood as no-death.

Birth is an expression complete this moment. Death is an expression complete
this moment. They are like winter and spring. You do not call winter the
beginning of spring, nor summer the end of spring.

Because life and death, like spring and summer, are not *in* time, they are
timeless. In the *now* that is prior to objectified time, birth is no-birth because
no self is ever born. What was stated in chapter 1 about the self may here be
understood in terms of time. If there is no one nontemporal who is born and
dies, then there are only the events of birth and death. But if there are only
those events, with no one *in* them, then there is no real birth and death.
Alternatively, we may say that there is birth-and-death in every moment, with
the arising and passing away of each thought and act.

This seems to leave us only the present: not, of course, the present as usually understood—a series of fleeting moments that incessantly fall away to become the past—but a present which incorporates the past and the future. Yet
even such a present-that-does-not-fall-away becomes awkward if there is no
longer a past or a future to distinguish the present from. "If someone says,
only the present experience has reality, then the word 'present' must be redun-
dant here, as the word 'I' is in other contexts. For it cannot mean present as
opposed to past and future. . . . Something else must be meant by the word,
something that isn't in a space, but is itself a space" (Wittgenstein).[34]

Something that isn't in time, but is itself time. This completes time's
deconstruction. If there is no past or future, then the present is refuted also,
and we are (in) Boehme's eternity-that-is-the-same-as-time. Without an objective past or future to contrast itself with, the no longer fleeting *now* cannot be
grasped or retained, and I myself can never become aware *of* that *now* because
I am not other than it. When the sense of *lack* at my core transforms into an
openness no longer defensive, the "I" changes from a wound that flees itself to
become the *now* that can never be lost. Without the reflexivity of a fixed self
to measure it, the moment expands to become everything and just as much
nothing, for it disappears as the stage of that objectified theater which we
construct and then find ourselves trapped within.

For life in the present there is no death.

If by eternity is understood not infinite temporal duration but non-temporality, then it can be said that a man lives eternally if he lives in the present. (Wittgenstein)[35]

When the Buddha was asked why his disciples, who lived such simple lives with only one meal a day, were so radiant, he replied: "They do not repent of the past, nor do they brood over the future. They live in the present. Therefore they are radiant. By brooding over the future and repenting the past, fools dry up like green reeds cut down [in the sun]."[36] Irvin Yalom makes the same point from the psychoanalytic perspective: Not the future but the present is the eternal tense.[37] Contrary to Heidegger, the man afraid of death does not hide in such a present; he is in hiding from such a present, for "to live in the present above time is to have no future, and to have no future is to accept death—yet this man cannot do. He cannot accept death and therefore neither can he live in the Now; and not living Now, he lives not at all."[38]

We have seen why this is so. In the *now* that does not come or go there is no security and no hope of filling up our *lack* but a groundlessness that, because it mocks the ambitions of the sense-of-self, is the source of our anxiety. The *now* gives us nothing to cling to, for when we cling we are not (in) the *now*.

Nunc fluens. Dōgen says that time does not arise or pass away, yet it does "flow." Thus far only the first part of that statement has been clarified. But how does being-time—the *now*—flow? Isn't that a contradiction?

This allows us to make amends to Heidegger. A man afraid of death may hide from the present, but as Heidegger emphasizes it is also possible to hide in the present. If the first is a person who never is where he is because he is always hurrying somewhere else, the second is the person who never goes anywhere. A Buddha is a Tathāgata, "one who does not come or go," yet the same phrase may point to the problem with someone who is psychologically ill. The French existential psychiatrist Minkowski commented on the "levelled-off" sense of time that depressive schizophrenics experience: "Each day life began anew, like a solitary island in a grey sea of passing time."[39] Someone obsessed with death-terror may deny all possibilities rather than acknowledge the one that cannot be coped with. But what Minkowski calls the "blocking of the future and fragmentation of the present" is not the being-time that Dōgen describes, for what is defective about this sense of time is that time does not flow. Notice the dualism in Minkowski's image: a solitary island in a sea of passing time, the present as that which resists the current. The difference may be illustrated by two ways of watching the second-hand of a clock. One may be paralyzed by the sense of time passing, mesmerized by the loss of all those moments which cannot be stopped from passing-away; or one may be liberated by the realization that the second-hand is going around *now*.

There is nothing mystical about this, just the simple fact that it is always now. It has always been now and always will be now, for there is something about this now which does not change, something that becomes obvious when we stop trying to get something from the now. This immutability is impossible to comprehend as long as we understand the present as a succession of fleeting now-moments, which implies that the only way the now could become eternal is by freezing one of those moments. Once we realize we are time, however, we experience something that sounds paradoxical when we try to express it: The *now* does not change (it is always now) but flows (that now never ceases to transform). While the *now* is immutable in the sense that it is always the same *now*, rather than a series of fleeting nows, nevertheless there is transformation, although experienced differently once one *is* the transformation rather than an observer of it. Such nondual change is smoother than we are accustomed to, more the continuous flowing that Dōgen refers to, for when not motivated by *lack* the mind does not try to fixate itself by jumping from one perch to another, staccato-fashion, always trying to fixate itself.

In one way, nothing becomes different: One still gets up in the morning, eats breakfast, goes to work, and so on. Yet there is something timeless about these activities. In place of the apparently solid self that does them and feels them to be lacking something, there is a groundless and therefore indisturbably peaceful quality to them. This double-dimension of changing-yet-not-changing is expressed in the Taoist concept of *wei-wu-wei*, the "action of nonaction" paradox also found in Buddhism and Vedānta:

> To learn, one accumulates day by day.
> To study Tao, one reduces day by day.
> Less and less is done until *wu-wei* is achieved.
> When *wu-wei* ['nonaction'] is done, nothing is left undone. (*Tao Tê Ching*)[40]

> Although while thus quiescent there is cognition of motion, nevertheless the mind, having attained its own cognition of rest or calmness and being indifferent to the motion, the state is called "The state wherein falleth the partition separating motion from rest."
> Thereby one recognizeth one-pointedness of mind. . . .
> One cometh to know that neither is the "Moving" other than the "non-Moving," nor the "Non-Moving" other than the "Moving." (From a Mahāmudra text of Tibetan Buddhism)[41]

> No-mind is that which is in action; it is that constant action which does not act. (Niu-t'ou Fa-yung, a Chinese Buddhist)[42]

> He who in action sees no-action, and in no-action action, he is the man of understanding among men; he is the controlled, acting perfectly. Having cast off attachment to the fruit of action, contented ever and dependent on none, though he engages in action yet he acts not at all. (*Bhagavad-gītā*)[43]

We end up with a *nunc* both *stans* and *fluens*: a now which does not change in the sense that it is always now, yet nonetheless flows serenely from just-this-one-thing to another just-this-one-thing. "Time is not the image of eternity," insists Berdyaev; "time is eternity which has collapsed into ruin."[44] But the eternity that transcends time, that time itself seeks, turns out to be time itself: that is, the actual nature of time, which also happens to be our own lacking-nothing nature, if the two are not delusively bifurcated. This breathes new life into Plato's definition of time in the *Timaeus*:

Wherefore he [the Demiurge father and creator] resolved to have a moving image of eternity, and when he set in order the heaven, he made this image eternal but moving according to number, while eternity itself rests in unity, and this image we call time.[45]

Time is the moving image of eternity, provided that we do not read into this any dualism between the moving image and the immovable eternity. In Buddhist terms, life and death are nothing other than the moving image of nirvāṇa.

<blockquote>

If no one else, the dying
must notice how unreal, how full of pretense,
is all that we accomplish here, where nothing
is allowed to be itself. Oh hours of childhood,
when behind each shape more than the past appeared
and what streamed out before us was not the future.

we take the very young
child and force it around, so that it sees
objects—not the Open, which is so
deep in animals' faces. Free from death.
We, only, can see death; the free animal
has its decline in back of it, forever,
and God in front, and when it moves, it moves
already in eternity, like a fountain.
    . . . it feels its life as boundless,
unfathomable, and without regard
to its own condition: pure, like its outward gaze.
And where we see the future, it sees all time
and itself within all time, forever healed.

</blockquote>

(Rilke, *Duino Elegies*)[46]

Appendix

The following schema summarizes the parallels regarding the relationships among death, the self, care, and time. It seems to put Heidegger on the same footing as the other two, but his conception is opposite because the arrows symbolize a different process. For Becker and Buddhism the arrows refer to mental-construction: for example, the psychoanalytic need to repress death-terror leads to the creation of symbolic immortality projects, and the Buddhist view of self as sense of *lack* leads to various projects to make ourselves real. For Heidegger, however, resolute care is based on authentic, future-oriented temporality. This means that, with Becker and Buddhism, our mental condition creates its corresponding temporality, but for Heidegger the sense of self is grounded in temporality.

DEATH → SELF → CARE → TIME

Becker

Mentally-ill: terror of death → damage to ego-structure → paralysis, partial (neurosis) or severe (psychosis) → objective time schema disintegrates.
Normal: denial of death → "healthy" ego-structure represses fear → transference, symbolic immortality projects → objective time schema necessary to expiate guilt.

Heidegger

Inauthentic: flight from death → dispersed self → distracted by everyday affairs → "vulgar" time as a series of levelled-off passing moments.
Authentic: awareness of death → pulls self together, accepts guilt → authentic care: anticipatory resoluteness → care grounded in authentic temporality, past and present united by concern with future.

Buddhism

Deluded: intuition of groundlessness, unconscious fear of nonbeing → sense of *lack* at core manifesting as death-fear, anxiety, etc. → various attachments and projects to make ego-self real → subject-object dualism—sense-of-self strives to real-ize itself in objectified spatio-temporal world.
Enlightened: the Great (Ego) Death: letting-go, evaporation of sense-of-self and collapse back into no-thing-ness → grounded in groundlessness: "from the very beginning, nothing was ever lacking" → freedom: no subjective need to real-ize self, so able to respond appropriately to situations → now which flows (Dōgen's *being-time*); self and world nondual.

3

The Pain of Being Human

When Samuel Johnson was asked, "I wonder what pleasure men can take
in making beasts of themselves?" he answered: "He who makes a beast of
himself gets rid of the pain of being a man."

—(*Murray's Johnsonia*)

The painful truth may be that Dr. Johnson's remark also gets at why we anesthetize
ourselves with alcohol, television, and so many other addictions; and, as he
knew all too well, the alternative to anesthesia is likely to be depression.[1] Today we have caught up with his insight: Existentialism highlights the anguish
of the human condition and psychoanalysis traces neurosis, including the low-
grade neurosis called normality, back to anxiety. Yet why is it so painful just
to be a human being? What causes our anguish and anxiety? Can the analysis
be carried any farther?

Chapter 1 presented the existentialist perspective on psychoanalysis: our primary repression is not sexual desire but death, and that denial returns to consciousness in distorted, symbolic ways which haunt us individually and collectively.
My critique shifts the focus from the terror of future annihilation to the anguish of a groundlessness experienced now. This groundlessness usually manifests in our consciousness as a gnawing feeling of *lack*, the conscious or repressed
sense each of us has that "something is wrong with me." On this account,
even fear of death and desire for immortality symbolize something else. They
become symptomatic of our vague intuition that the ego-self is not a hard core
of consciousness but a mental construction, the axis of a web spun to hide the
void. Those whose constructions are badly damaged, the mad, are uncomfortable to be with because they remind us of that fact. This reveals our deepest
longing to be ontological: the self wants to be *real*. Nothing less than *being*
can satisfy us.

In chapter 1, however, such a reinterpretation could only be adumbrated.
Chapter 2 explored the implications of this for time. Although *Being and Time*
argues for much the same relations among death, self, guilt, care, and temporality,
Heidegger reaches opposite conclusions, for he dis-covers the nature of Being

51

to be future-oriented temporality. Norman O. Brown's pregnant remark—that time is a schema for the expiation of guilt—suggested how to turn Heidegger's analysis upside-down. Since the understanding of finitude in *Being and Time* does not allow for the possibility of escape from the duality of life-versus-death, its distinction between inauthentic and authentic existence accounts only for the difference between unconscious and conscious awareness of death. Heidegger does not see how the return of the repressed can manifest itself even in resoluteness, as symbolic immortality projects, for example. The second part of chapter 2 presents a Buddhist deconstruction of time which argues for the possibility of a different way of experiencing time: a *being-time* that does not change but nonetheless flows, when the present is not a series of falling-away moments but always *now*.

Becker and Heidegger start with death as an irreducible datum and build their theories of finitude on that. We have seen that Becker is hardly more optimistic than Freud, for facing the truth of the human condition without psychological defenses leads to mental paralysis, partial (neurosis) or severe (psychosis). To hide from this fact is to find security in a world of projections and transferences. The best we can hope for is to integrate a little more of the fear of death into our lives, to learn to cope with a little more anxiety, and in that way become a little more aware of our transferences, so we choose less dangerous illusions, like God, over more dangerous delusions like fascism.

The early Heidegger is more resolute, as befits a philosopher who believes he has torn away the veil of everydayness to expose the meaning of Being; and he was deluded by fascism. Heidegger is interested in death as always outstanding possibility, for that possibility can transform my existence now. If, however, our problem with death is neither the threat of its actuality nor even its implications as impending possibility, but a *dualistic way of thinking*—a no-win game that the ego cannot stop playing because it is constituted by that game—there is another possibility: to end that game by ending the ego, in some yet-to-be-clarified way. Then the issue becomes: How is it possible to "die before you die"?

This chapter will explore that possibility further. In accordance with the three sources of our argument—psychotherapy, philosophy, and Buddhism—there are three overlapping sections.

First, we need to take a closer look at what psychology has discovered about guilt, anxiety, and transference, to see if they may be different symptoms manifesting the same problem: a repressed sense-of-*lack* that is intrinsic to the sense-of-self.

Second, we must evaluate those Western philosophers who have also described the human condition in terms of *lack*. Schopenhauer traces man's essential *lack* back to a blind will that ceaselessly strives without any possibility of finding satisfaction; our only hope is to extinguish ourselves by denying our will. Sartre's dualism in *Being and Nothingness* is no less pessimistic: "Human reality is by nature an unhappy consciousness with no possibility of surpassing its unhappy state, since our desire to be is a *lack* [*manque*] and since the for-itself is the being which is to itself its own lack of being." The for-itself of consciousness cannot help wanting to become what it can never become, the being of in-itself. Both thinkers deny the possibility of ending *lack* because they ground our sense-of-*lack* in basic metaphysical categories. Their challenge to wishful thinking must be taken seriously.

This chapter concludes by developing the Buddhist interpretation of *lack*, which agrees with much of the psychotherapeutic perspective yet suggests a way to resolve our unhappy state. Buddhism traces human suffering back to desire and ignorance, and relates all of them to our lack of self. The sense-of-self is analyzed into sets of interacting mental and physical phenomena, whose relativity leads to post-structuralist conclusions: The supposedly simple self is an economy of forces. The Buddhist solution to its *lack* is simple although not easy: If it is nothingness we dread, then we should become no-thing. As with other bipolar dualisms, the dichotomy between being and nonbeing can be conflated by yielding to the side we have been rejecting. In ceasing to deny my groundlessness I discover, paradoxically, that complete groundlessness (nonbeing) is equivalent to groundedness (being). This reveals that from the very beginning there has never been any *lack*, because there has never been any self-existing self apart from the world. The problem of desire is solved as the "bad infinity" of unsatisfiable *lack* transforms into a "good infinity" which needs nothing and therefore can freely become anything.

Psychological Anxiety

Guilt. Guilt has become an immense problem for modern man and it seems to be getting worse. In *Civilization and Its Discontents*, Freud understands a heightening sense of guilt as the price we pay for advances in human culture, but that price is so high that guilt has now become "the most important problem in the development of civilization." Norman O. Brown sees social organization as a structure of shared guilt: The burden is so heavy it must be shared in order to be expiated collectively. According to Otto Rank, contemporary man is neurotic because he suffers from a consciousness of sin just as much as premodern man did, but without believing in the religious conception of sin, which leaves us without a means of expiation. In the rituals of archaic man a sense of indebtedness was balanced by the belief that the debt could be repaid; today we are oppressed by the realization that the burden of guilt is unpayable.[2] Even the possibility of expiation is denied us because we are not aware that what is bothering us is guilt. Hence unconscious guilt accumulates individually and collectively, with consequences that periodically become disastrous. Is this the price of progress, or do we have a bad conscience about what we are doing to each other and to the earth? Or is there another possibility: Can the source of our guilt be distinguished from the reasons we invent to rationalize it?

Freud traced guilt back to the biologically transmitted memory of a prehistoric primal deed, sons banding together to kill their autocratic father. With each generation this process is internalized anew in the Oedipal complex; the same instinctive wishes recur and cannot be concealed from the superego, producing guilt. The child has death-wishes toward parents yet is also dependent upon their love. Freud saw a parallel between the libidinal development of an individual and the socializing process of civilization. Both require the internalization of a superego, leading to inevitable conflict with instinctual urges. At its best, this frustration is sublimated into creative activities, but even then there will be resentment which, introverted back against the self, becomes guilt.

It is fascinating to observe the primal deed reenacted with Freud as psychoanalytic father and Jung, Adler, Rank, and others as the rebellious sons. Becker's analysis of Freud's character, demonstrating his possessiveness toward the psychoanalytic movement as his own immortality project, implies that Freud's own unanalyzed motivations helped to make his deepest fears come true. Just as striking is that Freud, a secularized Jew, locates the beginnings of our "original sin" in a moral infringement against the Father which occurred at the beginning of history and has been passed down biologically since then. As in the Old Testament, we are not personally at fault for the initial violation, yet we inherit the consequences. Likewise, we cannot help it that in infancy we develop death-wishes toward our parents, but, given that such hostility arises toward the ones who nurture us, guilt is an understandable reaction. Both myths explain the origin of guilt feelings by giving us moral reasons which parallel the way guilt is believed to operate in everyday life: When we do (or want to do) something wrong, we feel bad about it. The mechanism is presumed to be the same. Original sin may be proto-historical, biologically inherited, pre-conscious, but it is only a repressed version of what happens whenever we infringe against the natural order. In terms of the distinction that the next paragraph will make between neurotic and ontological guilt, all guilt is neurotic for Genesis and Freud because we have all sinned.

Chapter 1 has described how existential psychology transforms the Oedipal complex into an Oedipal project: the attempt of the individualizing child to become father of him/herself. The Buddhist perspective makes this more than a flight from death. It is the sense-of-self's attempt to become self-grounding, to end its dependence on others by becoming autonomous, that is, *self*-conscious. If this is the primary meaning of the Oedipal situation, then the guilt that arises need not be traced back to ambivalent wishes, for it has a more primordial origin in the sense of *lack* inevitably deriving from the repressed intuition of self-consciousness that it does not self-exist. Such basic "guilt" is not neurotic but ontological. It is not a consequence of something I have

done, but the fact that I am—yet only "sort of." Ontological guilt is the contradiction between this sense that *I am* and the suspicion that *I am not*. Their
clash is the sense-of-*lack*, which generates the *I should be*. . . The tragedy is
that I "awaken" into being only to be confronted by my lack of being. Schizophrenics feel guilty just for existing because this contradiction is less repressed
for them.

The prehistories of Genesis and Freud's primal deed mythologize the fact
that this mode of awareness is not some natural way of experiencing the world
but historically conditioned. According to Erich Neumann, the full emergence
of the ego abolishes the original paradisal situation; this "is experienced as
guilt, and moreover as original guilt, a fall."[3] The evolution of *Homo sapiens*
into self-consciousness alienated the human species from the rest of the world,
which became objectified for us as we became subjects looking out at it. This
original sin is passed down to every generation as the linguistically conditioned
and socially maintained delusion that each of us is a consciousness existing
separately from the world.

The fact that this is a conditioning raises the possibility of a reconditioning
or a deconditioning. However, Kierkegaard and Heidegger understand ontological guilt as a datum to be accepted by those who become aware of their
finitude and attempt to live authentically. For Heidegger, we are guilty because guilt is the necessary attribute of a finite being who is constituted by a
"not." Acknowledging this pulls my dispersed life together and motivates me
to acknowledge my existence as a perpetual task. For Kierkegaard, the greater
one's genius the more profoundly one discovers guilt, because guilt is "the
opposite of freedom." "The relation of freedom to guilt is anxiety, because
freedom and guilt are still only possibilities." His understanding of their relationship is striking: freedom and guilt polarizing out of anxiety—in the same
way that the sense-of-self and sense-of-*lack* polarize? Kierkegaard sees that anxiety
wants to become guilt: "As soon as guilt is posited, anxiety is gone and repent-
ance is there."[4] He celebrates such guilt as the realization of sin and the possibility of faith. Yet there is another possibility. Perhaps even the "purest" guilt
is a device whereby ontological anxiety escapes from its dread-of-nothingness
by finding an object to worry about—in this instance, one's own objectified
sense-of-self. If so, even ontological guilt can be deconstructed back into something
more primordial—anxiety (an issue taken up in the next section). If depth of
ontological guilt is proportional to sense of self, such pure unprojected anxiety
may be so difficult to endure because it consumes the sense-of-self; even ontological guilt is preferable, for to feel bad about the sense-of-self is another way
to maintain it.

Why do we need to feel guilty, and accept suffering, sickness, and death as
condign punishment? What role does that guilt play in determining the meaning
of our lives? As so often, the best answer comes not from Freud but from an

existentialist. "Original sin: a new sense has been invented for pain" (Nietzsche).[5] Even the feeling of wrongdoing gives us some sense of control over our own destinies, because an explanation has been provided for our sense of *lack*. "The ultimate problem is not guilt but the incapacity to live. The illusion of guilt is necessary for an animal that cannot enjoy life, in order to organize a life of nonenjoyment" (Brown).[6] In *The Genealogy of Morals*, Nietzsche observes that man will suffer readily if he is given a reason for his suffering. Since nothing is more painful to endure than formless, unobjectified *lack*, we need to project it onto something, because only thus can we get a handle on it. This is the foundation of our two "blaming systems." Sense of *lack* seeks an object; if that object is found outside we react with anger, if directed inside it becomes guilt (introjected anger, according to psychoanalysis). In "Some Character Types Met with in Psycho-Analytic Work" (1916), Freud describes "criminals from a sense of guilt," whose guilt feelings are so powerful that committing a misdeed actually brings relief—which makes sense, if what they crave is something specific to feel guilty about and to be able to atone for. "Guilt implies responsibility; and however painful guilt is, it may be preferable to helplessness."[7] We are all too familiar with collective examples of the other blaming system: racism, anti-semitism, nationalism. If social organization is a structure of shared guilt, what better solution to one's communal sense of *lack* than to project it onto a common scapegoat? This is the *ressentiment* that Nietzsche detected in the soul of modern man:

> *The spirit of revenge*: my friends, that, up to now, has been mankind's chief concern; and where there was suffering, there was always supposed to be punishment.
>
> As far as man has thought, he has introduced the bacillus of revenge in things. He has even made God ill with it, he has *deprived existence* in general of its *innocence*.[8]

This reveals the problem with postulating an original sin as the ultimate cause of our suffering. Instead of helping us end our sense-of-*lack*, it reifies our *lack*—makes it self-existing—by providing it with a pedigree. It also empowers those institutions, religious and otherwise, that claim to have control over its absolution.

In contrast, Buddhism does not reify the sense of *lack* into an original sin, even though our particular problems with attachment and ignorance are historically conditioned. This is an important way nondualisms like Buddhism differ from theism. If you believe in an all-loving, all-powerful God, our suffering can be justified only by postulating a primal act of disobedience against Him. Śākyamuni Buddha declared that he was not interested in the metaphysical issue of origins, and emphasized that he had one thing only to teach: *duḥkha* and the end of *duḥkha*, the fact of our suffering now and the path to end that suffering. This means the Buddhist path is nothing other than a way to resolve our sense of *lack*. Since there was no primeval offense and no expulsion from the Garden, there is nothing that needs to be gained. Our *lack* turns out to be the sense that there is a lack, which does not mean we can simply deny or try to ignore that sense. For Buddhism our problem turns out to be paradoxical: The actual problem is our deeply repressed fear that our ground-lessness/no-thing-ness is a problem. When I stop trying to fill up that hole at my core by vindicating or realizing myself in some symbolic way, something happens to it, and to me.

This is easy to misunderstand, for the letting-go that is necessary is not directly accessible to consciousness. The ego cannot absolve its own *lack* because the ego is the other side of that *lack*. *In terms of life and death*, the ego is that which believes itself to be alive and fears death; hence the ego, although only a mental construction, will face its imminent disappearance with horror. Uncovering that repression, recovering the denial of death for consciousness, requires the courage to suffer. Our struggle against death is usually redirected into symbolic games of competition, as the urge to defeat our opponent or at least be a little better than our neighbor. To free us from the paralysis of death-in-life, the energy which is distorted into such symptomatic activities must be translated back into its more original form, the terror of death, and that terror endured. In contrast to Heidegger, the Buddhist path is not reso-luteness but simple awareness, which Buddhist meditation cultivates. One does not do anything with that anguish except develop the ability to dwell in it or rather *as* it; then the anguish, having nowhere else to direct itself, consumes the sense-of-self. Since the sense-of-*lack* is the other pole of the sense-of-self—tails to its head, but one coin— primordial *lack*-as-anguish devours not only the ego-self but itself. It is like the matter and anti-matter of quantum physics collapsing back into each other and disappearing, to reveal the ground they polarized out of.

The above account in terms of life and death may also be expressed in terms of *lack*-experienced-as-guilt. When ontological guilt is experienced more "purely"— as the amorphous feeling that "something is wrong *with me*"—there seems to be no way to cope with it, so normally we become conscious of it as the neurotic guilt of "not being good enough" in this or that particular way. The guilt expended in these situations can be converted back into ontological guilt, and that guilt must be endured without evasion; again, the method for doing this is awareness. The result is that one becomes profoundly guilty and feels completely worthless, not because of anything one has done but simply be-cause one *is*. Letting go of the mental devices that sustain my self-esteem, I stand alone and vulnerable. Such guilt, experienced in or rather as the core of one's being, cannot be resolved by the ego-self; there is nothing one can do with it except be conscious of it and bear it. James Hillman makes a similar point about dealing with depression: "Depression is still the Great Enemy. More personal energy is expended in manic defenses against, diversions from, and denials of it than goes into other supposed psychopathological threats to society. . . . It reminds of death. *The true revolution begins in the individual who can be true to his or her depression.*[9] Such a revolution also begins in those who are true to their ontological guilt.

Accounts of guilt abound in theistic mysticism, but it is easy to go astray by understanding ontological guilt as neurotic guilt. The dualism between man and God, the one as lowly and "stinking with sin" as the other is lofty and perfect, encourages this. Even so enlightened a text as *The Cloud of Unknowing* falls into the trap of encouraging self-loathing: "And no wonder if thou loathe and hate to think on thyself, when thou shalt always feel sin a foul stinking lump, thou knowest never what, betwixt thee and thy God: the which lump is no other thing than thyself." The "over-abundant love and worthiness of God in himself" is contrasted with "the filth, the wretchedness, and the frailty of man, into the which he is fallen by sin, and the which he must always feel in some degree the whiles he liveth in this life, be he never so holy."[10] The problem with drawing such theological conclusions is that our sense of ontological guilt is vindicated as something we deserve; this transforms it back into a neurotic guilt and we end up aggrandizing the wretched ego-self in the guise of attacking it.

It is difficult to avoid such comparisons as long as one distinguishes between God and man, for "if you keep the opposition between God and man, then you finally arrive, whether you like it or not, at the Christian conclusion . . . that all good comes from God, and all evil from man. With the absurd result that the creature is placed in opposition to its creator and a positively cosmic or daemonic grandeur in evil is imputed to men" (Jung).[11] Buddhism denies both God and ego-self, for in the duality of autonomous self and the great Self of monotheism ("I am what I am") each pole feeds off the other. Therefore Buddhism is able to offer another alternative to such invidious comparisons. The point is neither to flee from the pure-guilt-as-anguish by objectifying it in some fashion, nor to identify with it by abasing oneself, but to let it burn itself out, like a fire that exhausts its fuel, which in this case is the sense-of-self. If we cultivate the ability to dwell *as* it, then ontological guilt, finding nothing else to be guilty *for*, consumes the sense-of-self and thereby itself as well. Since this devours one's compensatory self-importance, one becomes a completely ordinary person, who feels no different from anyone else and no need to be different from anyone else. Contrary to Heidegger, this is the end of experiencing our existence as a burden to be shouldered, inasmuch as the heavy weight of life originates in the need to secure or vindicate ourselves. According to Buddhism, the ego-as-*lack* dissolves in the experience of one's true nature as a groundlessness which has nothing to gain and nothing to lose, and is therefore free.

What is the seal of freedom attained? No longer to be ashamed of oneself. (Nietzsche)

Anxiety. It can be no coincidence that everything said above about guilt must now be restated in terms of anxiety. The first seems to be a more limited case of the second. Even ontological guilt has an object: one's own sense of self, for it is the self that the self feels bad about. In anxiety, however, *lack* attains its originary form, which is formless. Cultivating such objectless anxiety is the most direct route to realizing our groundlessness.

Freud gradually realized that anxiety is at the heart of the humanization process. He first understood anxiety as a byproduct of repression but soon reversed himself. "It was not the repression that created the anxiety; the anxiety was there earlier and created the repression." This makes ego rather than libido the locus of anxiety. Although Freud emphasized that his concept of the unconscious was derived from the theory of repression, he never succeeded in answering to his own satisfaction why there is repression in the first place. In neurotic phobias the symptom has been constructed in order to avoid an outbreak of anxiety, which traces neurosis and repression back to anxiety. But that just pushes the problem back a step: "We have once more come unawares upon the riddle which has so often confronted us: whence does neurosis come— what is its ultimate, its own peculiar *raison d'etre?* After tens of years of psycho-analytic labors, we are as much in the dark about this problem as we were at the start."[12]

Among the next generation of psychoanalysts, Karen Horney and H. S. Sullivan had the most interesting things to say about anxiety. Horney's distinction between *Urangst* and basic anxiety seems to parallel the above distinction between ontological and neurotic guilt. *Ur-angst*, or "primal anxiety", is prior to the instinctive drives; it is normal, indeed unavoidable, in such situations as the threat of death. When, due to a variety of possible influences, a child is not permitted to grow according to his own needs and possibilities, he may develop "a profound insecurity and vague apprehensiveness, for which I use the term basic anxiety. It is his feeling of being isolated and helpless in a world conceived as potentially hostile." Living in a competitive society, such a child will usually develop an urgent need to rise above others. His idealized image of himself is transformed into an idealized self, which becomes more real to him than his real self, resulting in "the search for glory." The other side of this basic anxiety is basic hostility, and other neurotic trends are security measures arising out of that hostility.[13]

Is there anyone, child or adult, without this well-named "basic" anxiety? Horney's basic anxiety is the basic situation for all of us, due not to some adverse influences that happen to affect all of us but to the basically anxious nature of the ego. If a solution is to be found to the predicament that psychoanalysis has discovered, it is not in repairing the ego but in recognizing the basically uncomfortable nature of that ego and discovering the origin of that discomfort. For Horney, "anything may provoke anxiety which is likely to jeopardize the individual's specific protective pursuits, his specific neurotic trends," but this puts the cart before the horse, as Freud realized, for why do we have protective pursuits and neurotic trends?

Harry Stack Sullivan saw a more essential connection between anxiety and the formation of the self. Anxiety originally arises out of the infant's apprehension of the disapproval of significant persons in his world. Like Freud, Sullivan viewed anxiety as "cosmic," something that invades us totally, and the self is formed out of the infant's necessity to deal with such anxiety-creating experiences, to defend against that anxiety. The self "comes into being as a dynamism to preserve the feeling of security." This pertains not only to behavior but to awareness itself: "The self comes to control awareness, to restrict one's consciousness of what is going on in one's situation very largely by the instrumentality of anxiety, with, as a result, a dissociation from personal awareness of those tendencies of the personality which are not included or incorporated in the approved structure of the self."[14]

We could not ask for a formulation more in harmony with the self *as lack*: It is not merely that something is denied, for that denial is what constitutes the self. So much for the nobility of Cartesian ego-consciousness: The sense-of-self is reduced from the locus of rationality to a pattern of evasions. No wonder it feels so uncomfortable, for coping with discomfort is its role, and no wonder we never realize who or what we are, for such a consciousness has no being, only a function. This makes the sense-of-self into a double *lack*: an *ungrounded* awareness whose task is to *repress* anxiety.

Just as ontological guilt wants to become a more specific fault, so I can get a handle on what is wrong with me, anxiety wants to become fear. Freud distinguished between anxiety (in which there is no object threat) and fear (in which there is), but psychotherapists since him have found that distinction difficult to maintain in practice. According to Rollo May, "anxiety is the basic underlying reaction . . . and fear is the expression of the same capacity in its specific, objectivated form." Anxiety "is objectless because it strikes at that basis of the psychological structure on which the perception of one's self as distinct from the world of objects occurs."[15] It is formless, nonspecific anxiety regarding the nature of the self that takes form in all fear, in which case Stekel was almost right when he said that all fear is fear of death. According to my Buddhist interpretation, such pure anxiety reflects the ego-self's intuition of its own unreality; how reassuring, then, to project this outside as the threat posed by an external object. If the self is constituted by the denial of anxiety, as Sullivan seems to say, to objectify anxiety into fear will also subjectify the sense-of-self as that which copes with the fear—and as *that which needs to be protected from the threat.* It is another variation on the vicious circle mentioned in chapter 1: The stronger my defenses become, the greater my sense that there is something weak which needs to be protected. How carefully it needs to be guarded if we do not know what it is; and how obsessively so if it is nothing! Then no defense less than total control of any situation can long satisfy us.

Self-observation.—Man is very well defended against himself, against being reconnoitred and besieged by himself, he is usually able to perceive of himself only his outer walls. The actual fortress is inaccessible, even invisible to him, unless his friends and enemies play the traitor and conduct him in by a secret path. (Nietzsche)[16]

If the objectification of anxiety into specific fears also subjectifies the self that fears, then ending anxiety (if that is possible) also implies ending the sense-of-self as something autonomous and self-grounding. Freud saw that anxiety invades us wholly, and said that what the ego fears in such anxiety "is in the nature of an overthrow or extinction." Rollo May adds that in anxiety "the security base of the individual is threatened, and since it is in terms of this security base that the individual has been able to experience himself as a self in relation to objects, the distinction between subject and object also breaks down."[17] No Buddhist could express it better. For psychoanalysis, such breakdown is a definition of psychosis. For Buddhism, it may describe enlightenment:

Where there is an object there is a subject, but not where there is no object. The absence of an object results in the absence also of a subject, and not merely in that of grasping. It is thus that there arises the cognition which is homogeneous, without object, indiscriminate and supermundane. The tendencies to treat object and subject as distinct and real entities are forsaken, and thought is established in just the true nature of one's thought. (Vasubandhu)[18]

The issue becomes whether the subject-object distinction can break down in different ways: if the mystic can swim in the same sea that drowns the psychotic.

In sum, the Buddhist critique of ego-self implies that anxiety is essential to the ego because it is the ego's response to its own groundlessness, something more immediately threatening than fear of death sometime in the future. This theme is familiar in existential philosophy as well but evidently not in psychotherapy. In *Existential Psychotherapy*, Irvin Yalom discusses what he calls the "ur-anxiety" of groundlessness, yet concludes that, unlike death anxiety (to which he devotes almost half his book), anxiety about groundlessness is not evident in our daily experience.[19] Is such anxiety so hard to recognize because it is so rare—confined, perhaps, to abstracted philosophers—or because it is so well-repressed? If even Freud was unable to recognize death-repression in his patients, because he did not resolve it in his own life, we should be cautious in answering this question.

Otto Rank's influential essay "Life Fear and Death Fear" divided anxiety into two opposed but complementary fears. Life fear is anxiety in the face of standing out from nature, thereby losing connection with a greater whole. Death fear is anxiety in the face of extinction, of losing individuality and dissolving back into the whole. "Whereas the life fear is anxiety at going forward, becoming an individual, the death fear is anxiety at going backward, losing individuality. Between these two fear possibilities, the individual is thrown back and forth all his life."[20] In a thought-provoking section of *Existential Psychotherapy*, Yalom develops this into his own dual paradigm of death-denial through individuation or fusion. The psychological defense of *specialness* is trying to become different and better than everyone else, thus deserving of a better fate. The defense of *fusion* is hiding in the group, which includes expecting to be taken care of by others and fantasizing about being rescued. Yalom employs these defenses against death to explain the behavior of his clients, despite the fact that many of them display little if any obvious death anxiety.

My point is that Yalom's paradigm need not be limited to the use Yalom finds for it, for specialness and fusion may work even better as defenses against a sense of ontological *lack*. Whether one is the President or a perfect mommy's boy, it is difficult to overlook completely the fact that one is going to die. What is less obvious is how much each of us is motivated by the need to resolve our sense-of- *lack*, in which case one can be more hopeful about the success of Yalom's dual strategies. If I am driven by an unacknowledged intuition of my groundlessness, I can try to compensate for that by becoming someone special who stands out from the crowd, and thereby hope to become more real by being acknowledged by the crowd. Conversely, I may try to resolve my sense of *lack* by fusing with others, which gains the security of anonymity: "There's nothing wrong with me; I'm just like everyone else." In the first case I compensate by striving to become more real than others, in the second I reassure myself by becoming no less real than others seem to be.

Traditionally, a communal version of the latter has been the more important. Society may well be a structure of shared guilt, as Brown says, but it is more obviously a structure of shared anxiety. Today our problem with anxiety is greater for at least two reasons: A more individualistic society produces people with a stronger sense-of-self, therefore with stronger anxiety, and it provides fewer effective ways to cope with that anxiety. Religion is the traditional consolation because it reassures me that my anxiety will be put to rest, my *lack* filled in, my groundlessness grounded in God or nirvāṇa. If this is our deepest need, the death of God will only result in the search for a secular equivalent. The more individuated can try to deify their own egos, but we have seen why it is difficult to become one's own sun. Most people require a more collective deity. Herein lies much of the appeal of nationalism, and socialism's claim to embody "the will of the people." "If modernization can be described as a spreading condition of homelessness, then socialism can be understood as the promise of a new home."[21] Herein, too, is a key to understanding many of the horrors of the twentieth century.

> Totalitarianism is a cultural neurotic symptom of the need for community— a symptom in the respect that it is grasped as a means of allaying anxiety resulting from the feelings of powerlessness and helplessness of the isolated, alienated individuals produced in a society in which complete individualism has been the dominant goal. Totalitarianism is the substitution of collectivism for community, as Tillich has pointed out. (Rollo May)[22]

When the anonymity of mass man within modern bureaucratic societies destroys the securities of localized community, it leads to an accumulation of anxiety that seeks a collective outlet. Without such a psychotherapeutic understanding, sociological explanations like Hannah Arendt's "the banality of evil" are incomplete.

In the passage from which the above quotation is taken, Rollo May looks no further than the need for community; he does not consider whether that need might express something else. This is no minor issue if our rapidly evolving "global village" means there is no return to the small towns that sustained almost all of us until a few generations ago. Nostalgia may mythologize those communities, but they provided the security of a common world-view and the hope of redemption in one symbolic form or another. Without that possibility, the question becomes whether there is another alternative to mass collectivism, a different type of community, in which individuals are able to take more personal responsibility for coping with increased anxiety and resolving their own ontological *lack*.

That brings us back to the possibility of ending anxiety. Again, most of what was said earlier about ending guilt also applies here, transposed from a minor to a major key. But, what is more noticeable in terms of anxiety (and it has already been noticed in chapter 1) is the almost unanimous agreement among existentialists and psychologists that anxiety cannot be eliminated; therefore the goal must be to reduce it and keep it in its proper place. Tillich traces ontological anxiety back to the self-awareness of the finite that it is finite. We cannot hope to end it, for no finite being can escape its finitude. All that psychotherapy can do is remove the more compulsive forms of anxiety and control the frequency and intensity of fear. Many psychologists doubt that anxiety should be eliminated, viewing it as a spur to, or a necessary byproduct of, heightened awareness. Liddell notes that "anxiety accompanies intellectual activity as its shadow."[23]

For a different view we must turn again to religion, which confronts us with the task of demythologizing transformation from consolation, of distinguishing possibility from wishful thinking. For the role of anxiety in the religious life, I can find no better account than the short chapter with which Kierkegaard concludes *The Concept of Anxiety*. In a few unforgettable pages Kierkegaard delineates the paradox that, if there is to be an end to anxiety, it can be found only through anxiety. Understood and experienced in the right way (one who misunderstands this anxiety is lost, he says), anxiety is a school which roots out everything finite and petty in us, and only then takes us wherever we want to go. Just as we have seen with death and guilt, the path of integration is an awareness that does not flee anxiety but endures it, in order to recuperate those parts of the psyche which split off and return to haunt us in projected, symbolic form. *The way to integrate death is to become truly dead*: to face and finally accept that I am going to die, without the psychological defense mechanisms that deny it or divert my attention. *The way to integrate guilt is to be profoundly guilty*: to let go of my compensatory desire to be a hero (in order to qualify for a special destiny) until I recognize that I too am nobody, no different from anyone else who stumbles along the surface of this planet and therefore deserving of no special fate; until I seek no special fate, but embrace the possibilities that arise for me. Similarly, *the way to integrate anxiety is to become completely anxious*: to let formless, unprojected anxiety gnaw on all those "finite ends" I have attempted to secure myself with, so that, by devouring these attachments, anxiety devours me too and, like the parasite that kills its host, consumes itself.

To learn how to be anxious is to learn the ultimate, writes Kierkegaard. The school of anxiety is the path to true freedom, which is what remains after we have been purged of all the comforting hiding-places we automatically flee to whenever we feel insecure. Only such anxiety is "absolutely educative, because it consumes all finite ends and discovers all their deceptiveness." The curriculum of this school is *possibility*, "the weightiest of all categories." No matter what tragedies actually befall us, they are always far lighter than what could happen. When a person "graduates from the school of possibility, . . . he knows better than a child knows his ABC's that he can demand absolutely nothing of life and that the terrible, perdition, and annihilation live next door to every man."[24] It is an exercise in awareness: dredging up all the psychic securities we have hedged around us and then "forgotten," until we found ourselves in a secure but constricted little world. Consciousness of what could happen at any moment deconstructs this comfortable cocoon by reminding us, at every moment, of our mortality; in psychotherapeutic terms, this demolishes one's unconscious power linkages or supports.

Unlike Ortega y Gasset, Kierkegaard holds out no piece of driftwood for the drowning man to grasp. "He who sank in possibility . . . sank absolutely, but then in turn he emerged from the depth of the abyss lighter than all the troublesome and terrible things in life." Such a person no longer fears fate, "because the anxiety within him has already fashioned fate and has taken away

from him absolutely all that any fate could take away." This spiritual discipline stands in striking contrast to the sense of divine protection that is usually
taken to be a secular benefit of religious faith. Kierkegaard is no less interested
in faith, yet for him it does not come cheaply. Authentic faith is not a refuge
from anxiety but its fruit.

If the ego-self is a mental-construction whose function is to preserve a feeling of security (as Sullivan puts it), then such an exercise in deconstructing
security should eliminate that sense-of-self. Usually much of our mental activity is structured by the need to have reassuring boltholes, where we can flee
when our self-esteem is threatened. A trivial example: Having lost a chess game
to an opponent with a much lower rating, I automatically compensate—official ratings show that I am really the better player. Each of us finds his or her
own ways to rationalize the more serious shortcomings of our lives. Fixed by
repetition, the web of these and other automatizations constitutes my character and therefore my unfreedom: all the ways I habitually run away from open
encounter with the world. For Buddhism as well as Kierkegaard, I must let go
of these thought-props, which is to suffer. Without these defenses to self-esteem,
I die a thousand little ego-deaths—or walk on the edge of a thousand swords,
to use the Zen metaphor. In Kierkegaard's terms, such thought-props are the
finitudes which must be rooted out to reveal the infinitude that is our true
ground.

The crux of *The Concept of Anxiety* concerns the relationship between anxiety and freedom:

> Anxiety is the dizziness of freedom, which emerges when the spirit wants to
> posit the synthesis [of psychical and physical] and *freedom looks down into
> its own possibility, laying hold of finiteness to support itself. Freedom succumbs
> in this dizziness.* Further than this, psychology cannot and will not go. In
> that very moment everything is changed, and freedom, when it rises again,
> sees that it is guilty. Between these two moments lies the leap, which no
> science has explained and no science can explain.[25]

Kierkegaard describes what we define today as repression: to repress is precisely
to make one's self unaware of freedom.[26] Why would we want to forget our
freedom and "finitize" ourselves so that we experience the world closed up into
restricted possibilities? Freedom makes us dizzy because as the opposite of causal
determination it is by definition groundless, hence absolute—literally, "unconditioned." Such indeterminacy is terrifying: an abyss without a bottom,
an openness that in itself is nothing except the ability to actualize this or
that from the infinitude of possibilities which freedom liberates from our
automatizations.

> In turning inward, he discovers freedom. He does not fear fate, for he lays
> hold of no outward task, and freedom is for him his bliss, not freedom to
> do this or that in the world, to become king or emperor or an abusive

street-corner orator, but freedom to know of himself that he is freedom.[27] Although we crave this freedom—how could we not, if it is our nature?—we are also afraid of it, for the cost of such infinitude is also infinite. In order to be able to become anything, I must first become no-thing, "admit the void; accept loss forever."[28] Yet such "Holy Insecurity" (Buber's phrase) may not be incompatible with a deeper security, if we remember its original meaning: *se-cura*, "without care."

Projection. My discussions of guilt and anxiety will be incomplete unless these subjective phenomena are supplemented by some reference to their objectifications: projection and transference. The apparently objective world is unconsciously structured by the ways we seek to secure ourselves within it. We meet again the unfortunate paradox that precisely this attempt to ground ourselves in the world is what separates us from it.

In *The Ego and the Id*, Freud observed that the dynamically unconscious repressed is not capable of becoming conscious in the ordinary way. How does the unconscious become conscious? Freud suggests that "anything arising from within that seeks to become conscious must try to transform itself into external perceptions."[29] That insight is now taken for granted, yet the way Freud expresses it also takes for granted commonsense subject-object dualism even as the phenomena he refers to—projection and transference—raise questions about that dualism. Such formulations assume that the locus of the unconscious is someplace within me and that the objective world is what it appears to be, something external to me. Like most of us all the time and perhaps all of us most of the time, Freud takes for granted the objectivity of the world— a dangerous assumption, given Kant's Copernican revolution and the more recent discoveries of quantum physics and cognitive psychology. It is also a difficult assumption to become aware of, since we constitute the world in a manner which conceals the fact that we have constituted it.

> Perhaps the most potent defense of all [against death-anxiety] is simply reality as it is experienced—that is, the appearance of things. . . . appearances enter the service of denial: *we constitute the world in such a way that it appears independent of our constitution.* To constitute the world as an empirical world means to constitute it as something independent of ourselves. (Yalom)[30]

Why is this such a potent defense against death-anxiety? Why do we forget that we (for it is a social construction: we learn to perceive the world the way others do) have constituted the world? Yalom relates this to a repressed fear of groundlessness, which makes us try to secure ourselves by stabilizing the world we are *in*. We need a world of dependable, self-existing things, fixable in objective time and space and interacting in ways we can learn to manipulate. This "external" dependability of the world is just as important to us as "internal" psychic organization, for either without the other would be helpless. Once a predictable world has been automatized, we can concentrate on achieving our ends within that world. However, there is another reason for "forgetting" if the sense-of-self which is *in* that world is itself constituted at the same time. In that case these acts of constitution cannot be accessible to self-consciousness because they are also the foundations of self-consciousness. *Then to repress the fact that my objective world is constituted is also to repress the fact that I am constituted.*

The implication of this for projection and transference is that unconscious phenomena need not be sought in some undetermined mental place within me but are to be found embodied in my world. If I want to find my unconscious, I should look at the structures of my world, and if we want to locate our collective unconscious we must look to the shared structures of our social world. Both of these include our patterns of behavior in the world. "We may say that here the patient *remembers* nothing of what is forgotten and repressed, but that he expresses it in *action*. He reproduces it not in his memory but in his behavior; he *repeats* it, without of course knowing that he is repeating it" (Freud).[31]

> What really happens [in transference] is not that the neurotic patient "trans-fers" feelings he had toward mother or father to wife or therapist. Rather, the neurotic is one who in certain areas never developed beyond the limited and restricted forms of experience characteristic of the infant. Hence in later years he perceives wife or therapist through the same restricted, distorted "spectacles" as he perceived father or mother. The problem is to be under-stood in terms of perception and relatedness to the world. (Rollo May)[32]

This does not mean that developing into the less restricted forms of experience characteristic of most adults is a satisfactory solution. The "pathology of nor-malcy" (Fromm) or the "psychopathology of the average" (Maslow) are no answer, insofar as the child is father to the man and we remain children "blown up by age." The difference is that the infant's world is determined by his parents', but as we grow up our need for security becomes invested in wider social structures, which emphasize competing for socially agreed security and status symbols: money, prizes, power, and so forth.

Jung describes projection as leading to a dream-like experience of the world: "The effect of projection is to isolate the subject from his environment, since instead of a real relation to it there is now only an illusory one. Projections change the world into the replica of one's unknown face. In the last analysis, therefore, they lead to an auto-erotic or autistic condition in which one dreams a world whose reality remains forever unattainable."[33] If we all project, then we are all narcissists, constantly encountering our own faces without recogniz-ing them. Each of us dreams a world, and if our socially constituted symbols are the true archetypes of our collective unconscious, our fascination with manipulating them amounts to a collective dream, maintained by each of us striving in these symbolic ways to secure or realize oneself within that dream.

(Examples of this will be discussed in chapter 5.) In contrast, *the* Buddha is not a name but a title: literally "the awakened one."

Jung also notes that in the process of individuation people take their projections back into themselves. Chapter 2 presented the example of how our socially agreed and apparently objective temporal schema can be deconstructed back into an eternal now. To understand better the principles involved in such de-projection, we can benefit from the fifth and last part of Spinoza's *Ethics.* "Of the Power of the Intellect, or of Human Freedom" demonstrates how the way to human freedom may be realized through the proper employment of the intellect. This is less an intellectual than a psychotherapeutic path (as those terms are now understood), since the process involves gaining awareness of one's automatized motivations in order to become less determined by them.

Proposition three is: "An emotion which is a passion ceases to be a passion as soon as we form a clear and distinct idea of it." The distinction we make today between ideas and emotions does not apply here; for Spinoza, the important difference is whether these mental events are experienced in confused or clarified form. Do we passively suffer from the way our minds work[34] or are we "self-determined" because we understand how they function? Proposition two makes it clearer that, in psychotherapeutic terms, this is the difference between an unconscious transference/projection and the awareness of what we are doing to ourselves: "If we remove a disturbance of the mind or an emotion away from the thought of an external cause, and join it to other thoughts, then love or hatred toward the external cause, as well as waverings of the mind which originate from these emotions, are destroyed."

Earlier in the *Ethics,* Spinoza defines love and hatred as pleasure and pain, respectively, accompanied by the idea of an external cause. In a similar fashion, my argument in this chapter implies that fear might be defined as "anxiety accompanied by the idea of an external cause" and guilt as "anxiety accompanied by the idea of an internal cause (i.e., oneself)." The solutions are similar in each case: to break the association between the emotion and its supposedly external (or introjected, in the case of guilt) cause, which is exactly what this chapter has been recommending in order to experience pure ontological guilt and anxiety, unrelieved by any projection or introjection. If something about a person particularly bothers me, the psychotherapeutic approach uses that as an opportunity to learn something about myself, by inquiring into why that affects me. Perhaps an extreme version of this attitude is found in the Bodhisattva's Vow chanted by Zen students: "If someone becomes a sworn enemy of me, abuses and persecutes me, I will bow down to him with humble language, in reverent belief that he is a merciful incarnation of Buddha, come to liberate me from sinful *karma* that has been produced and accumulated over countless *kalpas....*"

Spinoza is pointing out that "passion" is our mental creation. If I suffer psychologically, it is because my own ways of thinking, alienated and pro-jected, have put me in a bind. Terrified of death, I strive compulsively to immortalize myself in some symbolic fashion—and find myself engaged in symbolic life-and-death struggles against everyone else trying to do the same. Efforts to real-ize myself symbolically mean I give power over myself to those persons and situations which can grant or refuse the symbolic reality that I hope will fill up my *lack*.

Spinoza, like Buddhism, believes that genuine freedom can be actualized by becoming aware of the repressed mental events we have projected. If, for ex-ample, I want to be respected by certain philosophers, whom I look upon as eminent (usually because others look upon them as eminent), this will natu-rally affect the nature of my world and the way I feel compelled to act within it. Spinoza shows me how to become more "self-determined" by realizing that the opinions of these philosophers do not have direct power over my state of mind, for I give these people power over me by my ways of thinking about their states of mind. In gaining a "clear and distinct idea" of my desire for their approbation—by becoming aware of it rather than just being motivated by it—I can distinguish that desire from my idea of those people ("the thought of an external cause") and notice instead the connections between that desire and other ideas of mine, such as my desire for symbolic immortality as a fa-mous thinker ("join it to other thoughts"). In this way I can free myself from those "waverings of the mind" arising from fear of their evaluation and the need to be esteemed ("loved") by them. This does not mean I should become indifferent to the opinions of others, but it allows me to respond in a more self-determined way, informed rather than affected by their comments.

This also happens in psychotherapy and in the relationship between spir-itual teacher and disciple. As in the above example, our "external cause" usu-ally relates directly or indirectly to the approval of others, for it is through the eyes of our fellows that we try to make ourselves real—no doubt because it was through others' eyes that we gained a sense-of-self which needs to feel real, during the socialization process. The therapist and master create situa-tions where the transferences and projections of the client/student become more obvious, since they are not reinforced by the conscious or unconscious compli-ance of the other. To that extent the psychotherapeutic situation and the Zen interview may work to resolve similar problems; but from a Buddhist perspec-tive, the psychoanalytic movement does not have as clear a conception of what it is working *toward*.

Freud saw early that normalcy is a low grade of pathology, and his goal of strengthening the ego ("where id was, there ego shall be") was making the best of a bad situation. Decades of Freudian and Neo-Freudian ego-psychology have not discovered any better criterion of mental health. Replacing sexual inhibi-tion with the existential repressions of death, groundlessness, and meaninglessness brings us closer to the wellsprings of human motivation, but what will we find if and when those repressions can be "fully" analyzed? If it is possible for a few intrepid souls to become aware of their terror of death and groundlessness, and "integrate" them in some fashion— according to Buddhism, by letting-go and dying to oneself—what will be the result? Might such people in the past have become sages and religious innovators? Is it enough to accept their teachings, or do we need to follow their example?

If the ego-self is the center of a web spun to hide the void, an ungrounded mental construct that dreads and tries to compensate for its suspected groundlessness, then no psychology of ego-strengthening can suffice, and I think psychotherapy is empirical enough that it is beginning to realize this. If so, psychology will be able to find no satisfactory definition of mental well-being until it discovers the possibility of "grounding" our consciousness in something besides libido, something that (according to Buddhism) we can realize only by yielding to our groundlessness.

Existential Anguish

The self as lack: What philosophers have held such a view? Much has been said about Kierkegaard, and more will be said about Nietzsche in the next chapter, but the two most important Western exponents of *lack* are Arthur Schopenhauer and Jean-Paul Sartre. In them we find the most disconsolate descriptions of man's tragic condition, unrelieved by any *deus ex machina*. If Buddhism wants to propose the possibility of a more hopeful conclusion, their critiques must be challenged.

Schopenhauer follows the metaphysical pattern that Nietzsche mocks: he begins by discovering the essential nature of reality in order to deduce how we should live. Yet in one important respect he breaks the pattern: his pessimism. Metaphysicians have been the great optimists of reason; in them, mankind's search for a synthesis of reality, truth, and meaning reaches an apogee. The order of things being revealed, the problem of life is also solved. We assume our proper place, at or near the top of the hierarchy of beings, and fulfill ourselves by fulfilling our function within the whole.

Schopenhauer's importance is that he put an end to that. Like many others before and since, he believed he had finally discovered the essence of reality, and for once the news was grim. Others had been discouraging. Gnostics and Neoplatonists despised creation as the malicious deed of a demiurge, but they saw that as only the first act of a play which would have a happy ending, when we learn to withdraw from the materialized world back into the spiritual realm wherefrom it emanated. Schopenhauer would have none of that. The inner reality of life and nature is blind, insatiable will, and the only alternative is nothingness. Not to be born is best; next to that, to die without being reborn.

The World as Will and Idea does not specifically describe the self as a *lack*, yet its account of the will amounts to the same thing; moreover, it extrapolated that sense-of-*lack* to the world as a whole. Will is the essence of everything, manifesting itself in all the animate and even the inanimate forms of the universe. The questionable advantage of humanity's exalted status is that we are able to know that our nature is unfulfillable will. If self-consciousness allows us to anticipate our death, so that we live and die more painfully, Schopenhauer rents the veil of existence to help us will more painfully, because more aware of our absurd situation. Given his influence on the intellectual climate of late nineteenth-century Europe (an undercurrent to its technological and evolutionary optimism), it is likely that his conception of the will influenced Freud's; and that influence is not difficult to find in Freud's concept of the libido, our basic instinctual psychic energy. No wonder the Freudian ego feels so uncomfortable, perched tenuously on top of a volcano whose flow it is supposed to direct.

Schopenhauer himself was much influenced by the noumenal-phenomenal dualism of Kant and tried to reduce Kant's twelve categories to one, causality. Causal relations (which for him include spatio-temporal connections) are the subjective conditions of experience, "a veil of Māyā" (his phrase) between ourselves and reality. But he is more hopeful than Kant about the possibility of experiencing the world as it is in itself, unconditioned by the epistemological structures of the subject. To know the thing-in-itself is to experience one's identity with it, a conception influenced less by Hegel or Schelling than by what Europe was beginning to discover about the nondualist Indian philosophies of Buddhism and Vedānta. When we come to know ourselves intuitively, in our inmost nature, we realize ourselves to be primordial, ungrounded, and blind will. "It always strives, for striving is its sole nature, which no attained goal can put an end to. Therefore it is not susceptible of any final satisfaction, but can only be restrained by hindrances, while in itself it goes on forever."[35] The lure of every temporary satisfaction turns out to be illusory, for we quickly become bored. Human life swings like a pendulum between the suffering of frustration and the duller pain of tedium.

Thus life is meaningless. Schopenhauer compares it to riding a raft through turbulent rapids, struggling to avoid every shoal and rock, only to reach an escarpment where one is hurled down to eternal nothingness. This contrasts nicely with the Zen story of a man chased by a tiger, who falls off a cliff yet manages to grab a bush. Above him the tiger, below the abyss, and the roots of the bush begin to loosen; but the bush has berries—and how sweet they are! Perhaps this story suits Schopenhauer's own life better, for the man who recommended that the will renounce itself was little inclined to do so himself.

Religion, the metaphysics of the masses, is man's attempt to deny the vanity of life. Our will to live can be satisfied only with the promise of endless life, and although that would only be endless dissatisfaction we conceive of immortality as the end of frustration as well. The Being of the philosophers also reveals our aspiration for eternity, to attain some goal that the intellect could serenely contemplate. A more satisfying although temporary consolation is art, in which the will contemplates the image of its own forms, and this is especially true of music, which

is distinguished from all the other arts by the fact that it is not a copy of the phenomenon, or, more accurately, the adequate objectivity of will, but is the direct copy of the will itself and therefore exhibits itself as the metaphysical to everything physical in the world, and as the thing-in-itself to every phenomenon. We might, therefore, just as well call the world embodied music as embodied will.[36]

For Schopenhauer our morality (or lack thereof) has three roots: egoism, malice, and compassion. Egoism needs no elaboration. Malice is the basis of immorality and exists only in human nature, being foreign to other creatures. In compassion the veil of Māyā parts as "I become you." Schopenhauer quotes the famous Vedantic formula for this, *tat tvam asi*, literally "that thou art."[37] In this act of self-overcoming, I grasp through the other and in the other the common reality, the will that unites all things. This is a temporary extinction of one's individual will, yet it points the way to the only possible salvation, in which the will turns back upon itself, to deny and finally overcome itself. Schopenhauer is rather vague about how this can happen, which may also reflect his own preference for aestheticism over asceticism.

This is a brief summary, but it raises the important issues. *The World as Will and Idea* was first published in 1819, yet the terrors and absurdities of history since then can hardly be said to refute it. Schopenhauer is no longer popular because monism of any sort is no longer intellectually respectable, and because his pessimism-of-will has been eclipsed by Nietzsche's less negative will-to-power. Psychotherapy does not so much replace his critique as sharpen it with more empirical tools. One could argue that they supplement each other: The return of the repressed in compulsive, symbolic form fits comfortably with Schopenhauer's analysis of the blind, insatiable will. The difference is the concept of repression itself, for repression implies the possibility of de-repression, of becoming aware again of what one has chosen to ignore. Repression explains our psychic compulsions by attributing mental causes to them, whereas Schopenhauer's compulsive will is primordial because not caused by anything else. This difference is crucial because of the different alternatives each allows. For Schopenhauer, we can choose only between compulsive will and escape into annihilation; for psychotherapy, there is either repression and its return as symptoms, or the difficult path of freeing oneself from compulsions by facing the truths we would rather not think about. This opens a door Schopenhauer does not, even if Freud and Becker do not open it very wide.

Schopenhauer's attitude toward music can help us understand this difference. The passage quoted above distinguishes music from the other arts: Music
is a reflection of the will itself and is therefore as metaphysical as the will. Yet
how can such contemplation of an insatiable will be so satisfying, even joyful,
if the operations of will itself are a perpetual source of dissatisfaction? Schopenhauer cannot claim that we aesthetically distance ourselves from the will, since
he notices that in our most cherished moments we tend to forget ourselves
and *become* the music, in a nondual fashion analogous with his explanation of
compassion. I think that what we most appreciate in music—more evident in
Mozart than in Schopenhauer's beloved Rossini—is not its willful but its playful quality, and we delight in this play not because it is a copy of will but
because it is the abeyance of will. To hear music most deeply is to regain the
no-longer-falling-away eternal now and forget past and future—because it is
also to forget the will, which is preoccupied with past and especially future.
When we are most one with music it is not in time but is experienced as
timeless-time, the *now* that flows. Insofar as we are constantly anticipating the
next note, we are not one with the music; when we are nondual with it, notes
no longer succeed each other and fall away but the same note dances up and
down. These different ways of hearing reflect the difference between will and
play, which is *lack*: If there is striving to reach somewhere or to gain something, there is a gap between me and the music, and that gap is a taste of the
lack that is will and its frustration.

The pleasure we experience in the tension-and-resolution of thematic development does not contradict this, for no-striving is not a matter of not-going-
anywhere but a going-of-not-going. When we stop trying to push the river, we
realize that the *now* flows by itself. I suspect we appreciate music so much
because it has become one of our main ways of attuning ourselves to that *now*.
Although we may not experience such moments often, they are the most cherished. Perhaps we hear the music of Bach and Mozart as spiritual because
there is something about it—a playful serenity without any sense-of-lack?—
that is especially conducive to such moments.

For Schopenhauer, our short-term choice is between the frustrations of blind
will and a more self-conscious subjective will temporarily contemplating the
objective will; yet my interpretation of music offers an alternative distinction
between the unsatisfiable *lack* that is will and a lacking-nothing playfulness.
Can this be extrapolated beyond music? Then to perceive the world as blind,
insatiable will is to project one's own mental state upon it. This striving is the
condition of that animal who can only live-toward-the-future, who is preoccupied with time as a flight from the now, which is painful because it exposes
our *lack*. In terms of death-repression, insofar as we are afraid of death we are
also afraid of life, for there is the need to extract something from present activity that will survive the impending (or at least always-outstanding) catastrophe.

The constant subliminal reminder that we have not found any such thing means there is no end to our striving. The same point can be made in terms of the self-as-*lack*. Instead of dreading something in the future, we are fleeing our own shadow, or running away from the groundlessness that keeps sucking on our feet, like quicksand, whenever we stop. Since in neither case are we able to dwell serenely in the here-and-now, we experience the essence of our lives as blind will and project that will onto the universe.

Without *that* veil of Māyā, what might we perceive? That will, like *lack*, is a function of self-consciousness, which is why other animals seem to lack our sense of *lack*. Since they do not dread death or suffer from their groundlessness, animals must experience the world, including their instincts, as *playful*.[38] They have no reason not to play, Humans are the only beings that die because the only ones that "know" they are alive, the only beings that try to make themselves real because the only ones that feel unreal. Other creatures are neither alive nor dead, neither real nor unreal, which means they have nothing to gain or lose. Since they do not search for a meaning to vindicate their existence, the meaninglessness of their world is no burden. Purposelessness allows their lives to be a dance.

Other criticisms of Schopenhauer follow from this. Malice is one of his three roots of (im)morality, accepted as an irreducible given. He notices that it exists only in human nature and not in other creatures, but he does not consider the implications. How, then, is malice related to our self-consciousness? If our way of maintaining self-esteem and gaining a sense of specialness is through the respect of others, competition takes on new meaning as symbolic life-and-death. Then, as Dr. Johnson delicately put it, there is something in the misfortunes of friends that is not displeasing to us. To diminish you is to elevate myself.

The most serious problem for Schopenhauer is how to overcome the will. Many critics have noted that the possibility raised at the end of *The World as Will and Idea*, of transcending the will, is inconsistent with everything else claimed about the will. If my inmost nature is will, how can that will turn back upon itself and overcome itself? There is a parallel problem in Zen practice, in the "gaining ideas" which obstruct many students. Instead of forgetting oneself by becoming absorbed in one's meditation, one strives to attain the state of mind in which there is no *lack*, an exercise that quickly becomes self-defeating. In this case the solution is not to strive, but to learn how to let go and allow oneself to be absorbed into the meditation. In such *samādhi* there is no will because there is no reflexive sense of ego-self. In contrast, Schopenhauer's will is absolute and irreducible, so there can be no end to it. Only if the will is not an *ur*-instinct, because it originates from something else—such as a repressed fear of death or groundlessness—can there be the possibility of deconstructing it back into that something else.

The question raised in all three of these issues is the same: whether the blind will is indeed primordial, or whether our experience of such a will is the effect of a to-be-uncovered repression and a to-be-exorcised cause. If the Freudian concept of libido is a modern version of Schopenhauer's will, the importance of this issue extends far beyond Schopenhauer's metaphysics.

At the very end of *The World as Will and Idea*, Schopenhauer gently chides the Indians, who evade nothingness with myths of *nirvāṇa* or reabsorption in Brahman. "Rather do we freely acknowledge that what remains after the entire abolition of will is for all those who are still full of will certainly nothing; but, conversely, to those in whom the will has turned and has denied itself, this our world, which is so real, with all its suns and milky-ways—is nothing." Given our human fear of nothingness, this seems a courageous conclusion, yet it is Schopenhauer's way of making the best of a bad thing, since will is worse. Then does Schopenhauer swing from one extreme to another? Whether we fear and shun nothingness or embrace it as the extinction of our suffering, we miss something about its nature, insofar as both cases presuppose the usual duality between being and nothingness. From the Buddhist perspective, that duality is the one which most needs to be deconstructed.

Sartre replaces Schopenhauer's monism of will with a dualism of in-itself and for-itself, to draw conclusions even more pessimistic—for, unlike Schopenhauer's will, consciousness cannot renounce itself. His existentialist version of Cartesianism declares that the self is *le manqué*, "the lack," and since that lack is ontologically based, Sartre concludes more consistently than Schopenhauer that there is no help for it. Because we are nothing we are free, but rather than something to celebrate this is something we are condemned to. Freedom turns out to be a poor substitute for being.

This absolute freedom of the for-itself was a realization that even Sartre was never quite comfortable with. Both his life and his work are tinged with nostalgia for security and objective meaning, which is the inevitable legacy of a self that can never overcome the gap between itself and the world. His grasp of man's predicament comes close to the Buddhist analysis I am offering, but his irremediable version of the subject-object dualism forecloses the Buddhist solution. I wonder if his Marxism was one consequence of this homesickness. Perhaps what attracted Sartre was not so much its theory as the shared commitment to something greater than self, the meaning which such a community of belief gives to a life emptied by freedom.

Being and Nothingness presents two ontologically primitive categories: being-in-itself and being-for-itself. Sartre avoids the Cartesian problem of how to relate subject and object by defining each in relation to the other. The for-itself is that which reveals the in-itself, and the in-itself is that which appears to the for-itself. "Consciousness is not what it is and is what it is not," for in knowing that something is a table I learn what my consciousness is: it is other than that table. Consciousness can never become an object, which points to the supreme sadness of the for-itself. Since the for-itself is empty, pure and mere transparency, it can never stabilize itself, either objectively in the world or subjectively in the self-reflexivity of ego. "What the for-itself lacks is the self—or itself as in-itself." Human consciousness is a hole or a fissure in being, through which nothingness comes into the world. This fissure is outside the causal order, thus completely free, but for Sartre there is little joy in that freedom. "Everything is permissible if God does not exist, and as a result man is forlorn, because neither within him nor without does he find anything to cling to."[39]

The problem is that this empty for-itself wants to become something, and that desire to be reveals our *lack* : "human consciousness, by its very nature, is a lack." In *The Words*, Sartre remembers that even as a young child he had an intuition of this. "How can one put on an act without knowing that one is acting? The clear, sunny semblances that constituted my role were exposed by a lack of being which I could neither quite understand nor cease to feel." Recounting his reaction to such adventure novels as *Michael Strogoff*, Sartre sees the connection between the child's sense of lack and his fantasies of heroism, whereby he will fill it up. "Heroism, absent and impossible, was the sole object of my passion; heroism, the blazing flame of the poor in spirit. My inner poverty and the feeling of being gratuitous did not allow me to renounce it entirely."[40] Later it became sublimated into writing.

As a *lack*, the for-itself wants to become in-itself, wants the solidity and security of objective existence. Yet, there is no such Being-in-itself-for-itself— except God, according to the classical definition, but that is an oxymoron for Sartre, which is why God cannot exist. This makes us the being whose hopeless project is to be God. Sartre's pessimism and nostalgia arise from the impossibility of renouncing this *passion inutile*. Running after itself in an interminable and futile pursuit, the for-itself generates time: "The for-itself is a flight and *I am this flight* out of the past and into the future."[41] The for-itself needs this "diaspora," and Sartre does not entertain the possibility of ending it. The contrast with Buddhism arises because Sartre believes "the for-itself must be its own lack." For Buddhism our sense-of-*lack* is not a basic metaphysical category but a conditioned effect and a continuing process, which allows for a possibility Sartre does not: a deconditioning that ends sense-of-*lack*.

Sartre emphasizes more than anyone else the absoluteness of our freedom, yet, ironically, realizing that absolute brings anguish. "The facticity of freedom is that freedom is not free not to be free"—the negative formulation betrays a Pyrrhic victory. The high price of that freedom, its burden, is revealed by a lingering desire for objective meaning to exist in-itself and in one's life. In *The*

Age of Reason, Sartre's protagonist Mathieu admits that he always longs to exchange his freedom "for a good sound certainty." Self-consciousness cannot help yearning to secure itself, even if only in the most abstract, symbolic way.

Many of us are in quest of the self, seeking to find out who or what we are, yet according to Sartre there is no answer in those terms. What is needed is not discovery but decision, and, as we know all too well, there is nothing irrevocable about many of our decisions. That we can and do change our minds means the creation of our lives is always ex nihilo, and my existence precedes my essence because I am the result of what I make of myself. It is no use looking for motives to determine my decisions, for in deciding I also choose the motives to be determined by. The clear awareness of this unalienable freedom is *angoisse*, "anguish," a more heartfelt term than the anxiety preferred by psychologists. My life is up to myself, and, like it or not, this remains true at every moment. Sartre gives the example of a gambler who has firmly resolved to quit but feels his resolve melting away as he is about to walk past the casino. Sartre's definition of "bad faith" supplements Rollo May's definition of repression. May points out that repression implies the possibility of freedom, Sartre that we hide from our absolute freedom by choosing to believe we are already determined. Because the for-itself can never become in-itself, we cannot *be* a waiter; we can only play at being a waiter. But since absolute freedom makes us absolutely uncomfortable, we sacrifice this playful quality for the security of thinking that we have become in-itself, that we are *real*. Ironically, however, once I become reified into my role, that restriction of possibilities tends to become uncomfortable and I begin to crave the freedom that I so willingly sacrificed before. As Rank said about life-fear and death-fear, between these poles we are tossed back and forth throughout our lives.

Since our sense-of-self is dependent on the complicity of others, the sense of reality we crave is largely socially determined. *Being and Nothingness* includes a famous analysis of the "look of the other." Sartre contrasts my looking through a keyhole, absorbed in the domestic drama within, with what happens when I suddenly realize that someone is observing *me*. In the flush of embarrassment my freedom escapes me and I become objectified to myself as well as by the observer. Elsewhere Sartre emphasizes how my self-identity depends on the struggle between myself and the other to determine who is in-itself and who is for-itself. From a Buddhist perspective, however, this contest presupposes the sense-of-self's sense of *lack*. It is because I feel myself to be a *lack* that should be real but is not, that should know what it is but does not, that I am so vulnerable to the other's look, fearing an evaluation that challenges my self-esteem and hoping the other will support my fragile sense-of-self. The look of the other materializes me by dissolving me, by reminding me that I am faking it, that my identity is an act I have learned to play and forgotten I am playing. That look catches me out by putting me back in touch with the sense-of-*lack*

I have been repressing. It frightens me because the other, at a distance, does not participate in the social rituals that reassure me of my being.[42]

In his first philosophical work, *The Transcendence of the Ego*, Sartre analyzed the reflexive structure of self-consciousness in a way which almost echoes the conclusions of Mahāyāna Buddhism. The important insight is that the ego-self is mentally constructed by the vain attempt of consciousness to reflect back upon itself and grasp itself. The moment I become aware that I am reading a book is very different from being absorbed in the book. "So long as I was reading, there was consciousness of the book, of the hero of the novel, but the I was not inhabiting this consciousness. . . . there was no I in the unreflected consciousness."[43] To become self-conscious afterwards is to reflect on my pre-reflective consciousness of reading, and the self I then become conscious of is neither the "I" that was reading nor the "I" that performs this act of reflection but a "me," a mental object that is constructed retrospectively by that act of reflection. For Sartre, following Husserl, consciousness is always intentional; and whatever we can become aware of *as* the self is never consciousness itself but another intentional object—an object that can be no more satisfactory than any other attempt of the for-itself to become in-itself. In my Buddhist terms, the sense-of-self, being mentally constituted in this way, can never ground itself, yet neither can I help wanting to ground myself so long as I think that I am that sense-of-self: hence my sense-of-*lack*. From this failure, Sartre later derived our need for self-expression, which sublimates the pursuit of self into symbolic expression such as works of art. Thus for Sartre, as for Freud and Lacan, symbolism is the result of frustration.

Quite early in his philosophical career, then, Sartre distinguished between two moments in the structure of consciousness, the intentional and the reflexive. Only later, however, did he finally see through the reflexive attempt of consciousness to consolidate a self and become fully convinced of his lack of identity,[44] to end up with almost a Buddhist understanding of the problem. That presents us with two strikingly different evaluations of apparently similar experiences: for Sartre the anguish of impersonal spontaneity, for Buddhism the liberation of impersonal spontaneity.

> Transcendental consciousness is an impersonal spontaneity. It determines its existence at each moment, without anything *before* it being conceivable. Thus each moment of our conscious life reveals to us a creation *ex nihilo*. Not a new arrangement, but a new existence. There is something anguishing for each of us, to experience directly this tireless creation of an existence of which we are not the creators.[45]

This passage would not be out of place in a work of Mahāyāna philosophy—until the negative evaluation of the last sentence. Since Sartre agrees with Buddhism that consciousness only retrospectively becomes self-conscious, whence comes the reflexive *we* at the end, to observe and devalue this pre-self-conscious experience? The impersonal spontaneity that is transcendental consciousness determines not only its existence at each moment, it determines *us*. As well as revealing a creation ex nihilo, we ourselves are created ex nihilo. Then who is experiencing "directly" this anguishing, tireless creation?

That inconsistency touches on the heart of the matter, which is the onto-logical difference between Sartre's subject-object dualism and the nondualism of traditions such as Buddhism. There are hints of the problem in Sartre's fictional protagonists. In *The Age of Reason*, Mathieu contemplates the fate of the fetus in his mistress: "A child: another consciousness, a little center-point of light that would flutter round and round, dashing against the walls, and never be able to escape." The trope protests against the prisonhouse of con-sciousness-versus-object dualism, but when there is an opportunity to conflate that dualism Sartre finds the experience repulsive. This is Roquentin's famous encounter with the "superfluous" (*de trop*) chestnut tree in *Nausea*: " I was the root of the chestnut tree. Or rather I was entirely conscious of its existence. Still detached from it— since I was conscious of it—yet lost in it, nothing but it." Notice the ambivalence: He *is* the root, yet his consciousness is also alien-ated from it. Sartre's dualism of consciousness and object makes it difficult for him to cope with this experience. The tree root is merely a material thing, he thinks, so the fact that he was conscious means he must still have been de-tached from it.

There is another way to understand what was happening. Roquentin's de-scription is quite comprehensible as the account of an aborted nondual experience. His consciousness begins to merge with the root, but his revulsion indicates his inability to let go of himself and fully *become* the chestnut root. As a result of this, Roquentin ends up distinguishing existence (repulsive because it is *de trop*) from the reality of a circle or a musical phrase. His duality is revealing; Plato could have done no better. Sartre likes consciousness to be pure and luminous, existence hard and objective. It is the middle ground between them that makes Sartre uncomfortable; his writings are replete with abhorrent reac-tions to anything soft or squishy, and de Beauvoir noticed his "allergy to chlo-rophyll." In Becker's dualism of man as half-animal, half-symbolizer, Sartre fits as someone who shuns the first to identify with the second. His pessimism realizes the problem with this alienated consciousness, but his dualism fore-closes the Buddhist solution.

For Sartre, the distinction between the intentional and reflexive moments of consciousness is based upon the irreducible dualism of the for-itself trying to become in-itself; for Buddhism the reflexivity of consciousness constitutes that dualism. That is the major difference between them. If the for-itself could give up the reflexive attempt of consciousness to grasp and solidify itself, for Sartre this would still leave the transcendence of transparent consciousness, no more or less a lack for abandoning that project. Even the first moment of intentional consciousness, before reflexivity, is dualistic for him; but the supposed onto-logical, primordial lack that Sartre attributes to the for-itself should not be confused with the *lack* of the reflexive "me," which is the sense-of-self's inability to real-ize itself. For Mahāyāna Buddhism, that act of reflexivity, conscious-ness doubling back upon itself, is what creates the dualism of interiority (subject) and exteriority (object) and thus the sense-of-*lack* such an alienation implies. Without this reflexivity there is no "I"-consciousness apart from the world, which implies what Dōgen claimed to have experienced: "I came to realize clearly that mind is no other than mountains, rivers, and the great wide earth, the sun and the moon and the stars." According to the Mahāyāna tradition, Śākyamuni Buddha attained enlightenment when he looked up from his meditations beneath the bodhi-tree and saw the morning star; at that moment he forgot both himself and the morning star as he *became* it. In Buddhism, this ability to forget oneself and let go of oneself is necessary for true freedom. The modern Zen master Hakuun Yasutani emphasized this point in an inter-view with a Western student:

> Usually when you hear a bell ringing you think, consciously or unconsciously, "I am hearing a bell." Three things are involved: I, a bell, and hearing. But when the mind is ripe, that is, as free from discursive thoughts as a sheet of pure white paper is unmarred by a blemish, there is just the sound of a bell ringing. That is *kenshō* [enlightenment].[46]

Kenshō is not a matter of me grasping my true nature, but realizing why I can never grasp that true nature: because when I do not try to grasp myself, or anything else, I *am* that star, that mountain, that sound. This possibility does not occur to Sartre: "If my consciousness were not consciousness of being con-sciousness of the table, it would then be consciousness of that table without consciousness of being so. In other words, it would be a consciousness igno-rant of itself, an unconscious—which is absurd."[47] Yet the alternative to reflex-ive consciousness is not unconsciousness but: the table. Not the table as an object, for that understanding assumes a for-itself that is conscious *of* it. In-stead, the table-as-much-mind-as-object, because experienced nondually when we let-go of the delusion of subject-object, according to Buddhism.

This approach also resolves a difficulty in Sartre's ethics. If there are no possible constraints on the absolute freedom of the for-itself, there is no rea-son why that for-itself, a "fissure" in the world, should take any responsibility for the world. Not only is there no difference between directing the course of nations and getting drunk in a bar (Sartre's example), but there seems to be no ethical reason not to kill anyone I want to, if I am prepared to accept the consequences or think I can escape them. I suspect the reason Sartre was in-clined to accept so much responsibility for the world (as his politics shows) is that he intuited something which did not fit very comfortably into his dualis-tic ontology: Evacuating consciousness to the point of realizing *I am nothing* is equivalent to identifying with the whole world as my own body, as the *Tao Tê Ching* puts it.

Sartre's dualism can also be challenged internally by contrasting his analysis of the Look with the master-slave dialectic in Hegel's *Phenomenology of Mind*. For Sartre, our choice is between the for-itself and the in-itself. The other's look allows the options of objectifying the other or being objectified by the other. Yet Hegel sees that my opposition to the other is also recognition of myself in the other, and vice versa. That is, my sense-of-self is not a hard core of consciousness (and *lack*) but socially-conditioned, arising dialectically in relation to the other. For Hegel, the struggle between me and the other is possible only because each of us conditions the other. This is not true of Sartre's dualism, which implies that I as for-itself can know the other only as object in-itself. Then how can any in-itself threaten my for-itself? In other words, Sartre's subject-object dualism cannot account for the struggle between the two consciousnesses because it cannot account for actual contact between two consciousnesses.

In sum, the fundamental problem is Sartre's fundamental dualism between for-itself and in-itself, which has the effect of irremediably alienating me from the world, including other people. Since we can never know anyone else directly but only by inference, we can never transcend the walls of self-consciousness dividing us. Our little center-points of light may flutter round and dash against the walls, yet they never escape their prison—which according to Buddhism is self-made. Buddhism agrees that the for-itself is a *lack* which condemns itself to the Sisyphean project of trying to ground itself in one way or another. However, it is possible to give up that project by dying to oneself, which means the death of the for-itself as a reflexive consciousness alienated from its world. Until I truly become nothing, whereupon I realize how I can become anything, I am not free. There is no such freedom for those who still experience themselves as a *lack*, and who therefore cannot help trying to objectify themselves in order to ground themselves.

Critiques of Sartre's absolute freedom often miss this point by focusing on the inevitability of external constraints or the sedimentation of habit. Yet Sartre's argument is directed precisely at the bad faith of habit, showing how we allow ourselves to be automatized into such routines rather than experience the anguishing creation of every moment ex nihilo. Such debates overlook the more fundamental bad faith of the person who believes himself to be free because he experiences himself as *pure* lack. The discussions of ontological guilt and anxiety earlier in this chapter have suggested another possibility: that such a sense-of-*lack*, which has been reduced to its unprojected, nonobjectified form—when I realize there is nothing I can do to eliminate it, because the I is the problem—is not the goal but an advanced stage on the way to eliminating sense of *lack*. If so, we see why the *lack* of Sartre's for-itself still lacks true freedom. Instead of genuine openness and spontaneity, everything is overshadowed by anguish from the contradiction between desire to make myself real and the realization that I can never do so, which becomes the burden of nostalgia for securities left behind.

Without that perpetual homesickness, what do we see? Sartre calls human consciousness a hole or a fissure in being, but this metaphor works against his dualism, for there is no such thing as a self-existing fissure or self-contained hole. A hole is always a hole *in* something; holes and fissures are spaces for something to arise in the world or disappear from it. However, I think Sartre is right when he says that the for-itself is beyond causality, for that points at one aspect of creativity. When the for-itself is not obsessed with grounding itself into an in-itself, it can realize the creative relation between them: the for-itself constantly creating in-itself by *becoming* in-itself, without ever exhausting itself in the process. The resolution of Rank's oscillation between life-fear and death-fear, between our desire for security and our need for freedom, is becoming the opening through which new meanings emerge into the world, as (in Buddhist terms) emptiness gives rise to forms. The no-thing-ness of such an opening is a groundlessness which, when no longer fled as a *lack*, opens up the space for such creative irruptions. The mystery of the for-itself is that when it stops trying to grab its own tail and reify itself in the world, it becomes a fountain from which life-giving water springs forth from an unfathomable source.

Schopenhauer is monistic and Sartre is dualistic, yet from the Buddhist perspective they make the same mistake: Both reify our sense-of-*lack* by building their ontology upon it. Schopenhauer's primordial and blind will can never achieve more than the briefest satisfaction; since we too are expressions of this insatiable craving, our lives can at best oscillate between the suffering of frustration and the duller pain of tedium. Sartre's for-itself cannot help wanting to be what it cannot be, hence its sense of *lack* is unresolvable. The pessimism of both thinkers rests on a lack which is built into the universe, but we have noticed enough problems with their arguments to raise doubts about their conclusions. Buddhism emphasizes our *lack* as much, yet is able to offer more hope because the Buddhist sense-of-*lack* is conditioned, like the sense-of-self it shadows. This opens up the possibility of deconditioning *lack* by deconditioning the sense-of-self, an alternative which has been repeatedly mentioned and must now be developed. The last section of this chapter presents the Buddhist analysis of our *lack* and how it may be ended.

Buddhist Duḥkha

A monk whose mind is thus released cannot be followed and tracked out even by the gods. . . . Even in this actual life, monks, I say that a released person is not to be thoroughly known. Though I thus say and thus preach, some ascetics and brahmins accuse me wrongly and baselessly, saying that "the ascetic Gotama is a nihilist and preaches the annihilation, destruction and non-existence of an existent being." That is what I am not and do not affirm. Both previously and now I preach duhkha and the cessation of *duḥkha*. (Sākyamuni Buddha)[48]

I am not aware of any Buddhist equivalent for the psychoanalytic concepts of repression and the return of the repressed as a symptom. Yet Buddhism does have a term which corresponds to the sense-of-*lack* as it has been used it in this book, and by no coincidence it is the most important concept in Buddhism: duḥkha. The Buddha repeatedly summarized his teachings into four truths: *duḥkha*, the cause of *duḥkha*, the end of *duḥkha*, and how to end *duḥkha*. What makes this an equivalent for *lack* is that Buddhism finds an integral relationship between our *duḥkha* and our delusive sense-of-self. In order to end *duḥkha*, the sense-of-self must be deconstructed.

Duḥkha is a Sanskrit term (Pali, *dukkha*) meaning suffering, pain, discomfort, dissatisfaction, frustration, and the like. The first truth redefines *Homo sapiens* as the dissatisfied animal. Without confronting the ultimate source of our *duḥkha*, any amelioration in one aspect of life will only shift the emphasis to another: from physical pain to psychological stress, for example. That is because, like the anxiety psychotherapy addresses, *duḥkha* is not something the self has but something the self is.

The early commentarial tradition distinguishes three kinds of *duḥkha*. All that we usually think of as suffering and discomfort is included in the first, which incorporates the trauma of birth, illness, worry, decrepitude, death-fear; to be bound to what one dislikes; to be separated from what one loves, etc. When momentarily free of such suffering we are able to contemplate the second type of *duḥkha*, that caused by *anitya*, impermanence. "Such is the state of life, that none are happy but by the anticipation of change: the change is nothing; when we have made it the next wish is to change again" (Dr. Johnson again). As long as there is *lack*, real life is always elsewhere. Thus passes away our life, says Pascal: We seek rest in a struggle against difficulties and when we have conquered them rest becomes insufferable. The sense of *lack* pervading both allows us to find solace in neither. We have seen how a similar psychological dialectic between two antithetical possibilities—looking for comfortable chains and then wanting to escape them—tosses us back and forth like a pendulum. From this perspective, perhaps the main achievement of our contemporary technological society is not reduction of our dis-ease but greater sophistication in the ways we are distracted from this truth about our condition. "The only thing which consoles us for our miseries is diversion, and yet this is the greatest of our miseries" (Pascal again).[49] Instead of helping us resolve this problem, modernity has aggravated it:

> On the one hand, modern identity is open-ended, transitory, liable to ongoing change. On the other hand, a subjective realm of identity is the individual's main foothold in reality. Something that is constantly changing is supposed to be the *ens realissimum*. Consequently it should not be a surprise that modern man is afflicted with a *permanent identity crisis*, a condition conducive to considerable nervousness. . . .
> The final consequence of all this can be put very simply (though the simplicity is deceptive): *modern man has suffered from a deepening condition of "homelessness."* The correlate of the migratory character of his experience of society and of self has been what might be called a metaphysical loss of "home." It goes without saying that this condition is psychologically hard to bear.[50]

This makes modern man somewhat like a Buddhist monk, for the traditional mark of a monk is not so much his robe or shaven pate as that he leaves home and cuts himself off from his ancestral family. According to a Zen saying, however, there are different ways to be a monk: "Although one has left home, he is not on the way; although the other is on the way he has not left his home." How can the way itself be a home?

The Buddha's second truth gives the cause of *duḥkha* : *tṛṣṇā*, literally "thirst" usually translated as desire. The basic problem is not that we crave this or that thing, but that it seems to be our nature to crave. For Schopenhauer, desire is how the unsatisfiable will manifests in the world; for Sartre, the fact of human desire is sufficient to prove that human reality is a lack. That desire is the crucial issue has more recently been emphasized, although more positively, by contemporary continental thinkers such as Lacan, Girard, Lyotard, Deleuze, and Derrida. "Taken in its absolute sense, desire is the aspiration to replenish a void; it is a force that pushes toward the conquest of an object the subject believes will abolish this lack and quell his desire. Thus all human activity is impelled by desire" (Vergot).[51]

If it is not possible to fill up that void, can it be resolved in some other way? Buddhism does not attempt to explain the historical origin of *duḥkha* and *tṛṣṇā*. Their beginning cannot be found, said the Buddha, choosing his words carefully, yet in any case metaphysics is a distraction when the important issue is ending them. The contribution of Buddhism to this chapter is how it relates these first two types of *duḥkha*—dis-ease and impermanence— to the structure of the sense-of-self. The third kind of *duḥkha* is that due to the "conditioned states," the physical and mental factors whose interaction constitutes the ego-self. The third truth of the Buddha claims that it is possible to end *duḥkha,* and the fourth truth outlines a path to do so, which culminates in *samādhi,* meditative absorption. It is possible to end sense-of-*lack* by forgetting oneself, whereby the sense-of-self lets-go of itself. The rest of this chapter explains this Buddhist deconstruction. The following section presents the ontological and epistemological deconstruction of the self according to Buddhist doctrine. The final section looks at that deconstruction more phenomenologically, according to Buddhist praxis, in order to understand how it solves the problem of our *lack.*

Buddhist deconstruction of the self. Buddhism deconstructs the sense of self in two ways: synchronically, into the five *skandhas,* literally "heaps," and diachronically, into *pratītya-samutpāda,* "dependent origination." These doctrines explain how the illusion of self is constituted and how it functions. They also imply how it may be ended.

The five *skandhas* are the physical and mental factors that compose the psychophysical personality. They are: form, which includes the material body with its sense-organs; feelings and sensations; perceptions; mental formations (or volitional tendencies), including habits and dispositions; and consciousness, usually understood here as the six sense-consciousnesses (including mental consciousness of mental events). These are also called "the five groups of grasping." All experiences associated with the sense of self can be analyzed into these five impersonal "heaps," with no remainder outside them. There is no persisting self or transcendent soul to be found over and above their functioning. The Buddha emphasized that these five do not constitute the self; their interaction creates the illusion of self. He compared form to a lump of foam, sensation to a bubble, perception to a mirage, mental formations to a banana trunk (which has no hardwood core), and consciousness to an illusion. Evidently this *skandha* doctrine was one of the earliest teachings of the Buddha. It appears in the second sutra he is believed to have preached, which emphasizes that each *skandha* is impermanent, unsatisfactory (*duḥkha*), and without self. The recommended attitude is to regard each *skandha* "with proper wisdom, according to reality, thus: 'These are not mine, this I am not, this is not my self.'" As a result, the "well-instructed noble disciple, understanding this, wearies of them, becomes passion-free, and is thereby emancipated. And, upon hearing this sermon, the five disciples became emancipated."[52]

Much more could be said about the *skandhas,* but that way of deconstructing the self has been overshadowed by and even subsumed into *pratītya-samutpāda,* by far the most important doctrine in Buddhism. The Buddha said that someone who understands *pratītya-samutpāda* understands his teaching, and vice versa. Dependent origination explains our experience by locating all phenomena within a set of twelve factors, each conditioned by and conditioning all the others. The twelve links of this chain (a later doctrinal construct which integrates

shorter chains that the Buddha elaborated on different occasions[53]) are traditionally understood as follows.

The presupposition of the whole process is (1) *ignorance* or ignore-ance,
because something about experience is overlooked in our usual eagerness to
gratify desires. Due to this ignorance, the other factors function, including (2)
volitional tendencies (the fourth of the *skandhas*) from a person's previous lifetime
which survive physical death and tend to cause a new birth. The original Sanskrit
term *saṃskārah* is notoriously difficult to translate; sometimes it is rendered
"*karma*-formations." Literally something like "preparation, get up," it refers to
the influence that the residues of previous mental activities have on our conative
acts. The persistence of these volitional tendencies explains how rebirth occurs
without a permanent soul or persisting self to be reborn: The *saṃskārah* survive
physical death to affect the new (3) *consciousness* that arises when a fertilized
egg is conceived. This survival does not imply that anything is eternal. Both
volitional tendencies and the resulting rebirth-consciousness are impermanent,
conditioned by earlier factors and conditioning later ones.

Conception causes (4) *mind-body*, the fetus, to grow, which develops (5) the
six sense-organs, including the mental organ of mind understood as that which
perceives mental objects. The sense-organs allow (6) *contact* between each organ
and its respective sense-object, giving rise to (7) *sensation*, which leads to (8)
craving for that sensation. Craving causes (9) *grasping* or attachment to life in
general. Such clinging is traditionally classified into four types: clinging to
pleasure, to views, to morality or external observances, and to belief in a soul
or self. This classification is striking because it ignores any difference in kind
between physical sense grasping and mental attachment; evidently the same
problematic tendency manifests in all four. Grasping leads to (10) *becoming*,
the tendency after physical death to be reborn, causing (11) another *birth* and
therefore (12) "decay and death, sorrow, lamentation, pain, grief and despair."
And so the cycle continues.

These twelve links are usually understood to describe three lifetimes: the
first two factors give causes from the past that have led to our present existence;
the next five are their effects in the present; the following three are causes in
the present life which will lead to another birth; the last two are their effects
in a future life. These three lifetimes have also been taken metaphorically, as
referring to the various factors conditioning and conditioned by every moment.
In neither case is ignorance a "first cause" that initiated the whole process in
some distant past, for there is no first cause. The twelve factors are interdependent,
each conditioning all the others, and there is no reference in Buddhism to
some pristine time before this cycle began operating. Even (8) craving, which
the second of the Four Noble Truths gives as the cause of *duhkha*, is here
explained as conditioned by (7) sensation, which in turn is conditioned by (6)
contact, and so forth. In response to the problem of how rebirth can occur

without a permanent soul or self that is reborn, rebirth is explained as a series of impersonal processes which occur without any self that is doing or experiencing them. In one Pali sutra, a monk asks the Buddha to whom belong, and for whom occur, the phenomena described in *pratītya-samutpāda*. The Buddha rejects that question as misguided; from each factor as its preconditions arises another factor; that is all. The karmic results of action are experienced without their being anyone who created the *karma* or anyone who receives its fruit, although there is a causal connection between the action and its result.

A chain is only as strong as its weakest link, which suggests the Buddhist solution to this cycle of suffering. "Through the entire fading away and extinction of this ignorance [the first factor], however, the *saṃskārah* [the second factor] become extinguished," an extinction which in turn affects the third factor, and so forth until all twelve factors have been extinguished. "Thus takes place the extinction of this whole mass of suffering." This formulation has encouraged many Buddhist as well as most Western commentators to understand Buddhism as nihilistic, yet Śākyamuni Buddha himself denied this, for that misunderstands the significance of the fact that from the very beginning there has never been any self to be annihilated.

This exposition of basic doctrines in early Buddhism may seem a digression from our earlier discussions of death, *lack*, and the return of the repressed. It is necessary to keep in mind, therefore, the connection that Buddhism emphasizes between such theoretical constructs and the praxis they underpin. All Buddhist doctrines may be viewed as heuristic, because they all refer back to the essential matter of resolving our *duhkha*. We need to learn how the chain that leads to *duhkha* functions in order to understand how to end it. We must realize how certain, largely automatized and unconscious, ways of understanding ourselves in the world perpetuate both our sense-of-self and the objectified world we find ourselves in; that this delusive way of bifurcating experience causes *duhkha*; and that what has thereby been constructed may also be deconstructed.

From this point of view, the important issue is not whether the five *skandhas* are the correct or the only synchronous way to analyze the sense-of-self, nor whether the Buddhist doctrines of *karma* and rebirth are valid. It has already been noticed that there is more than one way to interpret Buddhist claims about *karma* and rebirth, but that issue (and the methodological problem of how such claims might be evaluated) will not distract us because it is tangential to the main point: the essential relation between *duhkha* and the sense-of-self. Our discussion of that relationship is not yet complete, because the Buddhist understanding of *pratītya-samutpāda* changed radically with the development of Mahāyāna. Nāgārjuna's interpretation of *pratītya-samutpāda* constituted a "Copernican revolution" within Buddhism. As with Copernicus and Kant, the change of perspective is simple yet it transforms the way everything is perceived.

The Buddha appointed no successor: "Let the *dharma* [the teachings] be

88 LACK AND TRANSCENDENCE

your guide." Inevitably, then, his words were canonized. Because those teachings were voluminous and repetitive, a "higher dharma" (*abhidharma*) was abstracted from the Buddha's lengthy guidebook (a raft that can be used to cross the river of life-and-death and then should be abandoned, to use the Buddha's analogy). Since sense-of-self is due to interaction among the *skandha* "heaps," as explained by *pratītya-samutpāda*, the abhidharmikas concluded that reality is plural: What exists are these various elements, which they enumerated and classified. Unfortunately, this process of extricating a core teaching also transformed the Buddha's path of liberation into the sort of metaphysics the Buddha had warned against.

The Mādhyamika critique of all philosophical views was a reaction to this. The locus classicus of this approach is the *Mūlamadhyamikakārikās* (hereafter MMK) of Nāgārjuna, who is believed to have lived in the second century A.D. The MMK offers a systematic analysis of the important philosophical issues of its time, not to solve them but to demonstrate that any possible conceptual solution is self-contradictory or otherwise unjustifiable. This is not done to prepare the ground for Nāgārjuna's own solution: "If I were to advance any thesis whatsoever, that in itself would be a fault; but I advance no thesis and so cannot be faulted."[54] The best way to elucidate Nāgārjuna's argument is to consider separately what the MMK says about *śūnyatā* and *nirvāṇa*. In the contemporary context, it will also be helpful to compare his deconstruction with that of Jacques Derrida, for although their approaches have important similarities they reach somewhat different conclusions.

Sunyata

> The spiritual conquerors have proclaimed *śūnyatā* to be the exhaustion of all theories and views; those for whom *śūnyatā* is itself a theory they declared to be incurable.
>
> We interpret *pratītya-samutpāda* as *śūnyatā*. *Śūnyatā* is a guiding, not a cognitive, notion, presupposing the everyday. (MMK, XII:8, XXIV:11,18)[55]

The first verse of the MMK proclaims its thoroughgoing critique of *being*: "No things whatsoever exist, at any time or place, having risen by themselves, from another, from both or without cause." Paralleling the poststructuralist radicalization of structuralist claims about language, Nāgārjuna's argument merely brings out more fully the implications of *pratītya-samutpāda*. Dependent origination is not a doctrine about causal relations between entities, because the mutual interdependence of these twelve factors means they are not really entities. In Derridean terms, none of the twelve phenomena—which in Buddhism are understood to encompass everything—is self-present because each is infected with the traces of all the others. That none is self-present is the meaning of *śūnya* and its substantive *śūnyatā*, terms notoriously difficult to translate. They seem to derive from the root *śū*, which means "to be swollen," like a hollow balloon but also like a pregnant woman; therefore the usual English translation "empty" and "emptiness" needs to be supplemented with the notion of "pregnant with possibilities." Rather than *śūnyatā* being a negative concept, Nāgārjuna emphasizes that it is only because everything is *śūnya* that any change, including spiritual transformation, is possible.

Regardless of how we decide to translate it, the point of *śūnyatā* is to deconstruct the self-existence/self-presence of things. Although Nāgārjuna addresses the main philosophical theories of his day, his target is as much that unconscious, automatized metaphysics disguised as *the world we live in.* If philosophy were merely a preoccupation of academics one could ignore it, but we have no choice in the matter because we are all philosophers. The fundamental categories of everydayness for us are self-existing/self-present things which nonetheless originate, change, and eventually cease to be; in order to explain the relations among these things, the categories of space, time and causality must also be employed. The most important and problematical of these supposedly self-existing things is, of course, the self. The Buddhist notion of interdependent factors is thus diametrically opposed to the Cartesian notion of an autonomous, self-grounded consciousness. And the vehicle of this commonsense metaphysics, creating and sustaining it, is language, which presents us with a set of nouns (self-existing things) that have temporal and causal predicates (arise, change, and cease).

The corresponding danger with *śūnyatā* is that it will itself become re-appropriated into a privileged metaphysical category, so Nāgārjuna was careful to warn that *śūnyatā* was a heuristic, not a cognitive notion. Although the concept of *śūnyatā* is so central to Mādhyamika that the school became known as *śūnyavāda* ("the way of *śūnya*"), there is no such thing as *śūnyatā*. Here there is an obvious parallel with Derrida's *différance. Śūnyatā,* like *différance,* is permanently under erasure, deployed for tactical reasons but denied any semantic or conceptual stability. It "presupposes the everyday" because it is parasitic on the notion of things, which it refutes—thereby refuting itself at the same time. "If there were something not *śūnya* there would be something *śūnya*; but there is nothing not *śūnya*, so how can anything be *śūnya*?" (MMK XII:7). For Nāgārjuna as well as Derrida, *différance/śūnyatā* is valuable because it provides a "non-philosophical site" from which to question philosophy itself. Yet, as Derrida emphasizes, the history of philosophy is the metaphysical reincorporation of such non-sites. Nāgārjuna warned that *śūnyatā* was a snake which if grasped at the wrong end could be fatal (MMK XXIV:11), but that nonetheless happened in later Buddhism, which transcendentalized such categories as *śūnyatā, vijñaptimātratā,* and Buddhanature. If those for whom *śūnyatā* is itself a theory are incurable, the question why so many people are incurable—why we seem to need some such theory—must be addressed, and will be taken up in the next chapter.

Until recently, Western philosophy has been largely a search for the one within the many, the Same that grounds Difference. Our century has seen the end of this project. Perhaps the most dramatic refutation has come from psychology, in Freud's demonstration that our ego-consciousness is not autonomous but irretrievably split, buffeted by psychic forces it cannot control because it is a function of them. Others have questioned our supposedly self-sufficient self-consciousness by emphasizing the differences inherent within language. The Swiss linguist Saussure taught that meaning is a function not of any straightforward correspondence between signifier and signified, but of a complex set of phonetic and conceptual differences. More recently the French critic Roland Barthes has pointed out that each text is a tissue of quotations: not a line of words releasing the single "theological" meaning of an author-god but a multi-dimensional space where a variety of writings blend and/or clash. Today Jacques Derrida argues that the significance of such a multi-dimensional space can never be completely determined, for the continual circulation of signifiers denies meaning any fixed foundation or conclusion. *What would we end up with if we extrapolated these claims about textuality to the whole universe?*

Nāgārjuna's logical and epistemological analyses did not appeal to the Chinese, who preferred a more metaphorical way to express the interconditionality of all phenomena: the analogy of Indra's net described in the Avataṃsaka Sūtra and developed in the Hua-yen school of Mahāyāna.

> Far away in the heavenly abode of the great god Indra, there is a wonderful net that has been hung by some cunning artificer in such a manner that it stretches out infinitely in all directions. In accordance with the extravagant tastes of deities, the artificer has hung a single glittering jewel in each "eye" of the net, and since the net itself is infinite in all dimensions, the jewels are infinite in number. There hang the jewels, glittering like stars of the first magnitude, a wonderful sight to behold. If we now arbitrarily select one of these jewels for inspection and look closely at it, we will discover that in its polished surface there are reflected all the other jewels in the net, infinite in number. Not only that, but each of the jewels reflected in this one jewel is also reflecting all the other jewels, so that there is an infinite reflecting process occurring. . . . [I]t symbolizes a cosmos in which there is an infinitely repeated interrelationship among all the members of the cosmos. This relationship is said to be one of simultaneous mutual identity and mutual inter-causality. (Francis Cook)[56]

Every such "individual" is at the same time the effect of the whole and the cause of the whole, the totality being an infinite body of members each of which is sustaining and defining all the others. "The cosmos is, in short, a self-creating, self-maintaining, and self-defining organism." This world is non-teleological: "There is no theory of a beginning time, no concept of a creator, no question of the purpose of it all. The universe is taken as a given." Such a universe has no hierarchy: "There is no center, or, perhaps if there is one, it is everywhere."[57]

That *this* textuality extends beyond language means that right now you are reading more than the teachings of Mahāyāna Buddhism as interpreted by David Loy, for in this page is nothing less than the entire universe. The Vietnamese Zen master (and poet) Thich Nhat Hanh makes the point better than I can:

If you are a poet, you will see clearly that there is a cloud floating in this sheet of paper. Without a cloud, there will be no rain; without rain, the trees cannot grow, and without trees we cannot make paper. The cloud is essential for the paper to exist. If the cloud is not here, the sheet of paper cannot be here either. . . .

If we look into this sheet of paper even more deeply, we can see the sunshine in it. If the sunshine is not there, the tree cannot grow. In fact, nothing can grow. Even we cannot grow without sunshine. And so, we know that the sunshine is also in this sheet of paper. The paper and the sunshine inter-are. And if we continue to look, we can see the logger who cut the tree and brought it to the mill to be transformed into paper. And we see the wheat. We know that the logger cannot exist without his daily bread, and therefore the wheat that became his bread is also in this sheet of paper. And the logger's father and mother are in it too. . . .

You cannot point out one thing that is not here—time, space, the earth, the rain, the minerals in the soil, the sunshine, the cloud, the river, the heat. Everything co-exists with this sheet of paper. . . . As thin as this sheet of paper is, it contains everything in the universe in it.[58]

To emphasize Nāgārjuna's point, the metaphor of Indra's Net does not refer to our interdependence, for that would presuppose the existence of discrete things which are being related together. Rather, just as for Derrida every sign is the sign of a sign, so everywhere in the universe there are only traces, and those traces are traces of traces.

Can our *duḥkha* be explained in terms of Indra's Net? Buddhism relates our dis-ease to the delusive nature of the ego-self, which like everything else is a manifestation of Indra's net, *yet feels separate from it*. The basic difficulty is that insofar as I feel separate (i.e., an autonomous, self-existing consciousness) I also feel uncomfortable, because an illusory sense of separateness is inevitably insecure. It is an ineluctable trace of nothingness in my fictitious (because not really self-existing) sense-of-self that is experienced as a sense-of-*lack*; in reaction, the sense-of-self becomes preoccupied with trying to make itself self-existing, in one or another symbolic fashion. The tragic irony is that the ways we attempt to do this cannot succeed, for a sense-of-self can never expel the trace of *lack* that constitutes it insofar as it is illusory; while in the most important sense we are already self-existing, because *the infinite set of differential traces that constitutes each of us is nothing less than the whole net*. "The self-existence of a Buddha is the self-existence of this very cosmos. The Buddha is without a self-existent nature; the cosmos too is without a self-existent nature" (MMK XXII:16). What Nāgārjuna says here about the Buddha is equally true for each jewel in

Indra's Net; the difference is that a Buddha knows it. I think this touches on the enduring attraction of what Heidegger calls onto-theology and Derrida calls logocentrism, not just in the West but everywhere: Being/being means security to us because it grounds the self, whether that is understood as experiencing something Transcendent or is intellectually sublimated into a metaphysical principle underlying everything. We want to grasp Being by meeting God face-to-face, or by gaining enlightenment, yet the fact that everything is *śūnya* means we can never resolve our *duḥkha* in that fashion.

As long as I am motivated by sense-of-*lack*, I shall seek to real-ize myself by fixating on something that dissolves in my grasp, since not only texts but everything else too is an elusive trace of traces. Then the solution must have to do with not-catching, with no longer needing to bring these fleeting traces to self-presence. What that involves phenomenologically will be discussed later in this chapter.

Nirvana

There is no specifiable difference whatsoever between *nirvāṇa* and the everyday world; there is no specifiable difference whatever between the everyday world and *nirvāṇa*.

The ontic range of *nirvāṇa* is the ontic range of the everyday world. There is not even the subtlest difference between the two.

That which, taken as causal or dependent, is the process of being born and passing on, is, taken non-causally and beyond all dependence, declared to be *nirvāṇa*.

Ultimate serenity is the coming to rest of all ways of taking things, the repose of named things; no truth has been taught by a Buddha for anyone, anywhere. (MMK XXV:19, 20, 9, 24)

The climactic chapter of the MMK addresses the nature of *nirvāṇa* in order to demonstrate that, if there is no self-existence or self-presence, even *nirvāṇa* must be *śūnya*. The everyday world of *saṃsāra*, which is the process of things being born, changing, and passing away, is the world of our *duḥkha*. Nāgārjuna turns traditional Buddhism upside-down by asserting that there is no specifiable difference between this world and the Buddhist goal of *nirvāṇa*. There is, however, a difference of perspective, or a difference in the way they are "taken."

The irony of Nāgārjuna's approach to *pratītya-samutpāda* is that its use of causation also refutes causation. Having deconstructed the self-existence or self-presence of things (including us) into conditions and interdependence, causality itself disappears, because without any*thing* to cause/be effected, the world will not be experienced in terms of cause and effect either. Once causality has been used to refute the apparent self-existence of objective things, the lack of things to relate together refutes causality. If things originate (and change, cease to exist, etc.), there are no self-existing things; but if there are no such things, then there is nothing to originate and therefore no origination. It is because we see the world as a collection of discrete things that we superimpose causal relationships, to glue these things together. Therefore the victory of causality is Pyrrhic, for if there is only causality there is no causality.

The aporias of causality are well known in Western philosophy, mainly due to Hume's critique. Nāgārjuna's version points to the contradiction necessary for a cause-and-effect relationship: The effect can be neither the same as the cause nor different from it. If the effect is the same as the cause, nothing has been caused; if the two are clearly different, then the necessary relationship between them is lost and any cause should be able to cause any effect.[59]

This helps us appreciate the final stage of the Mādhyamika and Hua-yen deconstruction of self-existence. To say that an event (e.g., Śākyamuni Buddha's twirling a flower) is caused by everything in the universe *is finally equivalent to saying that the event is caused by nothing*. It is not self-caused; rather, the category of causality is in effect eliminated. This is *tathatā*, the thusness or just *this*!-ness which describes the way an enlightened being lives, according to Mahāyāna. The Buddha is the *Tathāgata*, the one who "just comes" and "just goes."

This transforms *pratītya-samutpāda* from a doctrine of dependent origination into an account of non-dependent non-origination. It describes not the interaction of things but the sequence and juxtaposition of appearances—or what could be called appearances if there were some non-appearance to be contrasted with. Origination, duration, and cessation are "like an illusion, a dream, or an imaginary city in the sky" (MMK VII:34). The *Diamond Sutra* concludes that "all phenomena are like a dream, an illusion, a bubble and a shadow, like dew and lightning," and the *Gaṇḍavyūha Sūtra* relates this to what became Hua-yen's doctrine of nonobstruction: "Having realized that this world is like a dream, and that all Buddhas are like mere reflections, that all things are like an echo, you move unimpeded in the world."[60] As soon as we abolish the real world, "appearance" becomes the only reality, and we discover "a world scattered in pieces, covered with explosions; a world freed from the ties of gravity (i.e., from relationship with a foundation); a world made of moving and light surfaces where the incessant shifting of masks is named laughter, dance, game" (Michel Haar).[61]

Our way of trying to solve a problem again turns out to be what maintains the problem. We try to peel away the apparent world to get at the real one, but that dualism between them *is* our problematic delusion, which leaves, as the only remaining candidate for real world, the apparent one—a world whose actual nature has not been noticed because we have been so concerned to transcend it. And without any effective dualism between real and apparent, the question of whether the world is real or apparent loses meaning.[62]

One such "appearance" is what is called a Buddha. Insofar as we strive to *become* a Buddha, we misunderstand the Buddha's teaching. The serenity (*śiva*) we seek is the coming-to-rest of all ways of taking things, the repose of named things (*sarvopalambhopaśamaprapañcopaśamah*), including those called "Buddhas" (MMK XXV:24). Nāgārjuna's most important commentator, Candrakīrti (seventh century), glosses this verse: "The very coming to rest, the non-functioning, of perceptions as signs of all named things, is itself *nirvāṇa*. . . . When verbal assertions cease, named things are in repose; and the ceasing to function of discursive thought is ultimate serenity."[63] The problem is not merely that language acts as a filter, obscuring the nature of things. Names objectify appearances into the self-existing things we perceive *as* books, tables, trees, you and me. In other words, the objective world of material things, which interact causally in space and time, is metaphysical through-and-through. It is this metaphysics that most needs to be deconstructed, according to Buddhism, because this is the metaphysics, disguised as commonsense reality, which makes me suffer, especially insofar as I understand myself to be one such self-existing being in time that will nonetheless die.

It is possible to end our *duḥkha* because the coming-to-rest of using names to take perceptions as self-existing objects can deconstruct the automatized inside-outside dualism between our sense-of-self and the "objective" everyday world. Since that world is as differential, as full of traces, as the textual discourse Derrida analyzes, the Buddhist response is to use those differences/traces to deconstruct that objectified world—including ourselves, since we sub-jects are the first to be ob-jectified. If there are only traces of traces, what happens when we stop trying to arrest those elusive traces into self-present things? "When there is clinging perception [*upadane*], the perceiver generates being. When there is no clinging perception, he will be freed and there will be no being" (MMK XXVI:7).

This explains how Buddhist doctrine deconstructs the self-existence of things, yet this is not sufficient for understanding how that deconstructs our sense-of-*lack*. The last section of this chapter will address that phenomenological deconstruction by considering how the most fundamental dualism of all— between my ungrounded sense of being and the nonbeing or no-thing-ness that threatens it—may be conflated.

Letting the mind come forth. By now it has become clear that, from the Buddhist perspective, our most problematic duality is not life against death but self versus nonself. In psychological terms, our primal repression is not denial of death-fear—which still holds the feared thing at arm's length by projecting it into the future—but the sense-of-self repressing its suspected nothingness right now. I have argued that we become aware of this most intimate threat as a sense-of-*lack* that haunts our sense-of-self. According to Andre Malraux, the greatest mystery of life is not that we find ourselves thrown randomly into the universe, "but that in this prison we can fashion images of ourselves sufficiently powerful to deny our nothingness." Yet why has it always been so important for us to deny our nothingness? Is it the need to deny our nothingness that makes us experience the universe as a prison?

This particular bipolarity infects much of our thinking. A good example is Paul Tillich's *The Courage to Be*. According to Tillich, ontological anxiety is anxiety about one's ultimate nonbeing, which for him means not being able to preserve one's own being. Since he believes this anxiety cannot be eliminated, his theological solution is for us to be accepted by the Power of Being, which gives us the courage to affirm being despite the threat of nonbeing. God is "the self-affirmation of Being itself which prevails against nonbeing." Perhaps it is reassuring to learn that God is not on the side of nonbeing—which is presumably why nonbeing does not rate a capital—but the Buddhist approach is different. As Yung Chia put it, "Being is not being. Non-being is not non-being. Miss this rule by a hair and you are off by a thousand miles."[64] Such conceptual paradoxes may not seem directly relevant to our lives, yet the speculations of theologians and metaphysicians are only the most abstract version of a game which touches our core, since the basic issue turns out to be the groundedness or groundlessness of that core. If our lives are a search for being, sublimated into one or another symbolic form, no problem is more intimate that the bifurcation of being from nothingness. Like the matter and anti-matter of quantum physics, they arise together in relation to each other, and therefore they should be able to disappear together by collapsing back into each other which cannot leave the nothingness we dread (for that is one of the two poles) but ... what?

In the *Samyutta Nikāya*, Śākyamuni declares that "the world is nothing in itself and for itself. ... therefore it is said that the world is nothing." What is this nothing? He says that it is the six organs of eye, ear, nose, tongue, body, and mind, their six sense objects, and the six corresponding types of sense-consciousness. Yet the Buddha also describes these same eighteen *indriyas* as *the all*: "Whosoever, O monks, should say: 'Reject this all, I will proclaim another all'—it would be mere talk on his part. ... Why so? Because it is beyond his scope to do so." The Buddha then provides "a teaching for the abandonment of the all": "The eye must be abandoned, visual-objects must be abandoned, eye-consciousness must be abandoned, eye-contact must be abandoned. That enjoyment or suffering or neutral state experienced which arises according to eye contact—that also must be abandoned." And so forth for all the other senses.[65] Since the Buddha has just said that these eighteen *indriyas* encompass everything, such a teaching seems odd: There is nothing else to become, nowhere else to turn. The solution is so obvious that we are likely to overlook it: It is simply to realize something about the *śūnya* "empty" nature of these phenomena, an approach that Mahāyāna later developed in detail.

As in psychotherapy, the Buddhist solution to bipolar dualisms involves recognizing the side that has been denied. If death is what the sense-of-self fears, the answer is for the sense-of-self to die. If it is no-thing-ness (i.e., the repressed intuition that, rather than being autonomous and self-existent, the "I" is a construct) I am afraid of, the best way to resolve that fear is to become nothing. In another passage from the *Genjō-kōan* fascicle of the *Shōbōgenzō* (quoted in previous chapters), Dōgen sums up this process:

> To study the buddha way is to study the self. To study the self is to forget the self. To forget the self is to be actualized by myriad things. When actualized by myriad things, your body and mind as well as the bodies and minds of others drop away. No trace of realization remains, and this no-trace continues endlessly.[66]

"Forgetting" ourselves is how we jewels in Indra's Net lose our sense of separation and realize that we are the net. Meditation is learning how to die by learning to forget the sense-of-self, which happens when I become absorbed into my meditation-exercise. If the sense-of-self is a result of consciousness reflecting back upon itself in order to grasp itself, such meditation practice makes sense as an exercise in *de-reflection*. Consciousness *un*learns trying to grasp itself, real-ize itself, objectify itself. Enlightenment occurs in Buddhism when the usually automatized reflexivity of consciousness ceases, which is experienced as a letting-go and falling into the void and being wiped out of existence. "Men are afraid to forget their minds, fearing to fall through the Void with nothing to stay their fall. They do not know that the Void is not really void, but the realm of the real Dharma" (Huang-po).[67] This process implies that what we fear as nothingness is not really nothingness, for that is the perspective of a sense-of-self anxious about losing its grip on itself. According to Buddhism, letting go of myself and merging with that no-thing-ness leads to something else: When consciousness stops trying to catch its own tail, I become no-thing, and discover that I am everything—or, more precisely, that I can be anything. Then, when I no longer strive to make myself real through things, I find myself "actualized" by them, says Dōgen.

An example of Zen meditation (which puts Hua-yen theory into practice, according to D. T. Suzuki) may be helpful here. In the Zen lineage that I am familiar with, a first *kōan*, such as Joshu's *Mu*, is treated more or less like a *mantram*. Putting all one's mental energy into "muuu . . ." (repeated mentally during breath exhalations) undermines the sense-of-self by letting go of the mental processes which sustain it. At the beginning of such practice, one attempts to concentrate on "muuu . . ." but is distracted by other thoughts, feelings, memories, desires, and intentions that arise. A later, more focused stage is when one can concentrate on "muuu . . ." without losing it: "Muuu . . ." effectively keeps other thoughts away. The stage when "both inside and outside naturally fuse" occurs when there is no longer the sense of an "I" that is repeating an objective sound; there is only "muuu . . ." This stage is sometimes described by saying that now "muuu . . ." is doing "muuu . . ." It is "muuu . . ." that sits, walks, eats, and so forth.

Sometimes this practice leads to a condition that has been described as hanging over a precipice. "Except for occasional feelings of uneasiness and despair, it is like death itself." (Hakuin). The solution is to throw oneself completely into "muuu. . . ."

> Bravely let go on the edge of the cliff
> Throw yourself into the abyss with decision and courage
> You only revive after death! (Po-shan)

At this point the teacher may help by cutting the last thread. An unexpected action, such as a blow or shout or even a few quiet words, may startle the student into letting go. "All of a sudden he finds his mind and body wiped out of existence, together with the *kōan*. This is what is known as 'letting go your hold'" (Hakuin).[68] One classical Zen story tells how a student was enlightened by the sound of a pebble striking bamboo. When the practice is ripe, the shock of an unexpected sensation can help it to penetrate to the very core of one's illusory sense of being—that is, it is experienced nondually. Is this being or nothingness? Groundlessness or groundedness? If each link of *pratītya-samutpāda* is a trace of all the others, if each jewel in Indra's Net mutually conditions and is conditioned by all the other jewels, then to become completely groundless is also to become completely grounded, not in some particular but in the whole web of interdependent relations. The supreme irony of my struggle to ground myself is that it cannot succeed because I am already grounded *in the totality*. Or, better: as the totality. Buddhism implies that I am groundless and ungroundable insofar as delusively feeling myself to be separate from the world; yet I have always been fully grounded insofar as I am not other than the world.

With that conflation, the no-thing at my core is transformed from sense-of-*lack* into a serenity that is imperturbable because nothing is there to be perturbed. "When neither existence nor non-existence again is presented to the mind, then, through the lack of any other possibility, that which is without support becomes tranquil" (Śāntideva).[69] We have already noticed this in the last verse of Nāgārjuna's *nirvāṇa* chapter: "Ultimate serenity is the coming to rest of all ways of taking things, the repose of named things."[70] As long as the sense-of-self needs to ground itself, the hole at my core is experienced as a *lack* threatening my fragile sense of being. To let go and become groundless is to realize that that hole is what grounds me: because it allows me to be grounded in the totality of interdependent relations.

How does this solve the problem of desire, the pendulum of frustration alternating with boredom? We find some help for this problem in an unlikely place. In an abstruse section of his Encyclopedia *Logic*, Hegel analyzes *schlechte Unendlichkeit*, literally "false endlessness" or "the bad infinite." He begins by defining determination as the particularizing characteristic of something, that quality which distinguishes it from other things. Such determination implies that the particularizing characteristic of each thing always has reference to other things: If a certain rose is unique because it is white, its uniqueness depends on all other roses being red, yellow, etc. We tend to see things as distinct from each other, but in such fashion each entity is dependent upon the others it is distinguished from, so much so that it might be said to have these others "within itself" as the conditions of its own determination. This, of course, is the argument Nāgārjuna uses to establish that things are *śūnya*, and the point Hua-yen makes with the metaphor of Indra's Net. Such interpenetration implies that the nature of every apparently distinct quality will vary as any of the others do. Hegel calls this *alienation* because it alienates each thing from itself: it is not really self-determining, if it is the sum of all the effects of all the others. This is a *bad infinite* insofar as a thing wants to free itself from such determination; all it can do is exchange one finite determination for another.

The reason for this excursus into Hegel's algebraic parable is that his resolution of the bad infinite involves the same reversal of perspective that Buddhist practice leads to. His bad-infinite expresses nicely the difficulty for an animal who endeavors to real-ize himself in ways which keep unravelling. As long as there is sense-of-*lack*, the sense-of-self cannot help trying to fixate itself, but what if *lack* comes to an end? A consciousness that seeks to ground itself by fixating on something dooms itself to perpetual dissatisfaction, for the impermanence of all phenomena means no such perch can be found. But since it is our *lack* that compels us to seek such a perch, the end of *lack* allows a different perspective. For Hegel too, true (as opposed to bad) infinity requires only a change of perspective. The solution is a different way of experiencing the problem: the "free-ranging variable" which always has some finite determination yet is not bound to any particular one. The bad infinite of *lack* transforms into the good infinite of a variable that needs to be nothing in particular. In Hegelian terms, this transforms the alienation of other-determination into the freedom of being-for-itself. In Buddhist terms, this transforms the alienation of a reflexive sense-of-self, always trying to fixate itself, into the freedom of an "empty" mind that can become anything because it does not need to become something.

The *Aṣṭasāhasrikā*, one of the most important *prajñāpāramitā* ("highest wisdom") sutras, begins by describing this "good infinity":

> No wisdom can we get hold of, no highest perfection,
> No Bodhisattva, no thought of enlightenment either.
> When told of this, if not bewildered and in no way anxious,
> A Bodhisattva courses in the Tathagata's wisdom.
> In form, in feeling, will, perception and awareness [the five *skandhas*]
> Nowhere in them they find a place to rest on.
> Without a home they wander, dharmas never hold them,
> Nor do they grasp at them. . . .
> But when he does not course in form, in feeling, or perception,

In will or consciousness, but wanders without home,
Remaining unaware of coursing firm in wisdom,
His thoughts on non-production—then the best of all the calming trances
cleaves to him.
The Leader himself was not stationed in the realm which is free from
conditions,
Nor in the things which are under conditions, but freely he wandered
without a home:
Just so, without a support or a basis a Bodhisattva is standing.[71]

"How is *prajñāparamitā* characterized?" asks Subhūti later in the same sutra. "It is characterized by non-attachment," replies the Buddha, who explains how defilement and purification are possible when there are no things to be defiled or purified:

To the extent that beings take hold of things and settle down in them, to that extent there is defilement. But no one is thereby defiled. And to the extent that one does not take hold of things and does not settle down in them, to that extent can one conceive of the absence of I-making and mine-making. In that sense can one form the concept of the purification of beings, i.e., to the extent that they do not take hold of things and do not settle down in them, to that extent there is purification. But no one is therein purified. When a Bodhisattva courses thus, he courses in *prajñāparamitā*.[72]

For Buddhism, the problem of desire is solved when, without the craving-for-being that compels me to take hold of something and try to settle down in it, I am free to *become* it. The Buddhist solution to the problem of life is thus very simple: the "bong!" of a temple bell, the "tock!" of pebble against bamboo, the flowers on a tree in springtime, to cite some Zen examples. Of course, becoming an object is precisely what we have been trying to do all along, yet in a self-defeating way, by compulsively seizing on our own objectifications in order to stabilize ourselves. But grasping at something merely reinforces the delusive sense of separation between that-which-is-grasped and that-which-grasps-at-it. The only way I can become a phenomenon is to realize I have always been it, according to Buddhism. When nothing is needed from the object to fill up my *lack*, it can be just what it is—the reverberating temple bell, and so forth: the cause and effect of everything, therefore just as much the cause or effect of nothing; neither reality nor appearance; and no longer frustrating because there is no longer anything lacking in me that I need to project as something lacking in my world.

If I *am* the object, however, it no longer makes sense to understand it as an object. When there is no sense-of-self that is supposed to be inside, there is no outside. In the "Sokushinzebutsu" fascicle of the *Shōbōgenzō*, Dōgen quotes the Chinese Ch'an master Yang-shan: Mind is "mountains, rivers, earth, the sun, the moon and the stars."

All the Buddhas and all sentient beings are nothing but the one mind, beside which nothing exists. This mind, which is without beginning, is unborn and indestructible. It is not green nor yellow, and has neither form nor appearance. It does not belong to the categories of things which exist or do not exist, nor can it be thought about in terms of new or old. It is neither long nor short, big nor small, for it transcends all limits, measures, names, traces and comparisons. It is that which you see before you—begin to reason about it and you at once fall into error. (Huang-po)[73]

The mind that Dōgen and Huang-po refer to is not some transcendental Absolute. It is nothing other than your mind and my mind, which is not green or yellow or big or small, because a free-ranging variable is not bound to any particular determination, which is why it can become green or yellow or big or small or. ... According to Buddhism, such a mind is *ab-solute* in the original sense of the term, unconditioned. Meditative techniques decondition the mind from its tendency to secure itself by circling in familiar ruts, in this way enabling its freedom to become anything. Such a mind is unborn and uncreated, yet it cannot real-ize this as long as it consciously or unconsciously understands its fundamental task as making itself real or finding some safe home.

Should your mind wander away, do not follow it, whereupon your wandering mind will stop wandering of its own accord. Should your mind desire to linger somewhere, do not follow it and do not dwell there, whereupon your mind's questing for a dwelling-place will cease of its own accord. Thereby, you will come to possess a non-dwelling mind—a mind which remains in the state of non-dwelling. If you are fully aware in yourself of a non-dwelling mind, you will discover that there is just the fact of dwelling, with nothing to dwell upon or not to dwell upon. This full awareness in yourself of a mind dwelling upon nothing is known as having a clear perception of your own nature. A mind which dwells upon nothing is the Buddha-Mind, the mind of one already delivered, Bodhi-Mind, Uncreate Mind ... you will have attained to understanding from within yourself—an understanding stemming from a mind that abides nowhere, by which we mean a mind free from delusion and reality alike. (Hui-hai)[74]

A mind that abides nowhere is free from both delusion and reality because the dualism between them—rejecting the one, grasping the other—is one of the more sublimated ways the mind seeks a secure dwelling-place, as will be discussed in chapter 4.

The most-quoted line from the *Diamond Sutra* encapsulates all this in one phrase: "Let your mind come forth without fixing it anywhere." This is believed to have precipitated the deep enlightenment of the sixth patriarch Hui-neng, acknowledged as the greatest Ch'an master. His own *Platform Sutra* emphasizes the same thing: "If we never let our mind attach to anything, we shall gain liberation." To obtain liberation is to attain what he calls "thoughtlessness." Thoughtlessness suggests blankness of mind, yet that is not what Hui-neng means: "Thoughtlessness is to see and know all things with a mind free from attachment. When in use it pervades everywhere, and yet it sticks nowhere.... When our mind works freely without any hindrance, and is at liberty to come or to go, we attain ... liberation." Such a mind "is everywhere present, yet it 'sticks' nowhere."[75]

Lacking nothing. This chapter has shown how Buddhism anticipated the reluctant conclusions of modern psychology: Guilt and anxiety are not adventitious but intrinsic to the ego. Schopenhauer and Sartre ground the self's *lack* in the metaphysical structure of the universe (a monism of unsatisfiable will, a neo-Cartesian dualism of objectified being and frustrated consciousness), yet we have seen reasons to doubt their pessimistic conclusions. The influence of Schopenhauer in late nineteenth-century Europe raises questions about the intellectual origins of Freud's libido theory. Does it discover the wellsprings of our behavior or import an unconscious metaphysical presumption that Freud was never able to question? In replacing repression of sexual wishes with repression of death-fear, later psychoanalytic theory has shifted its attention from libido to the ways we perceive ourselves in the world. This opens a door that Schopenhauer and Freud do not, for if those ways of perceiving have been learned, there is the possibility of a re-learning or un-learning.

According to my interpretation of Buddhism, our dissatisfaction with life derives from a repression even more immediate than death-terror: the suspicion that "I" am not real. The sense-of-self is not self-existing but a mental construction which experiences its groundlessness as a *lack*. We have seen that this sense-of-*lack* is consistent with what psychotherapy has discovered about ontological guilt and basic anxiety. We cope with this *lack* by objectifying it in various ways and try to resolve it through projects which cannot succeed because they do not address the fundamental issue. Chapter 5 will discuss some common examples of this, individual and collective projects that are historically conditioned although we now take them for granted as the normal preoccupations of life.

So our most problematic dualism is not life fearing death but a fragile sense-of-self dreading its own groundlessness, according to Buddhism. By accepting and yielding to that groundlessness, I can discover that I have always been grounded in Indra's Net, not as a self-enclosed being but as one manifestation of a web of relationships which encompasses everything. This solves the problem of desire by transforming it. As long as we are driven by *lack*, every desire becomes a sticky attachment that tries to fill up a bottomless pit. Without *lack*, the serenity of our no-thing-ness, that is, the absence of any fixed nature, grants the freedom to become anything.

4

The Meaning of It All

What does the self-as-*lack* imply about ethical values, the search for truth, and the meaning of our lives? To raise these issues in the Western tradition is to find ourselves in a dialogue with Nietzsche, the first (and still the most important) postmodernist, whose own texts resonate with many of the same concerns. Nietzsche realized that morality, knowledge, and meaning are not discovered but constructed: internalized games we learn from each other and play with ourselves. Perhaps the history of his own psyche reveals how momentous these discoveries were; inevitably his perceptions (like those of Freud and other intellectual revolutionaries) were somewhat distorted.

Nietzsche understood how the distinction we make between this world and a "higher" spiritual realm serves our need for security, and he saw the bad faith in religious values motivated by this anxiety. But he did not understand how his alternative, more aristocratic values, also reflects the same anxiety. Nietzsche ends up celebrating an impossible ideal, the heroic-ego which overcomes its sense of *lack*, because he does not see that a heroic ego is our fantasy project for overcoming *lack*.

Nietzsche realized how the search for truth is motivated by a sublimated desire for symbolic security; again, his solution reverses our usual dualism by elevating ignorance and "untruth" into conditions of life. Philosophy's attempt to create the world reflects the tyrannical will-to-power, becoming the most "spiritualized" version of the need to impose our will. But insofar as truth is our intellectual way to grasp being symbolically, those who no longer need to ground themselves can play the truth-versus-error game with lighter feet. Like Schopenhauer, Nietzsche overlooks a different reversal of perspective which could convert the bad infinite of heroic-will into the good infinite of truth-as-play.

What he considered the crown of his system—eternal recurrence—is actually its *denouement*. Having seen through the delusion of Being, Nietzsche could not let it go completely, for he still sought a Being *within* Becoming. "To impose upon becoming the character of being—this is the supreme will to power. . . . That *everything recurs* is the closest *approximation of a world of becoming to a world of being.*"[1] This may have been his self-conscious attempt to create a myth which might liberate us not from but into this world. If so,

102

it does not liberate us enough. Having exposed the bad faith of believing in eternity, Nietzsche is nonetheless able to affirm the value of this moment only by making it recur eternally. In place of the neurotic's attempt to rediscover the past in the future, he tries to rediscover the present in the future, yet (the basic problem) the eternal recurrence of the now can add something only if the now in itself lacks something.

Rather than the way to vanquish nihilism, Nietzsche's will-to-power turns out to be pure nihilism, for its eternal recurrence would ensure that our flight from *lack* could have no cloture. This is because nihilism is not the debacle of all meaning but our dread of that debacle and what we do to avoid it, compulsively seizing on certain meanings as a bulwark against that form of *lack*. If so, the only real solution to the dread of meaninglessness is meaninglessness itself, for only by accepting meaninglessness, by letting it devour the meanings that defend us from our no-thing-ness, can we realize a *meaning-free-ness* open to the possibilities that arise in our world.

In sum, when the *lack*-driven bad infinite transforms into a lacking-nothing good infinite, the dualisms of good-versus-evil, truth-versus-error, and meaningfulness-versus-meaninglessness are realized to be games. But do I play them or do they play me? As long as we do not understand what is motivating us, we play with the seriousness of a life-versus-death (or being versus no-thing-ness) struggle, for that is what the games symbolize to a self preoccupied with its *lack*. We are trapped in games which cannot be escaped yet cannot be won, since playing well does not resolve one's sense-of-*lack*. Realizing this much, without also understanding the possibility of ending *lack*, leads to cynicism, skepticism and despair. When there is no need to get anything from the game or gain cloture on it, then we can play with the seriousness of a child absorbed in its game.[2]

Qualifying for Immortality

"There are no moral phenomena at all, only a moral interpretation of phenomena" (*Beyond Good and Evil*).[3] That brings the issue back from some other "spiritual" world to this one, as we inquire into the genealogy of our moral interpretations. Why do we make the interpretations that we do? As we become more conscious of our motivations, what other interpretations become possible?

Nietzsche distinguishes two basic types of morality, master morality and slave morality. Master morality does not hesitate to affirm the exercise of power, whereas slave morality is based upon rejecting master morality as evil and valuing the opposite of that evil. Behind the piety of conventional Christian morals, Nietzsche detected the fear and *ressentiment* of the weak, who use ethical codes to control the strong. When this fear is projected onto the universe, it becomes a God who tells us to love each other even as he loves us, who will take care of us if we do and punish us if we do not. We may cower before such a God, yet this scheme gives us some grip on our fate—and, as Nietzsche emphasizes, a pretty good grip on our fellow man. We know who we are, what we can do, and where that is likely to get us. But this also destroys the innocence of our existence.

> That no one is any longer made accountable, that the kind of being manifested cannot be traced back to a *causa prima*, that the world is a unity neither as sensorium nor as "spirit,"—*this alone is the great liberation*—thus alone is the *innocence* of becoming restored.... The concept "God" has hitherto been the greatest *objection* to existence.... We deny God; in denying God, we deny accountability: only by doing *that* do we redeem the world. (*Twilight of the Idols*)[4]

We would be accountable to God because he would want to accomplish something through us. Nietzsche calls our bluff. We say we want to be free, yet who does not really want somebody, somewhere, to be watching and protecting us? If there is a correspondence between monotheism (a consciousness unifying and controlling the external world) and the ego-self (a consciousness unifying and controlling the internal), the issue is less accountability than ego-integrity: Without a God to keep us straight, who is strong enough to determine one's own direction? If God expires all is permitted, and the century that has passed since Nietzsche's proclamation has certainly fulfilled his predictions of nihilism.

Perhaps a period of chaos is unavoidable. "One interpretation has collapsed; but because it was considered *the* interpretation it now seems as if there were no meaning at all in existence, as if everything were in vain."[5] As with the adolescent forging an independent identity, some disorientation is inevitable before humankind matures enough to forego its projected parent and determine this-worldly criteria for moral interpretations. This would also explain the difficulty with Nietzsche's own solution, which understands the problem yet cannot quite escape it. He saw that the dualism of good-versus-evil is an internalized game we learn to play with ourselves. "In every ascetic morality man worships a part of himself as God and for that he needs to diabolize the other part." Since Christianity is the victory of pity over aristocratic values, his alternative is, in part, revaluing those aristocratic virtues. "The great epochs of our life are the occasions when we gain the courage to rebaptize our evil qualities as our best qualities."[6] This includes embracing the fact that "life itself is *essentially* appropriation, injury, overpowering of the strange and weaker, suppression, severity, imposition of one's own forms, incorporation and, at the least and mildest, exploitation."[7] Yet this famous passage is easily misunderstood out of context. Nietzsche idealizes the aristocrat insofar as the aristocrat lives more in this world. In psychological terms, readiness to defend one's honor implies a willingness to face death, and therefore a tendency to de-repress the fear of it. In principle, at least, such a person should be more alive when the issue is more obviously life and death.

The essential thing "in heaven and upon earth" seems, to say it again, to be a protracted *obedience* in *one* direction: from out of that there always emerges and always has emerged in the long run something for the sake of which it is worthwhile to live on earth, for example virtue, art, music, dance, reason, spirituality—something transfiguring, refined, mad and divine.[8]

Then the important thing about the true aristocrat (and much more the Over-man) is that he is master of his own "inward chaos." "You shall become mas-ter of yourself, master also over your virtues. Formerly they were your masters; but they must be only your instruments beside other instruments."[9] Yet, from a Buddhist perspective, the concept of self-mastery contains a problematic ambi-guity: Who is master of whom? If the ego-self is that which vainly tries to grasp itself, the project of self-*mastery* is not only questionable but impossible. That for the sake of which it is worthwhile to live on earth: Does that happen when I master myself or when I let go of myself?

These questions reduce to how our sense-of-*lack* may be overcome, and for Nietzsche that involves realizing the will-to-power, the closest thing to a metaphysical reality in his thought. Nietzsche's will is not Schopenhauer's will rechristened as good, for Nietzsche's is not a substratum; there is no such thing as "pure" will. Nor is it a faculty of the sort popular in eighteenth- and nineteenth-century psychology. The closest he comes to a definition is in *Beyond Good and Evil*, where "will is not only a complex of feeling and thinking, but above all an *emotion*: and in fact the emotion of command."[10] Retracing the genealogy of this, his master concept if he has one, will enable us to relate his will-to-power with the Buddhist sense-of-*lack*.

The will-to-power cannot be separated from its sublimation (or "spiri-tualization"), for Nietzsche discovered them together. Along with Burckhardt, he was among the first classicists to realize that the original Olympic games were a sublimated form of war. Nietzsche contended that Greek civilization was noble and sublime precisely because it had been so cruel and bloodthirsty; the "golden age" was created by bringing this original ferocity under control. "The thought seems to be: where there is 'the sublime' there must have been that which was *made sublime*—sublimated— after having been for a long time not sublime" (Hollingdale).[11] Having detected this phenomenon in ancient Greece, Nietzsche began to notice sublimated "base" impulses in many kinds of activity; for example, Wagner's ferocious will-to-power sublimated into the Bayreuth festival. This makes Nietzsche the first, as far as I know, to undertake a systematic study of repression. *Thus Spake Zarathustra* proclaims that the basic force opera-tive in all life is will-to-power. "Only where life is, there also is will: not will to life, but—so I teach you—will to power!" Everything good originates from sublimated will-to-power and everything bad from lack of this will or lack of its sublimation.

That Nietzsche's hypothesis originates in his study of Greece is fortuitous for relating it to *lack*. We trace the intellectual roots of Western civilization back to classical Greek culture because therein we find an exponential increase in human self-consciousness; just as striking from an anthropological point of view is that that increase is unaccompanied by any comparable religious sense of sin. Since religious expiation is the traditional way of coping with *lack*, this lack of sinfulness is significant. If *lack* is not absolved in that way it should manifest in some other way, and when we look for that other way it is not hard to find. Since Burckhardt and Nietzsche, the older classical view of the Greeks as tranquil and idealistic has been replaced by the realization that they were an anxious and striving people. "The Greeks shrank from suffering and delighted in the representation of youth and physical health; but in spite of their cult of euphoria there is a deep pessimism at the heart of classical literature, a longing turned back upon itself which is more terrible than any medieval dance of death because it is without hope."[12] What is the source of that pessimism and longing? If *lack* is the shadow of self, increased sense of self will also be increased sense that something is lacking. Nietzsche sees the sublimity of Greek culture as the sublimation of their original ferocity, yet here perhaps the genealogist of morals does not trace his genealogy back far enough. What makes us so ferocious? Can even the will-to-power, irreducible for Nietzsche, be deconstructed? What, after all, does power mean to us?

All power is in essence power to deny mortality. Either that or it is not real power at all, not ultimate power, not the power that mankind is really obsessed with. Power means power to increase oneself, to change one's natural situation from one of smallness, helplessness, finitude, to one of bigness, control, durability, importance.

We feel we are masters over life and death when we hold the fate of others in our hands, adds Becker,[13] and we feel we are real when the reality of others is in our hands, adds Buddhism. From that perspective, desire for power is on the same level as slave morality. Both become symptoms of our *lack*, equally frustrating inasmuch as we are motivated by something that cannot be satisfied in the way we try to satisfy it. No wonder Nietzsche's will-to-power can never rest, that it needs to increase and expand its horizons. And no wonder that morality for most of us has been a matter of collecting religious brownie points, so long as we think that is the way to get a grip on our eligibility for immortality—or being.

The whole basis of the urge to goodness is to be something that has value, that endures. . . . Man uses morality to try to get a place of special belongingness and perpetuation in the universe. . . . Do we wonder why one of man's chief characteristics is his tortured dissatisfaction with himself, his constant self-criticism? It is the only way he has to overcome the sense of hopeless limitation inherent in his real situation. (Becker)[14]

When I realize that I am not going to attain cloture on that diabolical part of myself, it is time to project it. "The Devil is the one who prevents the heroic victory of immortality in each culture—even the atheistic, scientific ones."[15] As long as *lack* keeps gnawing, then, we need to keep struggling with the Devil, and as we all know the best devil to fight is one outside our own group. Evil is whatever we decide is keeping us from becoming real, and since no victory over any devil can yield the sense of being we seek, we become trapped in a paradox of our own making: Evil is created by our urge to eliminate evil. Stalin's collectivization program was an attempt to build a perfect socialist society. The Nazi's Final Solution was an attempt to purify the earth of its vermin. "Evil arises in the honored belief that history can be tidied up, brought to a sensible conclusion."[16] But if the only sensible conclusion is when we no longer feel *lack*, there will be no conclusion except perhaps an apocalyptic one.

"Buddhism already has—and this distinguishes it profoundly from Christianity— the self-deception of moral concepts behind it—it stands, in my language, *beyond good and evil*" (*The Antichrist*).[17] That is not because "Buddhism is a religion for the end and fatigue of a civilization" but because the Buddhist critique of *ressentiment* (as Nietzsche characterizes it) understands the self-deception involved in such dualistic thinking, when I identify with one pole and try to eliminate its interdependent other.[18] Buddhism gets beyond good and evil not by rebaptizing our evil qualities as our best, but with an entirely different perspective: Ethical behavior is not so much the means to salvation as the natural, spontaneous expression of genuine enlightenment. Hee-Jin Kim explains Dōgen's view of the Buddhist precepts as nothing other than *tathata* thusness:

> *Not-to-commit-any-evil* is neither the heteronomous "Thou shalt not" nor the autonomous "I will not," but is *non-contrivance*. . . . When morality becomes effortless, purposeless, and playful, it becomes a non-moral morality which is the culmination of Zen practice of the Way in which morality, art, and play merge together. When ought becomes is in the transparency of thusness, only then do we come to the highest morality. Moral excellence as such does not constitute absolute freedom and purity from the religious and metaphysical standpoint. Only when an ought becomes an expression of thusness, does it reach the highest morality.[19]

This is the non-moral morality of the Mahāyāna bodhisattva, who, having nothing to gain or lose, is devoted to the welfare of others. As long as we experience ourselves as alienated from the world and understand society as a set of separate selves, the world is devalued into a field-of-play wherein we compete to full-fill ourselves. That is the origin of the ethical problem we struggle with today: Without some transcendentalized ground such as God or Buddhanature, what will bind our atomized selves together? Again, there is an answer in Indra's Net. When my sense-of-self lets go and disappears, I realize my interdependence with all other phenomena in that all-encompassing net.[20] It is more than being dependent on them: When I discover that I *am* you, the

trace of your traces, the ethical problem of how to relate to you is transformed. We do not need a moral code to tie us together if we are not separate
from each other.[21]

Just as Hua-yen causality is too general to be efficient, so this provides no
simple yardstick to resolve knotty ethical dilemmas. If (as we shall see in the
next section) non-abiding implies that there is no governing Truth to Grasp,
there is also no single Right Way to Act. Yet, more important, I think, is that
this absolves the sense of separation between us which usually makes those
dilemmas so difficult to resolve, including the conceit that I am the one who
has privileged access to transcendental principles. Loss of self-preoccupation
entails the ability to respond to others without an ulterior motive which needs
to gain something, material or symbolic, from that encounter. The recent history
of American Buddhism shows how danger of abuse remains when one's nondual
experience is not deep enough to root out those dualistic tendencies that incline
us to manipulate others. As long as there is sense-of-self, therefore, there will
be need to inculcate morality, just as infants need training wheels on their
bicycles. In Buddhism, however, ethical principles approximate the way of relating
to others that nondual experience reveals. As in Christianity, I should love my
neighbor as myself— in this case because my neighbor *is* myself. But in contrast
to the "Thou shalt not—or else!" implied in Mosaic law, the Buddhist precepts
are vows one makes not to the Buddha or to someone else but to one's to-be-
realized-as-empty self: "I vow to undertake the course of training to perfect
myself in the area of non-killing," and so forth. If we have not developed to
the degree that we spontaneously experience ourselves as one with others, by
following the precepts we endeavor to act as if we did feel that way. Yet even
these precepts are eventually realized not to rest on any transcendental, objectively
binding moral principle. In the Zen school of *kōan* practice that I am familiar
with, the last ten *kōan* examine the ten Mahāyāna precepts from the enlightened
point of view, to clarify what has by then become apparent: The precepts too
are spiritual training wheels. There are, finally, no limitations on our freedom—
except the dualistic delusions which incline us to abuse that freedom in the
first place.

Such freedom comes from realizing my place in Indra's Net, which entails
my interdependence with all other phenomena. Goethe noticed the paradox:
You have only to consider yourself free to feel bound, you have only to consider
yourself bound to feel free. We understand freedom as self-determination, that
is, determination by one's *self.* If there is no such reflexive self, freedom needs
to be understood differently. Why have questions of free will and liberty been
so central in the Western tradition, to the extent that the pursuit of freedom
might be considered our paramount value—and myth? Freedom is the crucial
issue for a sense-of-self *because it naturally understands its basic problem as lack
of autonomy.* So, we trace the origins of Western civilization back to the Greek

"emancipation" of reason from myth. Since the Renaissance, there has been a progressive emphasis, first on religious freedom (the Reformation), then political freedom (the English, American, French revolutions), followed by economic freedom (the class struggle), racial and colonial freedom, and most recently sexual and psychological freedom (psychotherapy, feminism, gay rights; deconstruction as textual liberation, etc.). Each of these struggles has dovetailed into its successors and each has been pursued with a religious fervor, for what is ultimately at stake in all of them is the right of the self to determine itself.

The sad fact is that it is much easier to fight for freedom than to live freely. Absolute freedom for an ego-self is impossible, since our lack of self-existence ensures that we never experience ourselves as free enough: Something is always felt to constrain us. As important as it is, the myth of freedom has been correlative to the project of self-grounding the ego-self, which seeks to eliminate all the ties that limit it so it can be truly self-determined. If such self-groundedness is not possible, what, then, can the search for freedom mean? When even the most absolute freedom does not end *duḥkha* but usually aggravates it (e.g., the last years of Howard Hughes), our struggle for freedom can be fulfilled only by transforming into a different quest. The ambiguity of the term enlightenment is fortuitous. The legacy of the eighteenth-century Enlightenment project—in social and scientific terms, that which liberates us from absolutism, dogmatism, and superstition   must dovetail into the enlightenment that frees me from me. Goethe's statement implies that the greatest freedom comes from losing self-preoccupation and assuming responsibility for all things: not just for our family or our nation, but for the whole of Indra's Net. And present social and environmental conditions increasingly make such a commitment necessary.

Grasping the Symbols that Grasp Reality

How much one needs a *belief* in order to flourish, how much that is "firm" and that one does not wish to be shaken because one clings to it, that is a measure of the degree of one's strength (or, to put the point more clearly, of one's weakness).[22]

Dr. Johnson's definition of remarriage, "the triumph of hope over experience," also fits our beliefs: We soon find others to replace those we have become disillusioned with. Fenelon thought that the most dangerous illusion is the one by which people try to avoid illusion, but doesn't that make the most dangerous illusion the search for truth? If one's final delusion is the belief that one has lost all delusions, and if there is no greater delusion than the one that eliminates all others, mustn't that delusion be . . . *the truth*?

"*What* really is it in us that wants 'the truth'?" begins *Beyond Good and Evil*, a question that echoes throughout Nietzsche's writings. The value of truth must be called into question. Perhaps no one yet has been sufficiently truthful about what truthfulness is—in which case we should be careful, for that may be for good reason. Nietzsche warns that one might get hold of the truth about truth too soon, before humankind is strong enough to give up the need for truth. "Look, isn't our need for knowledge precisely this need for the familiar, the will to uncover under everything strange, unusual, and questionable, something that no longer disturbs us? Is it not the instinct of fear that bids us to know? And is the jubilation of those who attain knowledge not the jubilation over the restoration of a sense of security?"[23] For Freud, desire for knowledge is "at bottom an offshoot, sublimated and raised to the intellectual sphere, of the possessive instinct."[24] Then, what might truth become for a person who no longer seeks to restore the feeling of security, who does not want to be its possessor? We need to ask what we want from our truth.

Nietzsche saw the relationship between our will-to-truth and our need for being:

> Man seeks "the truth": a world that is not self-contradictory, not deceptive, does not change, a *true* world—a world in which one does not suffer; contradiction, deception, change—causes of suffering! . . . Obviously, the will to truth is here merely the desire for a world of the constant. . . . The belief that the world as it ought to be is, really exists, is a belief of the unproductive who do *not desire to create a world* as it ought to be. They posit it as already available, they seek ways and means of reaching it. "Will to truth"— as the impotence of the will to create.[25]

The problem with this form of the will-to-truth is when it merely thinks the world rather than creates it. " *Actual philosophers, however, are commanders and law-givers.* . . . Their 'knowing' is *creating*, their creating is a law-giving, their will to truth is—*will to power*."[26] Even basic logical categories reflect our need to perceive things in a stable way, according to Nietzsche. That some things are equal, that there is such a thing as matter, that things naturally fall into categories: These are fictions, even if more or less indispensable in daily life. Such instrumental truths work to preserve us and give us a grip on our situation. In his later writings, when Nietzsche saw through the illusion of a unitary ego-self, he realized that these truths derive from the sense-of-self objectifying its own self-image.

> Man projected his three "inner facts," that in which he believed more firmly than anything else, will, spirit, ego, outside himself—he derived the concept "being" only from the concept "ego," he posited "things" as possessing being according to his own image, according to his concept of the ego as cause. No wonder he later always discovered in things only *that which he had put into them*!—The thing itself, to say it again, the concept "thing" is merely a reflection of the belief in ego as cause.[27]

Then, what would happen if we could cease believing in ego as a self-determining cause? If we cling to these "facts" for survival, can those who let-go of themselves let go of them? Nietzsche does not consider this Buddhist possibility but he contemplates "the most extreme form of nihilism," which might also be called " *a divine way of thinking*": the view "that every belief, every considering-something-true, is necessarily false because there simply is no *true world*. Thus: a *perspectival appearance* whose origin lies in us (insofar as we continually need a narrower, abbreviated, simplified world)." Nietzsche describes this as another reversal: Just as our rebaptized evil qualities trade places with our best qualities, so *truth becomes lie*—

Truths are illusions about which one has forgotten that this is what they are.

Truth is the kind of error without which a certain species of life could not live. The value for *life* is ultimately decisive.[28]

—and *lie becomes a kind of truth*, for this makes the will to appearance, even the will to deception, "deeper, more metaphysical, than the will to truth" insofar as that will-to-truth is motivated by the need for security. Nietzsche accordingly calls his own philosophy "inverted Platonism: the further it is from actual reality, the purer, more beautiful, and better it becomes. Living in illusion as the ideal."[29] There are no objective facts, no Immaculate Perception, no ultimate revelation of truth. Everything becomes a matter of perspective since "there is no solely beatifying interpretation."[30] Like eternal recurrence (discussed in the next section), perspectivism is a test and an intensification of our will-to-power. Perspectives gain in power by competing with each other. Superior perspectives develop by refuting or refining lesser ones. In this way the will continually surmounts itself, as each individual develops according to it's own ability.

Ernest Becker also believes that illusion is necessary:

If transference is a natural function of heroism, a necessary projection in order to stand life, death, and oneself, the question becomes: What is *creative projection*? What is *life-enhancing* illusion? . . .

Man needs a "second" world, a world of humanly created meaning, a new reality that he can live, dramatize, nourish himself in. "Illusion" means creative play at its highest level. Cultural illusion is a necessary ideology of self-justification, a heroic dimension that is life itself to the symbolic animal.[31]

"The essence of normality is the refusal of reality," a refusal that Becker too justifies as psychologically necessary. Yet, he too goes for what Nietzsche calls the bloody truths, peeling away repressions to arrive at "the potentially most liberating question of all, the main problem of human life: How *empirically true* is the cultural hero system that sustains and drives men?"[32] Thus Becker ends up with a double-tiered truth similar to Nietzsche's, between a life-enhancing illusion and the truth about this illusion, too painful for most of us to cope with. From the first perspective, the important truths for Becker too are the ones that defend my existence, all the more important if they can help me qualify for eternal existence (or self-being). That helps us understand the obsessions of medieval society: the virulence of its theological disputes, the necessity for inquisitions, the motivation behind religious wars to eradicate heresy. From the second and deeper perspective, however, the question is how much truth we can bear.

It is no coincidence, I think, that Buddhism also has a two-truths doctrine which distinguishes the usual truth of the everyday world from a higher truth that is not only difficult to understand but dangerous to misunderstand. The paradigmatic formulation is in chapter 24 of Nāgārjuna's MMK:

> The teaching of the Buddhas is wholly based on there being two truths: that of a personal everyday world and a higher truth which surpasses it.
>
> Those who do not clearly know the true distinction between the two truths cannot clearly know the hidden depths of the Buddha's teaching.
>
> Unless the transactional realm is accepted as a base, the surpassing sense cannot be pointed out; if the surpassing sense is not comprehended *nirvāṇa* cannot be attained.
>
> The feeble-minded are destroyed by the misunderstood doctrine of *śūnyatā*, as by a snake ineptly seized or some secret knowledge wrongly applied.
>
> For this reason the mind of the enlightened one was averse to teaching the Truth, realizing how difficult it would be for those of feeble insight to fathom it. (MMK XXIV: 8–12)

In this version, the higher truth that is fatal to the feeble-minded is *śūnyatā*. Candrakīrti's commentary on this passage explains that someone who misunderstands *śūnyatā* will reject the self-existence of things only to fall into the opposite extreme of believing that everything is merely illusion, and will get into trouble by ignoring the physical and moral law of cause-and-effect. Yet the higher truth is bloodier than that. Buddhism is more than a philosophy that refutes self-existence. It is a practice which deconstructs our sense-of-self, and letting go of ourselves in order to realize our own *śūnyatā* is seldom easy. If normality is the refusal of reality, it is because few are ready to face the truth about our lack of self-existence and the social games whereby we reassure ourselves. For many, the alternative to self-illusion is not Becker's creative play but a nihilism that no longer sees any reason to live. No wonder, then, that after his enlightenment Śākyamuni Buddha hesitated to teach what he had realized, according to the traditional account. The problem is not only that we are unable to understand such a difficult doctrine "beyond the reach of reason"; we resist it, for it does not grant us the kind of salvation we want, a grounding for the ego-self.

The other danger is that we will cling to *śūnyatā* by accepting it as the correct description of the way things are. So, as we have already noticed in chapter 3, Nāgārjuna emphasizes that the concept is relative to the self-existing things it refutes: Having fulfilled that function, *śūnyatā* refutes itself. *Śunyatā* is "the exhaustion of all theories and views," and those who make *śūnyatā* into a theory are "incurable" (MMK XIII:8). This would seem to undercut even Nāgārjuna's own view about the correct way to understand Buddhist teachings, but Nāgārjuna embraced its full implications and insisted that he had no view of his own. While Nietzsche ends up with an infinity of possible perspectives, Nāgārjuna seems to conclude with none, since *śūnyatā* is merely a heuristic device. Are these really contradictory, or does the exhaustion of perspectives liberate us for the polyvalence of many perspectives?

"Ultimate serenity is the coming to rest of all ways of taking things, the repose of named things; *no Truth has been taught by a Buddha for anyone, anywhere*" (MMK XXV:24). If truth is a matter of grasping the symbols that grasp reality, all truth is error on the Buddhist path. When *nirvāṇa* is the end of all ways of taking things, the game of truth-and-delusion is turned upside-down. There is no truth to be taught because nothing needs to be attained; instead, delusion is something to be *un*learned. In the *Diamond Sutra*, Subhūti asks the Buddha if his realization of supreme enlightenment means that he has not gained anything. "Just so, Subhūti. I have not gained the least thing from supreme enlightenment, and that is called supreme enlightenment." Buddhism does not provide a metaphysical system to account for reality but shows how to deconstruct the socially conditioned metaphysical system we know as everyday reality. It does not give us truths but shows how to become aware and let go of the automatized truths we are normally not aware of holding. Buddhism agrees with Nietzsche's and Becker's insight that our truth consists of illusions which we have forgotten are illusions, yet the Buddhist path is predicated on the possibility of deconstructing the ones that cause us to suffer: most of all, the ones that maintain our delusive sense-of-self.

Nāgārjuna's thunderbolt reverberates through subsequent Buddhism. The *Hsin Hsin Mei* of Seng-ts'an, the third Ch'an patriarch, points the way beyond truth:

If you want the truth to stand clear before you, never be for or against
The struggle between for and against is the mind's worst disease. . . .
There is no need to seek Truth; only stop having views.[33]

In place of *tertium non datur*, the logic of excluded middle, this celebrates the freedom of a mind that is not afraid of contradiction and so is able to dance in a coincidence of opposites, which is the way our minds naturally work when they do not "stick." According to the *Cheng-tao Kê* of Yung Chia, a man of the Way "neither avoids fantasy nor seeks truth"; to reject delusion and grasp the truth "mistakes a thief for one's own son." Yet, this advice will not help as long as my quest for enlightenment remains a sublimated attempt to ground myself. We seek some thing to fixate on, but the Buddhist solution is to take away: to keep pulling the rug out from beneath us until we let go of that need for solid ground and discover that groundlessness is not so bad, after all. "If I tell you that I have a system of law [*Dharma*, teaching] to transmit to others, I am cheating you," declared the sixth patriarch, Hui-neng. "What I do to my disciples is to liberate them from their own bondage with such devices as the case may need."

> Only those who do not possess a single system of law can formulate all systems of law, and only those who can understand the meaning [of this paradox] may use such terms. It makes no difference to those who have realized the essence of mind whether they formulate all systems of law or dispense with all of them. They are at liberty to come or to go. They are free from obstacles or impediments. They take appropriate actions as circumstances require. They give suitable answers according to the temperament of the inquirer.[34]

Hui-neng's revolutionary approach marks the beginning of Ch'an because it showed how to turn Nāgārjuna's philosophical deconstruction into a practice. His dharma-successors blazed a new trail, especially Ma-tsu, who seems to have initiated the unconventional and illogical techniques used to startle a monk and make him let go of whatever he has been clinging to: shouting in his ear, tweaking his nose, pushing him down, hitting him with a stick, or merely repeating what he had said—anything that might knock the ladder out from beneath a ripe aspirant. More violent methods were developed by Huang-po and especially his student Lin-chi. The gentler "zen of lips and mouth" was perfected by Nan-chuan and his successor Chao-chou.

Chao-chou did not begin to teach until he was a frail monk of eighty, so his method replaced blows with a few soft-spoken words that could penetrate to the core. This raises the question of how words can free us from words. Even if we accept that a sudden shout or blow might startle someone who is ready to let go of himself, what can words do except substitute one concept for another? Chao-chou's approach alerts us to a possible problem with Nāgārjuna's recommending the coming-to-rest of all ways of taking things: It may reinforce the dualism we already make between words and things, between thought and world, both of which are versions of our commonsense yet delusive bifurcation between mind and matter, according to Buddhism. If we understand words/ thought as a filter that needs to be eliminated in order to experience things/ the world more immediately, we reconstitute the problem of dualism in the means chosen to overcome it. On this issue too, Dōgen is insightful: "It is truly a pity to be unaware that discriminating thought is words and phrases, and words and phrases liberate *discriminating* thought."[35] The point is not to avoid discriminating thought but to *liberate* it.

> Words are no longer just something that the intellect manipulates abstractly and impersonally but something that works intimately in the existential metabolism of one who uses them philosophically and religiously in a special manner and with a special attitude. They are no longer mere means or symbols that point to realities other than themselves but are themselves the realities of original enlightenment and the Buddha-nature. (Kim)[36]

For Dōgen, symbols (and language generally) should not be understood merely as means of edification, for each can be experienced as an end in itself, like everything else. If a concept or symbol is how an intellectual mind tries to ground itself, why blame the victim? "Metaphor in Dōgen's sense is not that which points to something other than itself, but that in which something realizes itself." If the symbol is not used to compensate for my own *lack*—which makes me try to get something *from* it—it can be a way my mind consummates itself. Then, there is free interplay between mind and symbol: Although symbols can be redeemed only by mind, the mind does not function in a vacuum but is activated by symbols.[37]

The point of the Buddhist critique of truth is that letting go is neither a process of refuting error and grasping truth, nor is it a matter of rejecting language/thought. The crucial issue is whether our search for truth is another attempt to ground ourselves by fixating on certain concepts that are believed to give us an effective fix on the world. When there is this compulsion, certain ideas become seductive, that is, they become *ideologies*. The difference between *saṃsāra* and *nirvāṇa* is that *saṃsāra* is Indra's Net experienced as a sticky web of attachments which seem to offer something we feel the lack of: a grounding for the groundless sense-of-self. Intellectually, that seductive quality manifests as a battleground of conflicting ideologies competing for our allegiance. Ideologies offer the mind a sure grasp on the world: Now we know how the world is meaningful and what our role in that meaning is. Ideology is "the assumption that since the beginning and end of history are known there is nothing more to say. History is therefore to be obediently lived out according to the ideology" (Carse).[38] If there is no specifiable difference between nirvana and the everyday world (MMK XXV.19), then very different ideologies such as religions, metaphysical systems, nationalism, racism, Marxism, and psychoanalysis are in the same dimension insofar as they serve the same psychological function: trying to resolve the sense-of-self's intellectually experienced sense-of-*lack* by identifying with a belief-system. The problem is that they tend to become computer-viruses of the mind: When we assent to them—let them in—they take over the mind and fill it up.[39]

One of the more important issues in contemporary philosophy and critical theory is to what extent rationality itself amounts to such an ideology. Rather than myth being primitive reasoning, does our understanding of logical thinking make reason into a literalized, one-dimensional myth? "Has reason constituted itself to be the ruler of philosophy?" asks Heidegger. "If so, by what right?"[40] From our usual perspective, his questions may seem ridiculous, because self-refuting, but they also challenge that perspective. Certain types of postmodern thought may be viewed as subverting this socially constructed myth of rationality, and, just as in Nāgārjuna's painstaking refutation of all philosophical solutions, it is reason that is deconstructing itself.

What, then, is truth? A mobile army of metaphors, metonyms, and an-
thropomorphisms—in short, a sum of human relations which have been
enhanced, transposed, and embellished poetically and rhetorically, and which
after long use seem firm, canonical, and obligatory to a people: truths are
illusions about which one has forgotten that this is what they are: metaphors
which are worn out and without sensuous power; coins which have lost
their pictures and now matter only as metal, no longer as coins. (Nietzsche)[41]

As metaphors lose their sensuous power they gain another role, as emblems.
The freshness of the original meaning decays into tokens. Once objectified and
socially validated, a truth enters the exchange market. It can be gained, possessed,
and lost.

Explanations succeed only by convincing resistant hearers of their error. If
you will not hear my explanations until you are suspicious of your own
truths, you will not accept my explanations until you are convinced of your
error. Explanation is an antagonistic encounter that succeeds by defeating
an opponent. It possesses the same dynamic of resentment found in other
finite play. I will press my explanations on you because I need to show that
I do not live in the error that I think others think that I do.

Whoever wins this struggle is privileged with the claim to true knowledge.
Knowledge has been arrived at, it is the outcome of this engagement. Its
winners have the uncontested power to make certain statements of fact. They
are to be listened to. In those areas appropriate to the contests now concluded,
winners possess a knowledge that can no longer be challenged. (Carse)[42]

When sense *of lack* evaporates because sense-of-self evaporates, the seductive
web of *saṁsāra* transforms into the polyvalence of Indra's Net, where each
viewpoint is able to appreciate others because it no longer identifies with a
truth-project that is threatened by those others. This is not Nietzsche's
perspectivism, the competition among perspectives each trying to impress its
own will-to-truth upon the world, but a non-abiding wisdom that can wander
freely among truths since it does not need to fixate on any of them, for (as
Hui-neng put it) non-dwelling mind does not stick on any of the six sense-
objects, and that includes mind-objects.

Is this relativism, the bugaboo of all value theory? If so, this approach to
relativism defangs it of its poison in two ways. First, one of the main difficulties
with relativism is the danger of destructive ideologies such as racism, sexism,
and the like. We want to be able to say that they are false. Buddhism meets
this concern in a different way: When such ideologies lose their seductive quality
they are exposed as collective forms of ignorance and stupidity to be *un*learned.
They are attractive only because they offer an easy intellectual way to fill up
our sense-of-*lack*.

Second, even if all ideologies are competing in the same intellectual arena,
there are some important internal differences. Many ideologies are difficult to
escape once you are committed. An old-style Marxist who began criticizing

Marxism would be told to purge himself of his bourgeois tendencies; a psycho-analyst will tell the analysand that she is resisting. On the other side are what might be called *meta-ideologies*, because they are designed to self-negate: to free us from all ideologies including themselves. Derrida writes about the need to lodge oneself within traditional conceptuality in order to destroy it, which expresses nicely one of the reasons Nāgārjuna insists on two truths: The every-day transactional realm must be accepted in order to point to the higher truth that negates it.[43] According to Mādhyamika, *śūnyatā* is like a poison antidote that expels the poison from our bodies and then expels itself, for if the anti-dote stays inside to poison us we are no better off than before. The difference between ideologies and meta-ideologies rests on whether the sense-of-self's anxious groundlessness is to be resolved by providing something to identify with or by letting go of itself. Then the important issue is the liberating function of any truth or practice. The same thought that is liberating in one situation may be binding in another. Even the most valuable insights can lose their freshness and become "sticky" because they are now understood as something to cling to rather than a pointer to freedom; or rather, clinging to them is now misun-derstood as the path to freedom. This suggests that we should distinguish be-tween Buddhism as a path of liberation—a difficult path of dying to ourselves—and Buddhism as an institution providing cultural and psychologi-cal security, reassuring us of the meaningfulness of the Buddhist world view and our place within it.

The particular danger with Buddhist meta-ideology is the version of dualistic thinking that motivates it: the distinction between *nirvāṇa* and *saṁsāra*, enlightenment and delusion. Enlightenment includes (although is not limited to) realizing how the distinction we come to make between enlightenment and delusion is itself delusive; that enlightenment does not liberate us in the fashion we look to be saved. What makes the game of enlightenment-versus-delusion a meta-ideology is that this realization is essential to the game: "Those who delight in maintaining 'without the grasping I will realize *nirvāṇa*; *nirvāṇa* is in me' are the ones with the greatest grasping. When *nirvāṇa* is not [subject to] establishment and *saṁsāra* not [subject to] disengagement, how will there be any concept of *nirvāṇa* and *saṁsāra*?" (MMK XVI.9–10).

Psychoanalysis has been slow to discover these insights about truth because it soon became caught up in its own dogmas, heresies, and inquisitions. The fervor and rancor with which its theoretical controversies have been pursued testifies to how unsettling the psychotherapeutic message is and how deeply rooted our resistance to its liberative implications. Recently, however, some psychotherapists have been arriving at a similar realization. For example, in *Rethinking Psychiatry*, Arthur Kleinman emphasizes that what is important in therapy is not communicating the correct "symbolic order" but that both parties are committed to the same one:

In summary, then, what is necessary for healing to occur is that both parties to the therapeutic transaction are committed to the shared symbolic order. What is important is that the patient has the opportunity to tell his story, experiences the therapist's witnessing of that account, believes the therapist's interpretation of his problems, and comes to use the same symbolic vehicles of interpretation to make sense of his situation.[44]

At the end of *Existential Psychotherapy*, Irvin Yalom comes to the same conclusion about different psychoanalytic frames of reference: "Therapists may offer the patient any number of explanations to clarify the same issue. . . . *None, despite vehement claims to the contrary, has sole rights to the truth.* After all, they are all based on imaginary "as if" structures. . . . They are all fictions, all psychological constructs created for semantic convenience, and they justify their existence only by virtue of their explanatory power."[45]

That they are constructs is not problematic if they are, like Dōgen's metaphors, "not that which points to something other than itself, but that in which something realizes itself." The psychotherapeutic mind, as much as the religious one, does not function in a vacuum but is activated by these constructs. That brings us full circle, back to the approach of Śākyamuni Buddha, who was careful not to set up his teachings as the only truth: "It is not proper for a wise man . . . to come to the conclusion: 'This alone is truth, and everything else is false.'"[46] He compared his teachings to a raft that we may use to ferry ourselves across the river of birth-and-death (*samsāra*) to the "other shore" of *nirvāṇa* and then to be abandoned, not carried around on one's back. Rather than making faith a criterion of our enlightenment—presenting us with a dogma that we must believe, as part of the price of our salvation—Buddhist truths are like fingers pointing at the moon or a roadmap showing us the way to go.

Nihilism

The greatest weight.—What if some day or night a demon were to steal after you into your loneliest loneliness and say to you: "This life as you now live it and have lived it, you will have to live once more and innumerable times more; and there will be nothing new in it, but every pain and every joy and every thought and sigh and everything unutterably small or great in your life will have to return to you, all in the same succession and sequence. . . ."

Would you not throw yourself down and gnash your teeth and curse the demon who spoke thus? Or have you once experienced a tremendous moment when you would have answered him: "You are a god and never have I heard anything more divine." If this thought gained possession of you, it would change you as you are or perhaps crush you. The question in each and every thing, "Do you desire this once more and innumerable times more?" would lie upon your actions as the greatest weight. Or how well disposed would you have to become to yourself and to life *to crave nothing more fervently than this ultimate eternal confirmation and seal*? (*The Gay Science*)[47]

Eternal Recurrence. If everything manifests the will-to-power, why bother to sublimate? Nietzsche found his answer in eternal recurrence, which solves the problem ingeniously: not by grounding this life in some otherworldly eternity but by impressing the form of eternity on this life. Eternal recurrence has been celebrated as the capstone of his philosophy, yet I shall argue that, instead of vanquishing nihilism, eternal recurrence eternally defers it. That is because nihilism is not the always impending debacle of all meaning, but our fear of that debacle and flight from it—which perpetuates the debacle and gives it power over us. *The dread of nihilism*, which Nietzsche rightly saw as our collective shadow, the ghost that haunts Western civilization, *is the true nihilism.* Our problem is not nothingness but the ways we try to evade it.

This too puts Nietzsche in the same camp as Plato. If the Platonic invention of another Reality is an attempt to escape the *lack* we experience now, so too is Nietzsche's attempt to fill in the *lack* of that now by making the now recur eternally. The basic problem is that the eternal recurrence of the now can add nothing unless the now-as-now lacks something. Again we encounter sense-of-*lack*, here in its implications for meaning. This *lack* is not the meaninglessness of life but the threat of meaninglessness, and therefore it manifests itself as the devices we use to deny meaninglessness. In this way too, the repressed returns, sublimated into symbols/symptoms. Tillich believed that the problem of meaninglessness is the form in which nonbeing poses itself in our time, and that all human life can be interpreted as a continuous attempt to avoid despair.[48] He also gave the solution: The meaning of life must be reduced to despair about the meaning of life, in order to take more nonbeing of the world into ourselves. But one must despair in the right way.

How to overcome nihilism was the fundamental problem for Nietzsche, whose sensitive nose detected its stink almost everywhere. It is not a late development of Western civilization but man's normal condition, which is why the Overman is an overcoming of *man.* Then, does nihilism have an essential connection with *lack*, also humankind's normal condition? Nietzsche defines nihilism as increasing gloom, then terror, at the exhaustion of all meaning, a grand disgust directed at oneself as well as the world. Goals are missing, the desert grows. What Nietzsche the posthumous man predicted, we postmodern men are now living, and no one can say yet when or how this nihilism—today becoming recognized as a global problem—might be resolved.

At first nihilism disguised itself by creating Platonic-type values. Nihilism shows its disgust at life by creating a "true world" having all the attributes that life does not: unity, stability, identity, goodness, happiness. This invention of another world is the nihilistic act *par excellence* because it devalues this world. The incomplete nihilism which constitutes the development of Western civilization is the slow decomposition of that true world, and when it finally disappears we are left with this one, the "apparent" world that can no longer be considered apparent if there is nothing to juxtapose it with, yet nonetheless remains devalued and experienced as unsatisfactory.

Nietzsche's solution to nihilism is eternal recurrence. As many have noticed, the key to what is otherwise a peculiar doctrine seems to be the ethical motivation behind it. "The question, in everything you want to do: 'Is it such that I want to do it innumerable times?' is the greatest stress" because this thought would transform us in one way or the other: either crush us under its weight or prompt the supreme affirmation that Zarathustra makes, "Was *that* life? Well then! Once more!" This would be the great liberation that restores the innocence of Becoming because it makes one accountable only to oneself—which from a Buddhist viewpoint is still one too many.

Given Nietzsche's attitude toward truth ("Every philosophy also conceals a philosophy . . ."), this may have been his attempt to promulgate a myth. By what myth do you live? asked Jung. Well, this one is better than most. Like Heidegger's analysis of death in *Being and Time*, it can inspire us to live the way we want to live rather than let life pass by while we are making other plans. What *Being and Time* overlooks is the compulsive quality of a future-oriented life which may not be aware of what motivates its own symbolic immortality projects. We find the same future-directed tension in the will-to-power, since Nietzsche's will is by definition that which must always become more by surpassing itself. For Nietzsche as well as the early Heidegger, the future is necessary to focus us in the now, for otherwise we are diverted and scattered by chance possibilities. In *lack* terms, both try to resolve our sense-of-*lack* by making the sense-of-self more efficient. But if distractibility is a way of evading the anxiety of *lack*, their solutions replace one type of evasion with another.

Unamuno dismissed Nietzsche's eternal recurrence as "a sorry counterfeit of immortality," yet that puts the shoe on the wrong foot. The problem is not that it is a poor immortality but that it is an immortality, which still reflects a felt need to "stamp the form of eternity upon our lives." Eternal recurrence seems to exalt the now by refusing to evaluate it according to some other standard or to ground it in some other reality, yet here too the now is weighed and found wanting: Its *lack* can be filled up only by repeating it. The now as now—just *this*—is still not enough. A Buddhist may agree with Nietzsche that "*this* life is your eternal life!" but the eternity of this life must be understood differently, as a not-falling-away *eternal now* that, when it lacks nothing, may be discovered to be all we need.

Nietzsche calls eternal recurrence the basic conception of *Thus Spake Zarathustra*, yet it becomes a dominant theme only near the end of part four. Zarathustra teaches the Higher Men how to overcome the Spirit of Gravity, and at the beginning of "The Intoxicated Song" one of them declares: "For the sake of this day—I am content for the first time to have lived my whole life. . . . 'Was that—life?' I will say to death. 'Very well! Once more!'" At that moment Zarathustra hears the sound of the midnight bell and sings its song, "whose name is 'Once More,' whose meaning is 'To all eternity!'":

> O Man! Attend!
> What does deep midnight's voice contend?
> "I slept my sleep,
> "And now awake at dreaming's end:
> "The world is deep,
> "Deeper than day can comprehend,
> "Deep is its woe,
> "Joy—deeper than heart's agony:
> "Woe says: Fade! Go!
> "But all joy wants eternity,
> "—wants deep, deep, deep eternity!"

This roundelay is so important that it appears at the end of parts three and four; and the reason it is so important is that it reveals the origin of eternal recurrence to be *joy*. This joy wants to recur eternally, and because it is deeper than the heart's agony, such joy can even will that suffering to recur again too, if necessary for its own recurrence.

> Did you ever say Yes to one joy? O my friends, then you said Yes to *all* woe as well. All things are chained and entwined together, all things are in love; if you ever wanted one moment twice, if you ever said: "You please me, happiness, instant, moment!" then you wanted *everything* to return.[49]

Alas, for the failure of Nietzsche's moment of joy! However deep it was it was not deep enough, for he needed it again, and again . . . "Joy, however, does not want heirs or children, joy wants itself. . . . wants everything eternally the same."[50] This reaction is natural yet nonetheless ruinous. Ironically, that very desire for its recurrence is the worm which burrows in to destroy it, as in those most cherished musical moments that inspire us to think. "This is so beautiful, I wish it would never stop"—only to discover that the moment has ceased and cannot be recreated, destroyed by the self-consciousness which reflexively distinguishes itself from the music in order to enjoy enjoying it. Nietzsche yearns for that moment of joy again, because it absolves his sense of *lack*, but his desire for its recurrence is itself part of the problem that the deepest joy resolves. For, contrary to his roundelay, the *deepest* joy does not even will to recur: it wills nothing because it lacks nothing, if it is the deepest joy. By wanting to retain that joy, Nietzsche separates himself from it and thereby loses it into the past as a memory, then can only try to bring it back by willing the recurrence of everything—not realizing that his moment of pure joy was a temporary collapse of willing. Since the will-to-power always strives to overcome itself, it must project a future, which is why the only consummation it can attain is in eternal recurrence of such moments. However, striving to find the past in the future is less a formula for joy than a psychoanalytic definition of neurosis.

What is attractive about eternal recurrence is that it foregoes the need for any other Reality to compensate for the defects of this one. It is an affirmation of this world, yet this world not as let-go but as grasped-at, fixated by being brought back again and again. "Very well: Once more!" is his deep affirmation; yet deeper would be: "To all that has been: Thanks! To all that will be: Yes!" To say *yes!* to a single moment of joy, completely affirming it, is by definition an experience of no *lack*. At that instant, one wants nothing else, no void needs to be filled in or evaded, which means (if sense-of-*lack* is the shadow of sense-of-self) that this must be a moment of egolessness. Then one cannot have such a joy, one can only *be* such a joy. Blessed are those who have had or rather *been* such a moment, for it transforms all other moments as well— although not because of the entwined contingency that Nietzsche refers to. "An affirmation that is truly full and complete is also contagious: it bursts into a chain of affirmations that knows no limits" (Haar).[51] Yes, but this chain is not each contingent affirmation *causing* the next. Just the opposite: A complete affirmation breaks all causal chains. The joy of *just this!*—the Buddhist experience of *tathatā*, thusness—needs nothing, desires nothing, and thus reveals that the causal chain is a succession of *just this!* in an eternal now, where there is nothing to gain or lose. Paradoxically, when we experience the causal chain as such a succession, our experience is that there is no causal chain and no succession. It is the same way that Mādhyamika dependent origination refutes itself to become non-dependent non-origination. But when we experience the causal chain as a means to get somewhere else, we lose *just this!* and the eternal now. Life becomes joyous not when we get something from it, but when we become it.

So a moment of deepest joy does not banish woe by discovering the interdependence of joy with everything else, past and future. Rather, it reveals that what we thought was the means for solving *lack* is what maintains the problem. End of *lack* is not an effect that can be experienced at the conclusion of some causal chain, but the shattering of all causal chains insofar as they are our means for trying to overcome *lack*. Eternity is found not in the recurrence of time but in the evaporation of that objectified time whereby and wherein we hope to end our *lack*. This realization is embodied in Nāgārjuna's most important verse, which (MMK XXV.19 notwithstanding) distinguishes between *saṃsāra* and *nirvāṇa*: "That which, taken as causal or dependent, is the process of being-born and passing on, is, taken non-causally and beyond all dependence, declared to be *nirvāṇa*" (MMK XXV.9). *Nirvāṇa* cannot be caused and therefore cannot be attained. We might think of it as some kind of substratum pervading all our experience, but that is still too dualistic. It is simply the nature of our experience when there is not the sense of a self-conscious yet ungrounded self that *has* the experience and therefore feels something to be lacking in it. The joy of that experience is deeper than the heart's agony.

On this account, happiness in the form we seek it—"that too-hasty profit snatched from approaching loss" (Rilke)—cannot be gained. All we can do is realize that nondual "perspective" where nothing has ever been lacking. The *amor fati* Nietzsche celebrates is not accepting everything due to its interdependence with a moment of complete *Yes!* but the absence of any need to will that things be any different. The *amor* is not willing that everything be exactly the same, over and over again, but that everything be as it is; that, however, is not something which needs to be willed. Or, finally, which can be willed. In *The Birth of Tragedy*, Nietzsche came close to this. Only as an aesthetic phenomenon is existence justified, which amounts to saying that existence experienced aesthetically does not need to be justified. Are what we call "aesthetic experiences" tip-of-the-tongue tastes of something that has always surrounded us?

Instead of yielding to our groundless no-thingness, eternal recurrence is a last gasp at self-grounding Being, for it attempts to fill up *lack* by discovering a Being within Becoming. "To impose upon becoming the character of being—this is the supreme will to power. . . . That *everything recurs* is the closest *approximation of a world of becoming to a world of being.* . . ."[52] Nietzsche can find infinite value in the now only by having it recur infinitely. Therefore he ends up not with the end of nihilism but with another, more will-ful reconstitution of it. Nietzsche called his own philosophy inverted Platonism, yet eternal recurrence more correctly implies what Heidegger concluded, that Nietzsche is the most unbridled Platonist in the history of Western metaphysics.

For Buddhism, the problem of *lack* can be resolved only by ceasing to avoid it and instead becoming-one with it: letting go of oneself and falling into the void, in order to realize that the void is not really void but the realm of the Buddha-dharma, as Huang-po put it. What does this mean in terms of nihilism? To stop evading the debacle of all meaning and accept it, which means experiencing the meaninglessness of one's life-goals—an extreme of anguish not to be recommended lightly. Such an understanding of the solution also transforms our understanding of the problem, for this solution is usually understood as the problem. This implies that true nihilism is not the debacle of all meaning but our terror of that debacle and the ways we flee it, which include a compulsive need to find some meaning in life as a bulwark against that threat. If so, *nihilism is not our lack but the fear and denial of that lack, experienced in this instance as impending loss of meaning.* Insofar as Nietzsche's will-to-power is in flight from *lack*, then, the will-to-power *is* nihilism. Eternal recurrence insures that flight will have no cloture, for it tries to fill *up lack* by flight itself, by repeated recurrence of the passing moment. Thus eternal recurrence would not be final victory over nihilism but the final victory of nihilism: In grasping at the fleeting now by making it recur, it misses the now-that-does-not-fall-away. The need to pull ourselves together and willing-ly affirm our being, which Nietzsche and the early Heidegger both encourage us to do, deflects us from the opposite solution of yielding to the nonbeing we most dread, which we might discover to be not so dreadful after all.

Meaninglessness. We have seen that according to Buddhism the solution to the problem of death is to die. Only by ceasing to repress the dread of death, and then accepting my death, can I begin to live. Until then, my life is a kind of death-in-life, made compulsive by the need to overcome death in one or another symbolic fashion.

We have seen that it is possible to die before we die because fear of death symbolizes an even deeper anguish: the sense-of-self's fear of its own nothing-ness, also known as no-thing-ness, nonbeing, emptiness, unreality, groundless-ness. Put in these terms, the solution to the dread of nothingness is to become nothing. Only by ending the attempt to make myself real (the futile project of becoming self-grounded), only by accepting my groundlessness and letting go, can sense of *lack* come to an end in the lacking-nothing freedom of a no-thing that can be anything.

It comes as no surprise, then, that the problem of nihilism, which is the *threat* of life becoming meaningless, should follow the same pattern. If mean-inglessness is another version of *lack*, then denying the emptiness at the core of my being (which the ego-self project is an attempt to do) includes repress-ing a despair about life's lack of meaning. The compulsive meanings that fill up our lives are ways of evading a sense of meaninglessness we dread. The only way to resolve this repressed despair is to make it conscious: that is, to despair.

The "discovery" of objective meaning is one of our main ways of dealing with *lack*. As Zarathustra points out, man assigns values to things only to maintain himself. We can usually cope with anxiety and guilt as long as we know what the meaning of life is, for there is security in that even if we don't always do what that meaning implies we should do. However, such meaning-systems corrupt "the innocence of becoming," because in projecting and un-derstanding them as objective we repress the fact that these meanings are our own creations, socially constructed and validated. Insofar as they originate in *lack*, they are based on fear, so a test of our maturity is whether we are able to face that fear. "It is a measure of the degree of strength of will to what extent one can do without meaning in things, to what extent one can endure to live in a meaningless world *because one organizes a small portion of it oneself.*"[53] Who is strong enough to become his own sun? As Sartre experienced, the prospect of absolute freedom is enough to arouse anguish in the hearts of the bravest. "To say that we invent values means nothing else but this: life has no meaning *a priori* . . . value is nothing else but the meaning you choose."[54] The anguish of the forlorn for-itself that wants to be in-itself becomes, in terms of meaning, the nostalgia of freedom for a home of objectively existing purpose. If the ego-self's autonomy is a delusion, we can see why that is difficult. Commonsense subject-object dualism presumes the sense-of-self to be the locus of awareness; subjectivism goes further to make the subject the only source of value and meaning, which devalues the world into a field-of-activity wherein the self labors to fulfill itself. Apparently objective meanings paper over the problem of *lack* because they provide some objective security. But in order for that illusory self to feel secure, its meanings must be unconsciously projected. The sun that motivates me must not be realized to be my own creation, if I am to be inspired by it. When I am aware of constructing my own meaning, the absence of any external grounding for that meaning means I have nothing to lean upon. The natural response is a deepened sense of *lack*, experienced as anguish and ontological guilt: By what right do I create such meanings? Who am I to decide that this is the way to live?

Juxtaposing these two alternatives clarifies the Buddhist approach, which, contra Nietzsche, does not find a solution in strength of will. If the collapse of objective meaning exposes my sense of *lack*, that will be painful, yet it is nonetheless a problem to be desired, since becoming aware of my *lack* is necessary in order to eventually solve it. Then, realizing the subjectivity of meaning does not by itself resolve the matter, for it is a stage that must be endured in order to realize something else.

If despair is a stage, however, one must despair in the right way. Odd as it sounds, the danger with despair is that one will cling to it. In Kierkegaard's school of anxiety (recommended in *The Concept of Anxiety*), despair is the final exam. It dredges up our most cherished meanings and devours them, leaving us disconsolate. But we do not become completely empty unless despair devours us wholly *and also itself.* Despair (literally "no hope") is the reverse side of hope, and both are relative to the sense-of-self, for the ego-self alternates between the hope it will finally fixate itself and the dread it never will. Then, despair evaporates at the same time as the self. Yet often this does not happen, because when despair finally occurs, after a lifetime of avoiding it, it appears with a force that makes it seem *more real* than the meanings it roots out, which had been used to avoid it. From the Buddhist standpoint, the recurring thoughts and feelings that constitute despair are no more real and no less impermanent than any other thoughts and feelings. But when we despair, our usual psychological defenses fail and we identify with *self*-pitying thoughts and *self*-destructive inclinations. Then, instead of despair consuming the self, it reinforces the worthlessness of that self. We end up not becoming nothing but with a sense-of-self nourishing itself on self-disgust. This is the "reactive" tendency that so disgusted Nietzsche, and he saw what the problem is: "He who despises himself still nonetheless respects himself as one who despises."

Man would rather will nothingness than not will.[55] Yet the void Huang-po recommends is not something that can be willed.

When we despair in the right way, what happens? Abandoning the hope that we will eventually become something, we yield to our nothingness and discover that, from our vantage point in Indra's Net, we have always been everything. As Dōgen expressed it in *Genjō-kōan*, to forget oneself is to be enlightened by all things, which is to perceive oneself as all things. What does such mutual interpenetration imply about the meaning of life? For Buddhism, meaning too is neither objective nor subjective. Life is neither meaningful nor meaningless but what might be called *meaningfree*. According to the *prajñaparamitā* texts, emptiness is form: that is, *śūnyatā* is not experienced as something other than the things in the world, and to draw back from involvement in forms is criticized as "clinging to *śūnyatā*. " With end of *lack*, the long-sought freedom *from* becomes the concrete freedom *to*. To forget oneself and become nothing is to wake up and find oneself in or *as* a situation—not confronted by it but one with it—and if one is not self-preoccupied then meaning arises naturally within that situation. As Buber puts it, all real living is meeting. You start with yourself in order to forget yourself and immerse yourself in the world; you understand yourself in order not to be preoccupied with yourself.[56]

According to Buddhism, to become enlightened is to forget one's own suffering only to wake up in or *one with* a world of suffering. This experience is not sympathy or empathy but compassion, literally "suffering with." What will the meaning of life become for such a person, freed from the delusions of objective meaning and narcissistic self-preoccupation? What will that nondual freedom, which has nothing to gain or to lose, care to do? The career of the bodhisattva is helping others, not because one ought to, for the bodhisattva is not bound by dogma or morality, but because one *is* the situation, and through oneself that situation draws forth a response to meet its needs. Nāgārjuna described *nirvāṇa* as this world experienced noncausally and without dependence. The bodhisattva's deeds are examples of this because there is no ulterior motive behind them, and there is no ulterior motive because there is no need to ground or real-ize oneself through them. This avoids the consequentialist regress that occurs when we try to justify everything by relating it to something else.

> It is by no means an objective truth that nothing is important unless it goes on forever or eventually leads to something else that persists forever. *Certainly there are ends that are complete unto themselves* without requiring an endless series of justifications outside themselves. . . . If no means were complete unto themselves, if everything had to be justified by something else outside of itself which must in its turn also be justified, then there is infinite regress: the chain of justification can never end. (Yalom)[57]

From the Mahāyāna point of view, every act is an end complete in itself. This is less a rebuttal of philosophical utilitarianism than a critique of the utilitarian way we live our lives, in which everything becomes a means to something else. In his old age, W. B. Yeats reflected: "When I think of all the books I have read, wise words heard, anxieties given to parents. . . . of hopes I have had, all life weighed in the balance of my own life seems to me a preparation for something that never happens."[58] As our world becomes ever more rationalized (in Max Weber's sense), that becomes ever more true. One measure of our "fallenness" today is how little is done for its own sake, which puts more pressure on something when it is—sex, for example, which has become so important to us and so problematical.

As Yalom implies, existential psychotherapy has reached some similar conclusions about the problem of meaninglessness. Viktor Frankl maintains that asking for *the* task in life or *the* meaning in life is nonsensical, like a reporter interviewing a chess grandmaster: "And now tell me, maestro—what is the best move in chess?"[59] Yalom discusses the formidable problem posed by the "galactic" point of view, which seems to trivialize us and all our activities into microscopic specks flickering in the vast expanse of cosmic time. He points out that this renders life meaninglessness only from that perspective, a perspective that moreover is delusive from the Buddhist point of view. It abstracts me from my actual situation, but *there is no such Archimedean master perspective outside our various perspectives within Indra's Net*. The interpenetration of all the jewels in that net is not *sub specie aeternitatis*. Every jewel in Indra's Net is the whole net only by virtue of its own position within that net. We are free to experience and appreciate different perspectives, yet there is no perspectiveless perspective. Such situationlessness is no concern of man, as Buber said. Yalom makes this point eloquently at the end of *Existential Psychotherapy*:

> Frankl argues that pleasure is a by-product of meaning, and that one's search should be directed toward the discovery of meaning. I believe that the search for meaning is similarly paradoxical: the more we rationally seek it, the less we find it; the questions that one can pose about meaning will always outlast the answers.
> Meaning, like pleasure, must be pursued obliquely. A sense of meaningfulness is a by-product of engagement. Engagement does not logically refute the lethal questions raised by the galactic perspective, but it causes these questions not to matter. That is the meaning of Wittgenstein's dictum: "The solution to the problem of life is seen in the vanishing of the problem."
> Engagement is the therapeutic answer to meaninglessness regardless of the latter's source. Wholehearted engagement in any of the infinite array of life's activities not only disarms the galactic view but enhances the possibility of one's completing the patterning of the events of one's life in some coherent fashion. . . .
> The therapist's goal, then, is engagement. The task is not to create engagement nor to inspirit the patient with engagement—these the therapist

cannot do. But it is not necessary: the desire to engage life is always there within the patient, and the therapist's clinical activities should be directed toward removal of obstacles in the patient's way.[60]
Searching for the meaning of life is searching for something that enables us to stop searching. When *lack* comes to an end, then, so does the problem of meaninglessness. Freud believed that the best forms of engagement are love and work. Buddhism has no argument with that, yet offers a gloss: The best love requires egolessness. Realizing I *am* the other clears the way.

Creativity. Rank saw that the creative person stands out because he or she is outside the usual collective meaning-system. Something in your life makes you take the world as a problem that needs to be answered. If you cannot accept the socially given solution to the problem of life, then you must create your own. The artist's work becomes his own private religion, his attempt to justify his heroism directly, in concrete creation. Such a person must create or else risk "a dangerous kind of megalomania because the individual becomes too full with his own meanings. . . . The creative person is too full both of himself and of the world."[61] The neurotic is in the same situation without being able to objectify his meanings; they become bottled up inside him and he ends up unsuccessfully trying to validate his heroism in private fantasies.

Yet there is not that much difference between them, according to Becker. Whether they successfully objectify or not, the artist and the neurotic face the same problem: How can one create a *private* religion? "How can one justify his own heroism? He would have to be as God." The work of art is too conscious and therefore too unrepressed a transference-projection to satisfy the need for an objective meaning-system, so it cannot resolve the artist's sense of *lack*. Since the truly creative person fashions her own very personal gift to society, which is necessary to justify her heroic identity, it must always be aimed at least partly over the heads of her fellow men, for *they* cannot grant immortality. Or Being. Consequently, "there is no way for the artist to be at peace with his work or with the society that accepts it. The artist's gift is always to creation itself, to the ultimate meaning of life, to God." The only complete solution is complete renunciation, "to give one's life as a gift to the highest powers. Absolution has to come from the absolute beyond." What is true for transference generally is especially so here. The best solution is surrendering to the universe on the broadest, least-fetishized level, which frees us from the fetters of the consolations of our fellow men and of the things of this world.[62]

From a Buddhist point of view, the difficulty with this otherwise insightful account is the subject-object dualism it assumes. Without that dualism, we are able to recognize that the creative process is, at its best, not the act of an ego-self, which is then offered to the highest powers, nor even an act of the self in communion with those highest powers, but nondual, which is to say: a manifestation of those powers. This process is no more objective than subjective, for one must be attentive as well as receptive, a state perhaps best described as emptied. The hallmark of inspiration is this paradoxical synthesis of subjective freedom and objective necessity, both thereby intensified, as Nietzsche knew well and described well: "[Artists] know only too well that it is precisely when they cease to act "voluntarily" and do everything of necessity that their feeling of freedom, subtlety, fullness of power, creative placing, disposing, shaping reaches its height—in short, that necessity and "freedom of will" are then one in them."[63]

This casts another light on why artists can never be satisfied with their work or with the recognition of society. The artist's most important gift is not her work but herself, for the most creative work requires that she overcome herself, or more precisely forget herself. Then, one's sense-of-self is not the means but the obstacle, which is why the only solution is full renunciation that surrenders one's life to the highest powers. This makes the artist's religion no more nor less private than that of anyone who is truly religious. One's absolution is not a premonition of immortality but a temporary transformation in the way one's groundlessness is experienced, from the gnawing sense of *lack* we usually feel into the receptiveness of a spring through which a life-giving fountain gushes forth, from some fathomless source.

Yet, as Becker notices, the artist often bears more guilt than others. "Your very work accuses you; it makes you feel inferior. What right do you have to play God?"[64] For Becker, this follows from the impossibility of the artist justifying her heroism consciously, in concrete creation rather than repressed transference. But there is another way to look at it. Who suffers more, the person who has never known God or the person to whom God has appeared and then withdrawn? The more deeply you have experienced the fountain, the greater *lack* will you feel when more reflexive ego-consciousness returns. Creativity by itself grants not final absolution but only a taste of letting-go. That, of course, is no criticism of the taste.

The Seriousness of a Child at Play

> Mature manhood: that means to have rediscovered the seriousness one had as a child at play.[65]

For Derrida, like Nietzsche, the death of God unleashes limitless play. Derrida calls play the absence of the transcendental signified.[66] Yet, whether our God has died or not, we are already playing. The question is not whether we play but how. Do we suffer our games as if they were life-or-death struggles, because they are the means whereby we hope to ground ourselves, or do we dance with the light feet that Nietzsche called the first attribute of divinity? James Carse makes what amounts to the same distinction in his delightful and insightful *Finite and Infinite Games*:

There are at least two kinds of games. One could be called finite, the other infinite. A finite game is played for the purpose of winning, an infinite game for the purpose of continuing the play.

The rules of a finite game may not change; the rules of an infinite game must change.

Finite players play within boundaries; infinite players play with boundaries.

Finite players are serious; infinite players are playful.

Finite players win titles; infinite players have nothing but their names.

A finite player plays to be powerful; an infinite player plays with strength.

A finite player consumes time; an infinite player generates time.

The finite player aims to win eternal life; the infinite player aims for eternal birth.[67]

In terms of Indra's Net, the difference is between a player struggling to ground himself in the net and a player who plays with the net because she has realized that she *is* the net. In Derrida's terms, it is the difference between dreaming of deciphering a truth which will end play by restoring self-presence, and affirming the play which no longer seeks to ground itself. Nietzsche's philosophizing exceeds any system that can be constructed out of it, for (the will to power notwithstanding) it demonstrates how thinking can be such play. "I do not know what the spirit of a philosopher might wish more to be than a dancer. For the dance is his ideal, also his art, and finally also his only piety, his 'service of God.'"[68] A friend once complained to Samuel Johnson that he had tried to be a philosopher but cheerfulness kept breaking in; Nietzsche shows that the two need not be incompatible.

Zarathustra teaches three metamorphoses: from camel (a weight-bearing spirit) to lion (who captures freedom) to the child, who "is innocence and forgetfulness, a new beginning." Unless we become children, we shall not enter into the kingdom of heaven—which does not mean that children will enter therein, for they are already there, since they have not learned yet that life is a serious business, that death can lurk behind any corner, that symbolic death frustrates their every attempt to become real.

Of course, the normal child can soon distinguish easily and quickly between what adults call "real life" and "play." The more psychological way of stating the matter is to say that the child acts out his fantasies and seriously tries, through the play-situation, to resolve conflicts in which these fantasies play a part. But he normally recognizes reasonably well which of these selves and lives are *defined* as real by the adults around him; and he learns to go along with their game—until finally he is quite unaware that it was *their* game, for it is now his, too. (Hillman)[69]

One grows up by learning the socially acceptable ways to try to overcome *lack*. Joseph Campbell wonders if "the considerable mutual attraction of the very young and the very old may derive something from their common, secret knowledge that it is they, and not the busy generation between, who are concerned with a poetic play that is eternal and truly wise."[70] Those at the dawn and sunset of life are less likely to dualize it from night, and when life is not opposed to death it becomes play.

Adam should have been content to play with nature in paradise, says the Silesian mystic Jakob Boehme, and he fell when life became serious business, which turned nature from an end into a means. The Fall and all subsequent evil are due to self-will and desire; we become children of God again through an inward grace that regenerates us into childlikeness.

> This entire manifested or out-breathed universe is, he [Boehme] says, the expression of the divine desire for holy sport and play. The Heart of God enjoys this myriad play of created beings, all tuned as the infinite strings of a harp for contributing to one mighty harmony, and all together uttering and voicing the infinite variety of the divine purpose. Each differentiated spirit or light or property or atom of creation has a part to play in the infinite sport or game or harmony, "so that in God there might be a holy play through the universe as a child plays with his mother, and that so the joy in the Heart of God might be increased," or again "so that each being may be a true sounding string in God's harmonious concert."[71]

Boehme describes this divine melody as "the joyful play of eternal generation." The extended musical metaphor is so appropriate because music has no ulterior motives and no goal. It is *tathatā*. When it goes somewhere (e.g., in sonata-form development) it is not for the sake of getting there but for the sake of the going there. I can think of no better temporal analogy to complement the spatial metaphor of Indra's Net: the mutual interpenetration of musical instruments in the harmonic play of a symphonic concert.

What do madmen lack that sane men possess? "The ability to be careless and disregard appearances, to relax and laugh at the world," says Becker. The "need for legitimate foolishness" was the cure Otto Rank prescribed for neurosis. Like Nietzsche, they conclude that such childlike foolishness is the calling of mature men.[72]

Few of us seem ready to hear it. "So the grand destiny of man is . . . to *play?*" Does our incredulity reflect the absurdity of the proposal, or how far we have trudged from the Garden of Eden? Perhaps the negative connotations of the word reveal less about play than about us: our self-importance, our need to stand out from the rest of creation (and from the rest of our fellows) by accomplishing great things—which might just make us real. We are to play not because there is nothing else to do, not because the lack of some higher meaning means we just while away our time, but because we realize the nature of meaning and time. This is not inconsistent with the selfless service of the Bodhisattva, for loss of self-preoccupation is what makes true play possible, enabling the Bodhisattva to manifest the liberation he or she teaches:

To be playful is not to be trivial or frivolous, or to act as though nothing of consequence will happen. On the contrary, when we are playful with each other we relate as free persons, and the relationship is open to surprise; everything that happens is of consequence. It is, in fact, seriousness that closes itself to consequence, for seriousness is a dread of the unpredictable outcome of open possibility. To be serious is to press for a specified conclusion. To be playful is to allow for possibility whatever the cost to oneself. (Carse)[73]

The problem, ultimately, is "not enjoying yourself," Nietzsche's definition of original sin, which is as good a definition of *lack*. This fits nicely with an equally simple definition of Buddhism offered by the Vietnamese teacher Thich Nhat Hanh: a clever way to enjoy your life.

So this chapter will conclude by playing with Schopenhauer's conclusion to *The World as Will and Idea*. For those whose life is a struggle to feel real, this discussion of what remains after the evaporation of *lack* must seem childlike foolishness. But, conversely, to those who do not need to deny their groundlessness and make themselves real, the seriousness of adult preoccupations reveals itself to be—nothing but childish games. The next chapter looks at some of those games.

5

Trying to Become Real

If one looks with a cold eye at the mess man has made of his history, it is difficult to avoid the conclusion that he has been afflicted by some built-in mental disorder which drives him towards self-destruction.
—Koestler

Madness is something rare in individuals—but in groups, parties, peoples, ages it is the rule.
—Nietzsche

A century so full of war, revolution, genocide, and now ecocide testifies to the truth of these aphorisms but has yet to understand them. Why is group madness the rule? Is it because our self-destructive disorder is built-in, as Koestler speculates, or do we build it into ourselves by collectively repressing and projecting mental processes that we have not been able to cope with more consciously? If history is a nightmare from which we are trying to awaken, perhaps that nightmare began as a daydream more attractive than the pain of being human—until the dream took on a life of its own and an ugly turn, as we became trapped in our own objectifications. Then the key to this puzzle is why we prefer daydreaming to waking up, and that brings us back to *lack*. If the autonomy of *self*-consciousness is a delusion which can never quite shake off its shadow-feeling that "something is wrong with me," it will need to rationalize that sense of inadequacy somehow. Without a religious means of absolution, today we usually experience our *lack* as "I don't yet have enough of..." This chapter explores some of the more popular ways that we try to escape into the future.

My argument might seem to suggest conservative political and economic conclusions: Reformers are projecting their own *lack* when they see the short-comings that require radical solutions. Yet, the element of truth in that must yield to something of greater consequence: our individual lacks collectively objectified in social structures that return the favor and manipulate us. Hölderlin said that what makes the state a hell on earth is that man tries to make it his heaven. In *lack* terms, that becomes: By trying to resolve our sense-of-*lack*

133

collectively, we have compounded the problem, and such compounded *lack*-objectifications assume a life of their own. We need to look at the ways our personal senses of *lack* plug into the collective unconscious of our social behavior and institutions.

This chapter offers a new perspective on the supposed secularity of modern life by arguing that four historically conditioned forms of delusion/craving may be understood as our attempts to resolve such *lack*: the desire for fame, the love of romantic love, the money complex, and humanity's collective Oedipal project of technological development. These four tendencies are not limited to any particular time and place, of course, but they began to gain special importance in the West when Christianity began to decline. Burckhardt, Huizinga, and Aries all noticed a striking increase in death-preoccupation at the end of the medieval era. In psychotherapeutic terms, such an increase in death-anxiety requires stronger psychic devices to cope with it. In *lack* terms, the greater sense-of-self that began to develop then must have been shadowed by a greater sense-of-*lack*, leading to greater individual need to real-ize this self and more radical attempts to do so.

The pursuit of fame and money are attempts to real-ize oneself through symbols; romantic love tries to fill in one's *lack* with the beloved; technological progress has become our collective attempt to ground ourselves by "developing" the environment into our ground, until the whole earth testifies to our reality. As long as there was a truly catholic church, providing an agreed means to cope with *lack*, such projects did not seem spiritually necessary. Here we can benefit again from Nāgārjuna's denial of any difference between *saṃsāra* and *nirvāṇa*. If we do not presuppose the usual distinction between secular and sacred, we can see the same religious drive operating in each case: the conscious or unconscious urge to resolve our sense of *lack*. To the extent that these four are motivated by such a spiritual need, they may be considered secular heresies. Since they cannot fulfill that need, they tend to spin out of control and become demonic. Usually the secular/sacred dualism seems important to us insofar as we are wary of materialistic and psychologistic reductionism, yet there is another way to understand their nonduality. Rather than reducing the sacred to a function of the secular, this chapter goes the other way by suggesting that our modern worldly values (desire for fame, money, etc.) acquire their compulsiveness from a misdirected spiritual drive.

The Fever of Renown

Because the public image comes to stand as the only valid certification of being, the celebrity clings to his image as the rich man clings to his money—that is, as if to life itself. (Lewis Lapham)[1]

"How can he be dead, who lives immortal in the hearts of men?" mused

Longfellow, bestowing on Michelangelo our highest possible praise. "If his inmost heart could have been lain open," wrote Hawthorne of a character in *Fanshawe*, "there would have been discovered the dream of undying fame; which, dream as it is, is more powerful than a thousand realities." More powerful, because of such a dream is reality woven, and the nature of this dream ensures that there is no lack of historical testimony to its power. Unfortunately, seeing through one aspect of this delusion does not immunize us against others. Horace warned that the race for public honors traps men, for the urge to glory and praise ruins both wellborn and lowly: "Those who seek much, lack much." Yet this did not stop him from crowing at the end of his third ode: "I have wrought a monument more enduring than bronze, and loftier than the royal accumulation of the pyramids. Neither corrosive rain nor raging wind can destroy it, nor the innumerable sequence of years nor the flight of time. I shall not altogether die." Was Horace more vain than us or just more frank about his own motivations?

According to Alan Harrington, the urge for fame has only one purpose: "to achieve an imitation of divinity before witnesses." The gods are immortal, he says, but the rest of us will have to settle for a symbolic substitute, which requires witnesses. "*Being recognized before many witnesses* strengthens our claim to membership in the immortal company."² Yet Marcus Aurelius already saw the problem with witnesses: "Those that yearn for after fame do not realize that their successors are sure to be very much the same as the contemporaries whom they find such a burden, and no less mortal. What is it anyway to you if there be this or that far-off echo in their voices, or if they have this or that opinion about you?"³ What is the advantage of having one's own name on the lips of future generations, when their overriding concern will be the same as ours: to have *their* name on the lips of their successors. . . . How does that confer any reality on us? Nāgārjuna demonstrated the futility of such infinite regresses with his argument against dependent being. If there is no self-being there can be no dependent being either, inasmuch as dependent being requires the self-being of another. Yet we strive to become real through the eyes of others, who strive to become real through the eyes of others, who will strive. . . .

Nonetheless, in Western secular societies belief in an afterlife has been largely replaced by a craving for fame and the approval of posterity. Physical death may come, but such symbolic life can continue forever. Reputation—primarily through public deeds—was also paramount for the Greeks and Romans: "A culture whose afterlife offered so little comfort to the soul was obsessed with preserving the fame of the dead on the lips of the living."⁴ Like Derrida's elusive trace, however, genuine heroism is always receding if *true* greatness means achieving a sense of being without a sense-of-*lack*. A few generations ago, madhouses were said to be full of Napoleons, yet Napoleon was inspired by the example of Caesar, while Caesar lamented that he hadn't accomplished as much as Alexander, even as Alexander the Great modelled himself on Achilles. . . . When *lack* is "the origin of the origin," such traces become unavoidable. "If he was real, I can become real by imitating him"—unless *his* reality is a past that has never been present, in which case trying to recover the past in the future merely loses the present.

What little remains today of our discomfort with fame is a residue of the Judeo-Christian critique of Roman standards of public glory, for "in the wake of Jesus, public men of all sorts develop a kind of guilty conscience about their desire for achievement in front of an audience."[5] Christianity offered a different project to overcome *lack*. The success of this project accounts for the Middle Ages as we remember them; or, more precisely, that we remember so little about them. If history is what man does with death—a record of how humankind runs away from death—a society less preoccupied with death will make less history. It is no coincidence that at the end of the Middle Ages (when, according to Burckhardt, Huizinga, and Aries, man became more obsessed with death) man became more obsessed with symbolic immortality: "From the Renaissance until today men have been filled with a burning ambition for fame, while this striving that seems so natural today was unknown to medieval man" (Burckhardt).[6] The crisis in Europe's collective religious project to cope with *lack* opened the door to a proliferation of more individual projects, both secular and sacred (e.g., personal mysticism). The Reformation worked to de-institutionalize religion by shifting from a corporate orientation toward salvation (the Church as the body of Christ) to a more private relationship with God. If God is first and foremost the guarantor that our *lack* will be resolved, we can understand how God may be sought symbolically on earth—perhaps must be, if we no longer seek him in heaven.

In his comprehensive study *The Frenzy of Renown: Fame and Its History*, Leo Braudy traces the modern history of fame from late medieval glorification of the saint (e.g., St. Francis and Jeanne d'Arc) through the creative artist of the Renaissance (Michelangelo, da Vinci) and the writer of the nineteenth century (Byron, Dickens, Victor Hugo) to today's performer (Madonna, Michael Jackson). It seems to be a gradual descent from sacred to secular. Saints were believed to gain greater being from direct contact with God; Dante and Milton strove to be worthy of fame; today we have celebrities whose only claim to fame is that they are famous. Fame has become self-justifying as an end to be sought in itself.

According to Braudy, the eighteenth century (also singled out by Aries for its death-preoccupation) was a turning-point in the development of our modern preoccupation with fame:

[I]t is difficult not to characterize the latter part of the eighteenth century as a world in which the waning of belief in an afterlife has bred a twin obsession with posterity and death. . . . In a culture where talk of the afterlife was becoming less and less important to theology, let alone the ordinary believer, the hope of fame on earth was part of the expectation that one might be fulfilled, that is, recognized in one's lifetime. Hope of heaven, hope of immediate fame, and hope of fame in posterity were becoming difficult to distinguish.[7] This became tied up with the belief in progress (and, later, evolution): "The cult of progress, of growth, of achievement—the image of new dawns, new tomorrows, and a new sense of time so prominent in both the American and French revolutions—turned all eyes to the future, where perfection and understanding would be achieved on earth."[8] The decline in a sacred afterlife was accompanied by a rise in the importance of secular afterlife, for the need to project a *lack*-free time somewhere in the future remained. Diderot argued that in posterity fame will redeem one's work from the envy of the present, much as the Christian afterlife redeems the reputation of the virtuous from the persecutions of the wicked.

Gradually, however, this secularization of fame led to a decline of belief even in a secular afterlife. Hazlitt noticed that the young value posthumous fame because they don't yet believe in their own deaths, while the aged would rather have their celebrity on earth. Nowadays it has become more difficult to believe in any future, so we prefer our fame too on the installment plan. This profanation of salvation has eroded the distinction between good and bad fame. "How many times do I have to kill before I get a name in the paper or some national attention?" wrote a murderer to the Wichita police. Only with his sixth killing, he complained, had he begun to get the publicity he deserved. When it is believed that recognition by others is what leads to self-fulfillment, "fame promises acceptability, even if one commits the most heinous crime, because thereby people will finally know who you are, and you will be saved from the living death of being unknown."[9]

The living death of being unknown. When the real world becomes what's in the newspapers or on television, to be unknown is to be nothing. If my sense-of-self is internalized through social conditioning, that is, if others teach me that I am real, the natural tendency will be to cope with my shadow sense of unreality by continually reassuring myself with the attention of other people. Yet, if my sense of reality is gained by others' perceptions of me, then, no matter how appreciative that attention may be, I am constrained by those perceptions. "The difficulty arises when to be free is defined by being known to be free, because then one might be more known than free." This applies to anything that constitutes one's claim to fame: You can't use fame without being used by it. Part of this problem is the fan, who seeks to bask in the glory—share in the *being*—radiated by his or her heroes. "The audience . . . is less interested in what they [celebrities] think they 'really' are than what role they play in the audience's continuing drama of the meaning of human nature."[10] That drama may be dangerous, as John Lennon, Ronald Reagan, and many others have discovered.

"[T]he essential lure of the famous is that they are somehow more real than we and that our insubstantial physical reality needs that immortal substance for support. . . . because it is the best, perhaps the only, way *to be*." De Tocqueville, visiting America in the 1830s, noticed how democratic societies aggravate this tendency. Aristocracies fix one's social position so everyone knows who and where one is, while democracy engenders a need to stand out from the crowd. Democratic man usually has no lofty ambition, de Tocqueville said; he just wants to be first at anything.[11] Academics can readily recognize the consequences of this: "And hence this tremendous struggle to singularize ourselves, to survive in some way in the memory of others and of posterity. It is this struggle, a thousand times more terrible than the struggle for life, that gives its tone, colour, and character to our society" (Unamuno). To make matters worse, this struggle is not just with our contemporaries. "The heaven of fame is not very large, and the more there are who enter it the less is the share of each. The great names of the past rob us of our place in it; the space which they fill in the popular memory they usurp from us who aspire to occupy it. . . . If additions continue to be made to the wealth of literature, there will come a day of sifting, and each one fears lest he be caught in the meshes of the sieve."[12]

The importance of fame as a secular salvation has become so pervasive today that we no longer notice it, any more than a fish sees the water it swims in. It has infiltrated all the corners of contemporary culture, including Christmas carols ("Then how the reindeer loved him/ As they shouted out with glee/ Rudolf the red-nosed reindeer/ You'll go down in history!") and spaghetti sauce bottles (see the label on Newman's Own Spaghetti Sauce). The Guinness Book of World Records has become one of our most important cultural icons.

From a Buddhist perspective, the struggle between fame and anonymity is another self-defeating version of dualistic thinking. We differentiate success from failure, yet we cannot have one without the other because they are interdependent. Grasping one half also maintains the other. So our hope for success is equal to our fear of failure. And whether we win or lose the struggle for fame, we internalize the dialectic between fame and anonymity.

Just as the titles of winners are worthless unless they are visible to others, there is a kind of antititle that attaches to invisibility. To the degree that we are invisible we have a past that has condemned us to oblivion. It is as though we have somehow been overlooked, even forgotten, by our chosen audience. If it is the winners who are presently visible, it is the losers who are invisibly past.

As we enter into finite play—not playfully, but seriously—we come before an audience conscious that we bear the antititles of invisibility. We feel the need, therefore, to prove to them that we are not what we think they think we are. . . .

As with all finite play, an acute contradiction quickly develops at the heart of this attempt. As finite players we will not enter the game with sufficient desire to win unless we are ourselves convinced by the very audience we intend to convince. That is, *unless we believe we actually are the losers the audience sees us to be, we will not have the necessary desire to win.* The more negatively we assess ourselves, the more we strive to reverse the negative judgment of others. The outcome brings the contradiction to perfection: by proving to the audience they were wrong, we prove to ourselves the audience was right.

The more we are recognized to be winners, the more we know ourselves to be losers. . . . No one is ever wealthy enough, honored enough, applauded enough. (Carse)[13]

The more we are applauded, the more we feel our *lack.* If what I have sought for so long does not make me real, what can? "Many seek fame because they believe it confers a reality that they lack. Unfortunately, when they become famous themselves, they usually discover that their sense of unreality has only increased." Why? "The reception of the great work by the world can never satisfy the expectations its creator had for its own fame and his own."[14] When fame symbolizes my need to become real, such a disappointment is inevitable. No amount of fame can satisfy me if there is really something else I seek from it. From here there are two ways to go. One is concluding that I am not yet famous *enough.* Then, each achievement has to top the last one, for if I'm not going up I'm headed down; so this tends to become demonic. The other danger with becoming famous is that I might accomplish my project for overcoming *lack* without overcoming *lack,* with the effect of increasing my anxiety about being unreal. From a Buddhist standpoint, however, this second problem is also a great opportunity since it opens up the possibility of confronting my sense of *lack* more directly. Then the issue becomes how I deal with that heightened sense of pure *lack.*

All You Need Is Love

Few people would fall in love had they never heard of love. (La Rochefoucauld)

The English word "love" means too much and therefore too little. This section addresses only that historically conditioned form of attraction between the sexes called romantic love (defined by Madame de Staël as "self-love à deux"). It has been argued that this type of love verges on the ridiculous, like someone dying of starvation because he could not find any brussels sprouts. Then why does it so seldom seem ridiculous to us? Is it because romance has become one of the most widely accepted ways to overcome *lack*?

Our eagerness for both novels and films with their identical type of plot; the idealized eroticism that pervades our culture and upbringing and provides the pictures that fill the background of our lives; our desire for "escape," which a mechanical boredom exacerbates—everything within and about us glorifies passion. Hence the prospect of a passionate experience has come to seem the promise that we are about to live more fully and more intensely. We look upon passion as a transfiguring force, something beyond pain and delight, an ardent beatitude.[15]

This beatitude may transfigure pain, yet it remains dependent on it, since there is nothing more fatal to passion than the completion that brings lovers down to earth. The course of true love is hindered. Romance thrives on difficulties, misunderstandings, and forced separations, which postpone the complacency inherent in familiarity, when housekeeping emotions take over. Such a dismal encore to ecstasy being unendurable, suffering—the literal meaning of *passion*—comes to the rescue. The enmity between the families of Romeo and Juliet is necessary to challenge their attraction. Without it there would be no story to tell and (we have reason to suspect) no such grand passion.

As Diotima taught Socrates, love thrives on *lack*—or is it the reverse: Does our *lack* thrive on love? We are not unaware that passion means suffering, but we imagine that such passion is nonetheless exciting and vital in a way ordinary life is not. Therefore we revel in the pain, for all pain is endurable when we can see a reason for it and an end to it. Our formless sense of *lack* seeks to objectify itself into an object lacked, which grants the possibility of a project to gain the lacked thing.[16]

The Greeks and Romans were not unfamiliar with romantic love, yet for them it was the exception rather than the rule, and they looked upon it more as an illness. Plutarch called love a frenzy: "Some have believed it was a madness. . . . Those who are in love must be forgiven as though ill." Then how have we come to cherish this frenzy so highly? If salvation through romantic passion is a historically conditioned myth, what were its origins and why did it arise at the time it did?

Many of the answers are found in Denis de Rougemont's classic study *Love in the Western World*. It traces the myth back to the legend of Tristan and Iseult, a tale of unknown origins which became widespread in the twelfth century, about that time of the late Middle Ages singled out by Burckhardt and Aries as the turning-point in man's increasing awareness of death (and increasing awareness of *lack*). De Rougemont's analysis of the legend demonstrates that

> Tristan and Iseult do not love one another. They say they don't, and everything goes to prove it. *What they love is love and being in love. . . .* Their need of one another is in order to be aflame, and they do not need one another as they are. What they need is not one another's presence, but one another's absence.[17]

If absence gives us a project to overcome *lack*, presence must disappoint because it accomplishes one's goal without ending one's *lack*. Therefore each loves the other "*from the standpoint of self and not from the other's standpoint.* Their unhappiness thus originates in a false reciprocity, which disguises a twin narcissism." Narcissism, because the other is experienced not as he or she is, but as the opportunity to fill up one's own *lack*.[18] Of course, that is not the way Tristan and Iseult understand it. Like all great lovers, they imagine that they have been transported "into a kind of transcendental state outside ordinary human experience, into an ineffable absolute irreconcilable with the world, but that they feel to be *more real than the world*." De Rougemont concludes that Tristan and Iseult, unaware and in spite of themselves, desire nothing but death. The approach of death acts as a goad to sensuality, aggravating their desire. *Love in the Western World* begins by quoting Bedier's version of the legend: "My lords, if you would hear a high tale of love and death. . . . " We could listen to nothing more delightful, of course, for that is the fateful equation: "A myth is needed to express the dark and unmentionable fact that passion is linked with death, and involves the destruction of anyone yielding himself up to it with all his strength."[19] De Rougement dismisses this as anti-life but misses the point, if death is what most intimately symbolizes our fear of letting go of ourselves as well as our desire to let go of ourselves—which is the only way to overcome *lack*, according to Buddhism.

From a *lack* perspective, the most important aspect of de Rougemont's analysis is that he sees the "spiritual" character of romantic love: "The passionate love which the myth celebrates actually became in the twelfth century—the moment when first it began to be cultivated—a religion in the full sense of the word, and in particular a Christian heresy historically determined."[20] Again, it is unlikely to be a coincidence that the myth of salvation through romance arose just as the prevalent Christian myth declined, which cleared the way for more individualistic alternatives to develop, for more personal myths to overcome *lack*. De Rougemont relates the rise of the romantic heresy to the troubadours, who were probably under the influence of the Cathar heresy, itself likely to have been influenced by Manichaeism from eastern Europe. He thereby marginalizes the infecting virus into an external "other" invading pure Christianity, which perhaps reveals more about de Rougemont's anti-pagan bias than about the origin of the Cathars.

A famous twelfth-century judgment by a "court of love" in the house of the Countess of Champagne declared that love and marriage were incompatible, since the first is by choice and the second by duty. But their judgment was also opposed to any physical "satisfaction" of love: "Of *donnoi* [courtly love] he knows truly nothing who wants fully to possess his lady. *Whatever turns into a reality is no longer love*."[21] Because whatever love is consummated is no longer a way to become real? So the troubadours adored inaccessible ladies without hope of requital. The history of passionate love since then is the devolution of this courtly myth—still with strong spiritual overtones—into more "profane" love, "the account of the more and more desperate attempts of Eros to take the place of mystical transcendence by means of emotional intensity. But magniloquent or plaintive, the tropes of its passionate discourse and the hues of its rhetoric can never attain to more than the glow of a resurgent twilight and the promise of a phantom bliss."[22]

From spiritual transcendence through emotional intensity to . . . our present preoccupation with sexual fulfillment. Why has sex become so important to us? If we do not dualize secular from sacred, we can see the same urge functioning in each: Today we unconsciously seek a spiritual satisfaction from sex. *Spiritual* because we want sex to fulfill us and heal us—that is, to resolve our *lack*, yet that is to expect something it cannot provide except for the briefest of moments. "It is once more the aspiration towards the life sublime," says Huizinga, "but this time viewed from the animal side. It is an ideal all the same, even though it be that of unchastity."[23] And if we do not dualize the animal from the sublime, perhaps the main difference between troubadours and one-night stands is that the myth of sexual salvation is easier to see through. It is as easy as giving up smoking, which some people do twenty times a day. The logical and demonic culmination of this myth is Don Juan, who turns out to be motivated by the same project as the troubadours. Not lust but the inadequacy of sex as a religion—its obvious inability to satisfy *lack* for very long—is what drives him from one woman to another.

De Rougemont contrasts passion-love with life. The first "is an impoverishment of one's being, an *askesis* without sequel, an inability to enjoy the present without imagining it as absent, a never-ending flight from possession." Instead, he says, happiness depends on acceptance and is lost as soon as we try to gain it, since it pertains not to having but to being. "Every wish to experience happiness, to have it at one's beck and call—instead of *being* in a *state* of happiness, as though by grace—must instantly produce an intolerable sense of want."[24] Again, one can appreciate the wisdom in this without being satisfied with de Rougemont's solution, which is a return to more traditional Christian values, including a decision to keep troth. Religious faith and marital fidelity do not necessarily resolve the problem of *lack*, for they may simply replace one myth with another. Romantic passion is anti-life, insists de Rougemont, yet he does not see what impels the widespread fascination with anti-life: the *lack* - dissatisfaction built into life as we ordinarily experience it, a frustration that must be addressed one way or another.

None of the above is a critique of love in its spiritual, emotional, or physical aspects; it is rather an attempt to explain the widespread inability to find happiness in such relationships. Of course, the Western tradition has other and older myths about love. One profound example is the story of Psyche and Cupid; another is found in the *Phaedrus* and the *Symposium*. In these dialogues, Plato mentions a frenzied type of love that spreads from the body to infect the spirit with malignant humors, and contrasts that with a different kind of delirium conceived in one's soul by the inspiration of heaven (therefore to be called *enthusiasm*, "possessed by a god"). In the *Symposium*, Diotima teaches Socrates that erotic passion at its best is transformed into a love delighting in beauty of every kind. The lover who has ascended high enough will therefore experience the perfect form of beauty, which is the reality and substance that is *in* everything we perceive as beautiful.[25]

This Platonic account of pure love and everlasting beauty does not survive Nietzsche's scathing attack on all such Real worlds, yet it touches on something that does: the ability of love to transform our way of experiencing everything. We smile on the man for whom the whole world has suddenly become inexpressibly beautiful, simply because his beloved reciprocates. But who, he or we, experience the world more truly? Love shakes us out of the utilitarian, everything-for-the-sake-of-something-else way of seeing things, and therefore it opens up the possibility of an even deeper transformation. Ernest Becker wonders if "the reason that love is one of the principal sources of anguish in the higher primates is because it stands at the threshold of a this-worldly liberation."[26]

A wonderful example of such liberation is Etty Hillesum's love for Julius Speier, as recorded in her extraordinary diaries.[27] Soon after she met him in early 1941, Speier became the focus of her life and they became lovers, although he was more important as a "guru" figure for her. By the time that "dear spoilt man" died a year and a half later, however, her love had grown far beyond him, and during the Dutch Holocaust she devoted herself wholeheartedly to helping all those who were suffering. Survivors from Auschwitz confirmed that she was "luminous" to the last, doing everything she could to comfort others. I suspect that such love has nothing to do with narcissism. This implies that, instead of using the other to try to fill one's *lack*, one may participate in a deeper love that consumes self-love and self-preoccupation, and therefore their *lack*-shadow as well. Perhaps, like all bodhisattvas, Etty realized that when there is no self there is no other.

The Midas Touch

If there is to be a psychoanalysis of money it must start from the hypothesis that the money complex has the essential structure of religion—or, if you will, the negation of religion, the demonic. The psychoanalytic theory of money must start by establishing the proposition that money is, in Shakespeare's words, the "visible god"; in Luther's words, "the God of this world." (Norman O. Brown)[28]

What I want to see above all is that this remains a country where someone can always get rich. (Ronald Reagan)[29]

One of Schopenhauer's aphorisms says that money is human happiness *in abstracto*, consequently he who is no longer capable of happiness *in concreto* sets his whole heart on money. The difficulty is not with money as a convenient medium of exchange but with the money complex that arises when money becomes desirable in itself. That desire is readily understandable when money improves the quality of one's life, yet what about those many situations when its pursuit reduces the quality of our lives? How does this happen? Given our sense of *lack*, how could this not happen?

Money is the "purest" symbol "because there is nothing in reality that corresponds to it."[30] The coins and paper bills we pass around are in themselves worthless, as Midas discovered about gold. You can't eat or drink them, plant them, or sleep under them. At the same time, money has more value than anything else because it *is* value; it can transform into everything because it is how we define value. The psychological problem occurs when life becomes motivated by the desire for such pure value. We all sense what is wrong with this, yet it is helpful to make it explicit. To the extent that life becomes focused around the desire for money, an ironic reversal takes place between means and ends: Everything else is devalued in order to maximize a worthless-in-itself goal, because our desires have become fetishized into that symbol. "The crux of the matter is the general fact that money is everywhere conceived as purpose, and countless things that are really ends in themselves are thereby degraded to mere means."[31]

When everything has its price and everyone his price, the numerical representation of the symbol-system becomes more important—more *real*—than the things represented. We end up enjoying not a worthwhile job well done, or meeting a friend, or hearing a bird, but accumulating pieces of paper. To find the method in this madness we must relate it to the sense-of-self's sense-of-*lack*, whose festering keeps us from being able to fully enjoy that bird-song (just *this!*). Since we no longer believe in any original sin that could be expiated, what can it be that is wrong with us and how can we hope to get over it? Today the most popular explanation—our contemporary original sin—is that we don't have enough money.

The origin of money is puzzling. How did the transition from barter ever occur? How were human cravings fetishized into pieces of metal? The answer that Norman O. Brown provides is elegant because it reveals as much about the character of money now: Money was and still is literally *sacred*. "It has long been known that the first markets were sacred markets, the first banks were temples, the first to issue money were priests or priest-kings."[32] Simmel also noticed that Greek money was originally sacred because it emanated from the priesthood.[33] The first coins were minted and distributed by temples because they were medallions inscribed with the god's image and embodying his protective power. Containing such *mana*, they were naturally in demand, not because you could buy things with them but vice versa: Since they were popular you could exchange them for other things.

The consequence of this was that (as Becker puts it) "now the cosmic powers could be the property of everyman, without even the need to visit temples: you could now traffic in immortality in the marketplace." This eventually led to the emergence of a new kind of people, who based the value of their lives— and their hope of immortality—on a new cosmology focused on coins. In this way a new meaning-system evolved, which our present economic system continues to make more and more the meaning-system. "Money becomes the distilled value of all existence . . . a single immortality symbol, a ready way of relating the increase of oneself to all the important objects and events of one's world."[34] In Buddhist terms, beyond its usefulness as a medium of exchange, money has become modern man's most popular way of accumulating Being, of coping with our gnawing intuition that we do not really exist. Suspecting that the sense-of-self is groundless, we used to go to temples and churches to ground ourselves in God; now we work to secure ourselves financially.

Because the true meaning of this meaning-system is unconscious, we end up, as usual, paying a heavy price for it. The value we place on money rebounds against us. The more we value it, the more we find it used (and use it ourselves) to evaluate us. In *The Hour of Our Death*, Aries turns our usual critique upside-down. Today we complain about materialism, but modern man is not really materialistic, for "things have become means of production, or objects to be consumed or devoured . . . the ordinary man in his daily life no more believes in matter than he believes in God. The man of the Middle Ages believed in matter and in God, in life and in death, in the enjoyment of things and their renunciation."[35]

Our problem today is that we no longer believe in things but in symbols, hence our life has passed over into these symbols and their manipulation— only to find ourselves manipulated by the symbols we take so seriously, objectified in our objectifications. We are preoccupied not so much with what money can buy as with its power and status; not with the materiality of an luxurious car but with what owning a Lexus says about us. Modern man wouldn't be able to endure real economic equality, says Becker, "because he has no faith in self-transcendent, other-worldly immortality symbols; visible physical worth is the only thing he has to give him eternal life." Or Being. In this fashion our spiritual hunger to become real, or at least to occupy a special place in the cosmos, has been reduced to having a bigger car than our neighbors. We can't get rid of the sacred, because we can't get rid of our ultimate concerns, except by repressing them, whereupon we become even more compulsively driven by them.[36]

We tend to view the profit motive as natural and rational (the benevolent invisible hand of Adam Smith), but Brown's and Becker's summaries of the anthropological literature remind us that it is not traditional to traditional societies and in fact has usually been viewed with fear. For us, the desire for profit defines economic activity, yet in premodern societies there was no clear division between that sphere and others. "Man's economy, as a rule, is submerged in his social relationships. He does not act so as to safeguard his individual interest in the possession of material goods; he acts so as to safeguard his social standing, his social claims, his social assets. He values material goods only in so far as they serve this end . . . The economic system will be run on non-economic motives" (Polanyi).[37] Primitive people had no need for a financial solution to *lack*, for they had other ways to cope with it. Tawney brings this home to us by discovering the same truth in the history of the West:

> There is no place in medieval theory for economic activity which is not related to a moral end, and to found a science of society upon the assumption that the appetite for economic gain is a constant and measurable force, to be accepted like other natural forces, as an inevitable and self-evident datum, would have appeared to the medieval thinker as hardly less irrational and less immoral than to make the premise of social philosophy the unrestrained operation of such necessary human attributes as pugnacity and the sexual instinct.[38]

We are not surprised to learn that the crucial transformation evidently began at the end of the Middle Ages. Once profit became the engine of the economic process, the tendency was for gradual reorganization of the entire social system and not just of the economic element, since, as Polanyi implies, there is no natural distinction between them. "Capital had ceased to be a servant and had become a master. Assuming a separate and independent vitality it claimed the right of a predominant partner to dictate economic organization in accordance with its own exacting requirements."[39] The economic changes occurring now— for example, the concentration of the publishing industry and the expansion in banks' sphere of activity—remind us that this process of reorganization is still going on, while the individual money complex continues to supplant other personal meaning-systems.

"Happiness is the deferred fulfillment of a prehistoric wish," said Freud. "That is why wealth brings so little happiness: money is not an infantile wish." Then what kind of wish is money? "Money is condensed wealth; condensed wealth is condensed guilt."[40] "Filthy Lucre," the most brilliant chapter of Brown's *Life against Death*, develops this link between money and guilt. "Whatever the ultimate explanation of guilt may be, we put forward the hypothesis that the whole money complex is rooted in the psychology of guilt." The psychological advantage of archaic societies is that they knew what their problem was and therefore how to overcome it, according to Brown. Belief in sin allowed the possibility of expiation, which occurred in seasonal rituals and sacrifices. "The gods exist to receive gifts, that is to say sacrifices; the gods exist in order to structure the human need for self-sacrifice."[41] For Christianity, that sacrifice is incarnated in Christ, who "takes our sins upon him." Religion provides the opportunity to expiate our sense of *lack* by means of symbols—the crucifix, the Eucharist, the Mass—whose validity is socially maintained. In such a context we do feel purified and closer to God after taking Holy Communion.

But what of the modern "neurotic type" who "feels a sinner without the religious belief in sin, for which he therefore needs a new rational explanation"?[42] How do you expiate your sense of *lack* when there is no religious explanation for it? The main secular alternative today is to experience our *lack* as "not yet enough." This converts cyclic time (maintained by seasonal rituals of atonement) into future-oriented and therefore linear time (in which atonement of *lack* is reached for but perpetually postponed, because never achieved). The sense of *lack* remains a constant, yet our collective reaction to it has become the need for growth: an ever-higher "standard of living" (but *lack* means the consumer never has enough) and the gospel of sustained economic "development" (because corporations and the GNP are never big enough). The heart or rather blood of both is the money complex. "A dollar is . . . a codified psychosis normal in one sub-species of this animal, an institutionalized dream that everyone is having at once" (LaBarre).[43] Brown is almost as damning:

> If the money complex is constructed out of an unconscious sense of guilt, it is a neurosis. . . . The dialectic of neurosis contains its own "attempts at explanation and cure," energized by the ceaseless upward pressure of the repressed unconscious and producing the return of the repressed to consciousness, although in an increasingly distorted form, as long as the basic repression (denial) is maintained and the neurosis endures. The modern economy is characterized by an aggravation of the neurosis, which is at the same time a fuller delineation of the nature of the neurosis, a fuller return of the repressed. In the archaic consciousness the sense of indebtedness exists together with the illusion that the debt is payable; the gods exist to make the debt payable. Hence the archaic economy is embedded in religion, limited by the religious framework, and mitigated by the consolations of religion—above all, removal of indebtedness and guilt. The modern consciousness represents an increased sense of guilt, more specifically a breakthrough from the unconscious of the truth that the burden of guilt is unpayable.[44]

The result of this is "an economy driven by a pure sense of guilt, unmitigated by any sense of redemption," which is "the more uncontrollably driven by the sense of guilt because the problem of guilt is repressed by denial into the unconscious."[45] Nietzsche said that it is not only the reason of millennia but their insanity too that breaks out in us. Today our collective version of that insanity is the cult of economic growth, which is difficult to see through because it has become, in effect, our religious myth. "We no longer give our surplus to God; the process of producing an ever-expanding surplus is in itself our God. . . . Schumpeter agrees: 'Capitalist rationality does not do away with sub- or super-rational impulses. It merely makes them get out of hand by removing the restraint of sacred or semi-sacred tradition.'"[46]

If so, we can see what the problem is: Money and economic growth constitute a defective myth because they can provide no expiation of guilt—in Buddhist terms, no resolution of *lack*. Our new *holy of holies*, the true temple of modern man, is the stock market, and our rite of worship is communing with the Dow Jones Average. In return we receive the kiss of profits and the promise of more to come, yet there is no atonement in this. Of course, insofar as we have lost belief in sin we no longer see anything to atone for, which means we end up unconsciously atoning in the only way we know, working hard to acquire all those things that society tells us are important because they will make us happy; and then we cannot understand why they do not make us happy, why they do not resolve our sense that something is lacking. The reason can only be that we don't yet have *enough*. . . . "But the fact is that the human animal is distinctively characterized, as a species and from the start, by the drive to produce a surplus. . . . There is something in the human psyche which commits man to nonenjoyment, to work." It is a cruel parody of Heidegger's resolute preoccupation with the future. Where are we all going so quickly? "Having no real aim, acquisitiveness, as Aristotle correctly said, has no limit." Not *to* anywhere but *from* something, which is why there can be no end to it as long as that something is our own *lack*-shadow. "Economies, archaic and civilized, are ultimately driven by that flight from death which turns life into death-in-life."[47] Or by that flight from emptiness which makes life empty. If money, the purest symbol, symbolizes becoming real, the fact that we never quite become real means that we end up holding pure deferral in our hands. Those chips we have accumulated can never be cashed in, since if we were to do so the illusion that money can resolve *lack* would be dispelled and we would be left more empty and *lack*-ridden than before, because deprived of our fantasy for escaping *lack*. We unconsciously suspect and fear this; the only answer is to flee faster into the future.

All this points to the fundamental defect of our economic system, and any other that requires continual growth if it is not to collapse: What motivates it is not need but fear, for it feeds on and feeds our sense of *lack*. In sum, our preoccupation with manipulating the purest symbol, which we suppose to be the means of solving the problem of life, turns out to be one of the most pernicious symptoms of the problem.

Curiously, the best analogy for money may be *śūnyatā*. Nāgārjuna warns that there is no such thing as *śūnyatā*; it is a heuristic device demonstrating the interdependence of things, that nothing self-exists, but if we misunderstand this the cure is more dangerous than the disease. Although also nothing in itself, also merely a symbol, money is indispensable because of its unique ability to convert anything into another; but woe to those who grab this snake too by the wrong end.

Progress Is Our Most Important Product

While we think of ourselves as a people of change and progress, masters of our environment and our fate, we are no more entitled to this designation than the most superstitious savage, for our relation to change is entirely passive. . . . We talk of technology as the servant of man, but it is a servant that now dominates the household, too powerful to fire, upon whom everyone is helplessly dependent.[48]

Like the urge for fame, the profit motive and self-love à deux, we tend to think of scientific and technological progress as natural, which means, something that does not need to be explained. It is difficult to grasp the significance of any of these myths because they are too alive, too much *our* myths. Then might technological transformation be another case of mistaking nurture as nature? Is it natural to "progress" from the Wright brothers to a moon landing during one generation?[49] The importance of this question today means it can no longer be evaded; the ecological crisis impels us to determine the meaning of technology and progress for us.

At the end of his historical study of death, Aries comments on the belief that technology has no limits. "Technology erodes the domain of death until one has the illusion that death has been abolished." This suggests that technology might somehow be another symbolized, unconscious version of our attempt to avoid death. Heidegger seems to agree: "The self-assertion of technological objectification is the constant negation of death."[50] However, Heidegger's reflections led him to conclude that technological objectification is the main way Being discloses itself to contemporary man. The essence of modernity is the unfortunate technological tendency to reorganize everything into *Bestand*, a "standing-reserve." Rather than explain this in terms of something else, such as repression of death or groundlessness, Heidegger came to believe that we must accept this as the self-disclosure of Being today. In contrast, Buddhism, which does not refer or defer to any transcendental Being, can understand such problems according to its schema of desire based on ignorance. From a *lack* perspective, technology can be seen as our collective effort to create the ultimate security by transforming the entire world into our own ground. We try to make ourselves real by reorganizing the whole environment so that it supports and attests to our reality. "The purpose of the god-imitator is to subdue his environment absolutely. . . . The would-be god on earth never stops trying to incorporate the environment into himself."[51] This is another reason why people today can dispense with the consolations of religion: Now we have other ways to control our fate, or at least try to. If the world isn't "developed" enough yet to quell our *lack*, then it will have to be developed more. . . .

Part of our problem is how we understand the relation between science and technology. We celebrate the scientific quest for truth and subordinate technology

to the application of that truth. Heidegger and others have suggested that
their relationship is actually the reverse. "Technology is not applied science. It
is the expression of a deep longing, an original longing that is present in modern
science from its beginning. This is the desire of the self to seek its own truth
through the mastery of the object. . . . The power of technique is not to connect
thought effectively to nature; it alters nature to its own purpose. Its aim is to
master its being; to own it" (Verene).[52]

Another way to put it is that technology is our attempt to own the universe,
an attempt that is always frustrating because, for reasons we do not quite
understand, we never possess it fully enough to feel secure in our ownership.
Is that because the only genuine salvation is in being owned *by* it—that is, by
participating in something greater than us? "We now use the word Nature
very much as our fathers used the word God," John Burroughs noticed at the
turn of the century, "and, I suppose, back of it all we mean the power that is
everywhere present and active, and in whose lap the visible universe is held
and nourished." Nature can take the place of God because both fulfill our
need to be embedded in mystery; technology cannot because it is motivated by
the opposite response, attempting to banish the mystery by extending our control,
as if that can grant us the security we crave. Bill McKibben sums up his sombre
elegy on *The End of Nature*: "We can no longer imagine that we are part of something larger than ourselves—that is what all this boils down to. We used to be."[53]
Our success in "improving" nature means we can no longer rest peacefully in its
bosom. We cannot manipulate the natural world, in a collective attempt to self-
ground ourselves, and also hope to find in it a ground greater than ourselves.

In religious terms (and this whole book is an argument that in the end we
cannot avoid religious terms), the world-view implicit in technology has an
inadequate eschatology. It is a meaning-system without any ultimate meaning,
because lacking any vision of cloture between humankind and the cosmos.
This is a defect that is quite literally unendurable: A sense of purpose in the
universe must be and always is found somewhere. Then the issue is not how
hardheaded we are in our supposedly non-metaphysical materialistic realism,
but how repressed or conscious we shall be in our commitments. The technological
response to ultimate questions—those questions which because they are ultimate
can never be avoided—is to believe in . . . the future. What is the meaning of
life? Where are we all going so fast? Since we no longer have answers to those
questions, yet cannot live without answers, our answer is to defer the issue.
Until the last few years, our eschatology has been progress: Things are getting
better, or, when they obviously are not, things will get better. The ecological
crisis, which is no longer impending but something we are now well into,
signifies the end of this collective dream, although it remains to be seen whether
our collective psyche will recognize the fact in time. The supreme irony is that
our collective project to secure ourselves is what threatens to destroy us.

We have seen several examples of how, when our motivations are unconscious, we tend to pay an unexpected price: What we project rebounds back onto us. The modern Japanese philosopher (and Zen master) Hisamatsu put it well: That which has become an object to me is something that has captured me. What does this imply about technology, if technology is our attempt to objectify nature? For Buddhism, the problem with technological objectification is an extreme version of the problem with all objectification. Since we are nondual with the world, not separate from it, to objectify the world is to be objectified by it and in it. As the earth becomes reduced into a collection of resources for us to manage, the material and social structures created to do this do the same to us, and we find ourselves increasingly subjected to them. Nature, to be commanded, must be obeyed, said Bacon. But if we must obey in order to command, then our commanding is really obeying. The master becomes the slave, as in the dialectic of Hegel's *Phenomenology of Mind*:

The relationship of *Herrschaft* and *Knechtschaft* [master and slave] is the fable of technique, the inner structure of consciousness that makes the technological world function. It is the structure of technological desire. The self desires to assert its own truth over the object. It wishes to be certain of itself. Modern thought begins with the problem of the self, with the *cogito* claiming its own existence in Descartes. The self desires the external world. It desires to possess it as the object of its thought. To possess the object in thought implies not only knowledge at a distance, but the power to have the object actually as part of the self's sphere of action. Nature must be obeyed in order to be commanded. The self as master is born.

Real mastery requires a *means*. The self develops technique—the idea of work put into the hands of another agency held in bondage to the self. The agency in servitude that will allow the self to be free to enjoy the world is the machine. The machine is the first appearance of the form of technique. The machine is a process that once set in motion will continue to a desired end; the mechanical servant. The self now has, but does not realize that it has, another self. This is the human self that is tied to the machine. Once the machine comes onto the scene all must be reinterpreted in terms of the machine. *L'homme machine* is only the first crude idea of this servant-self. This self has experienced the absolute fear that it cannot own the external world. Work is the answer to the fear that the self may be nothing, have no more reality than the object it has the power to negate. Technique is the form this work takes. All before the self can become the subject of its work. All spheres of existence are subject to technical formation.

What rides the back of the servant-self is the fear that it is nothing. Its *Dasein* is governed by this fear. As Jaspers says, modern man is haunted by the sense that something is behind him. "A dread of life perhaps unparalleled in its intensity is modern man's sinister companion." (Verene)[54]

Perhaps the source of that dread is now clearer.

Conclusion. It is more than curious that the same karmic-like problem with objectification also infects the other three projects to resolve *lack*. One cannot use fame without being used by it. In *Being and Nothingness*, Sartre argues that in order to win and keep the love of the other, I must present myself as a fascinating object. Pursuing the purest and most important symbol of all, we become preoccupied with what it symbolizes about us. And insofar as the sense-of-self uses these projects to fill up its sense-of-*lack*, each tends to become demonic, for none can grant the reality we seek. No one is ever rich or famous enough to fill up the sense of emptiness at one's core; the myth of romance ends in Don Juan's joyless quest for sexual fulfillment; and today we are destroying the whole earth in order to save it, as we once did for Vietnamese villages.

Rather than being natural, as we tend to think, the contemporary importance of these four projects has been historically conditioned. Of course, there have been people in most times and places who were greedy, fell in love with love, sought glory, and tried to harness the resources of their environment. Yet the decline in corporate faith at the end of the Middle Ages cleared the soil for these to take root and grow into "heresies" that have assumed a more central role in our psychic struggle against death-anxiety and dread of groundlessness. We could say that today the weeds have taken over the garden, but what is the alternative? What would we rather cultivate in their place?

Another remarkable similarity among these four is that the modern history of each is a gradual devolution from (what might be called) sacred to secular. In the late Middle Ages, saints were the most respected people. St. Francis did not seek fame; it was a by-product of what was believed to be his more immediate relationship with God. Dante and Milton strove to be worthy of fame, but today fame is sought for its own sake and we celebrate celebrities. The troubadours adored noble ladies without hope of physical satisfaction or even the desire for it; later this became an emphasis on emotional intensity; today's version is sexual fulfillment. In exchanging the fruit of his labor for medallions with the god's image, archaic man used the god to protect himself by participating symbolically in the god's reality; later such cosmic powers were bargained for in the marketplace, and now in the stock market. When we look for the same pattern in the development of science and technology, an otherwise peculiar fact becomes more meaningful: the spiritual origins of Western science, the very inquiry we think of as defining secularity. Pythagoras was a mystic, the founder of a religious school whose sacred doctrine centered on numbers and their harmonies. The Harmony of the Spheres may seem absurd to us but it was important as late as Kepler. Some of this religiosity persists in the attitude of such great scientists as Newton and Einstein, who demonstrate and celebrate a non-utilitarian quest for understanding which still has spiritual overtones, yet that motivation has long been superseded by our desire for power and control over natural processes.[55] This answers the question of how our secular

Western civilization could evolve out of a non-secular society. It didn't. What we think of as secularity is still sacred, for our secular obsessions are symptomatic of our spiritual need. By trying to become real through them, we continue to seek Being although in a distorted, heavily symbolized fashion.

These conclusions give a new perspective on the Mahāyāna denial of any bifurcation between sacred and secular: "There is no specifiable difference whatever between *nirvāṇa* and the everyday world; there is no specifiable difference whatever between the everyday world and *nirvāṇa*" (MMK XXV.19). Without that dualism, how can Buddhism describe these four devolutions? The pattern translates into a movement from nondual *participation* in something greater than the sense-of-self (and therefore greater than the sense-of- *lack*) to a more dualistic relation in which the reified sense-of-self *uses* objects in its vain Oedipal project to fill up its sense-of-*lack*. The historical tendency is toward greater objectification, which is also subjectification, inasmuch as the sense-of-self is the first thing to be objectified. For Buddhism, however, "greater than sense-of-self" refers not to something transcendentally Other to this world but to the interdependence of Indra's Net. There is no appeal to another reality, just the need to come out from my private and delusive hiding-place—my sense-of-self—in order to realize *this* one, in order to experience the full implications of my integral interdependence with everything else.

Conclusion:
Transcendence East
and West

The concept of *lack* has helped to raise some fresh questions about the distinction we too easily make (or too easily deny) between sacred and secular. Insofar as *lack* remains a constant, and religion our means to resolve it, the development of the modern West has been characterized not by a decline in religious faith but by the replacement of a collective, socially agreed route to salvation with more individualistic attempts to cure oneself. If my argument is correct, much of the frenetic quality of our lives today is due to the fact that these quack cures keep promising to fill in our *lack* yet never quite do so, which encourages us to run ever faster from our shadow into an ever-elusive future.

If *lack* helps us understand the development of Western culture, can it also help us to understand other cultures? I conclude by speculating about the implications of *lack* for some important cultural differences. I shall offer a tentative theory which explains some of the distinctive features of Indian, Sino-Japanese, and Western cultures as different ways of responding to and acculturating our sense-of-*lack*. The first section will set the stage by challenging our usual stereotype about "the East." In order to compensate for that generalization, it argues not only that there is no such thing as *the* East, but that the contrasts between India and China/Japan are more significant than their similarities. This will amount to another stereotype, yet one useful for exploring the possibility that more is at stake here than dissimilarity.

The second section adumbrates the pattern in those differences, which reduces to differing attitudes toward *transcendence*. The distinction between this phenomenal world and another realm or dimension transcending it is one of the fundamental determinants of Indian civilization, whereas China and Japan are much more this-worldly in assigning primary value to—and thereby *sacralizing*—socio-political structures. In terms of our problem with *lack*, Indian culture postulates another aspect of reality which can fill in our *lack*, while both Chinese and Japanese cultures attempt to resolve groundlessness by grounding their members more tightly into a hierarchical social system. This section considers the various meanings and types of transcendence, and reflects on why an overtly transcendental dimension arose in certain places while not in others.

154

The third section reflects on where "the West" fits into this schema. One could argue, curiously, that India and Japan each have more in common with the West than with each other. That is because Western civilization, like Indian, originated with a strong sacred/secular bifurcation; yet the ostensible eclipse of the sacred has transformed Western societies into more secular nations, similar in many ways to China and Japan, which lack India's transcendental reference point. But this perspective is misleading, because, as we have seen, in the most important sense a transcendental dimension is unavoidable. When we do not apprehend or project a transcendental realm to fill in our *lack*, we end up sacralizing some aspect of the secular, for we do not escape the need to ground ourselves in one way or another. In east Asia, the transcendental dimension remained embedded in the *sacred authority* of social and political hierarchies, whereas in the West the transcendental has been internalized into the supposedly autonomous and self-directed *individual*. These basic cultural differences underlie many of the political and economic tensions between east Asia and the West today.

A New Stereotype

The following contrasts between India and China/Japan are so striking that the almost dialectical structure of these oppositions cannot be overlooked. Since so much relevant data could be cited, I mention only those differences that seem to me the most important.[1]

Universals and particulars. Traditional Indian culture displays a strong preference for universals over particulars. In Indian thought (as in the Sanskrit and Sanskrit-influenced languages) there is a preponderance of abstract notions, which are treated as if they were concrete realities. Emphasis is on the unity of things; the changing manifestations of the phenomenal world tend to be devalued if not dismissed as illusory. Accordingly, there is a lack of historical and geographical consciousness: little interest in calculating time or recording the specific details of locality, few historical or biographical works with accurate dates. Indian aesthetics does not analyze individual works of art, and books of classification lack illustrative case histories. In sum, not the specific but the generalization is important.

In contrast, traditional Chinese culture prefers particulars over universals. The Chinese language has a concrete flavor with an extraordinary number of similes and metaphors; for example, the philosophical concept of perfection is metaphorized as "round," and in Ch'an Buddhism one's true nature is "your original face." Chinese literature includes detailed geography, historiography, and biography, because specific places, historical events, and the people that made them are all important. The paradoxical dialogues of Ch'an do not offer abstract Buddhist teachings but concretize those teachings by responding appropriately to particular situations. The other side of this preference for the concrete is that Chinese culture (like Japanese culture) is poorer mythologically than the "fantastical" Indian imagination, which created the richest of the world's mythologies. Even the few Indian histories "are tinged with fantastic and legendary color."[2]

In a pattern that will become important as it recurs, Japanese culture may be viewed as extrapolating these Chinese traits, for it also emphasizes sensible and concrete events over abstract universals. Nakamura names this Japanese tendency *phenomenalism*. In contrast to the Indian inclination toward an Absolute transcendent to the phenomenal world, and Chinese understanding of the Tao as a more dynamic ground of changing phenomena, for the Japanese the phenomenal world may be said to *be* the absolute.[3]

Sacred and secular. India placed the highest value on the religious goal of one's individual self merging with the Universal Self, which is without personal differentiation. There was little discussion of the problems with social and political structures, for such concerns were subverted by the belief that one's individual self is ultimately nondual with other selves. This world was devalued into a means to prepare for another: "The ancient Indians led their life on this side of heaven with the expectation of a life after death." There was emphasis on introspective behavior and the subjective comprehension of one's personality (in contrast with modern Western emphasis on scientific, i.e., objective, comprehension of the personality). This bias toward introspection was accompanied by a preference for passive, forbearing behavior and a tendency to abstain from action.[4]

Traditional China was more worldly in placing the highest value on the family. Chinese people were less concerned to transcend this world, but identified with their family and worked for its welfare. Ancestors were worshiped in order to gain prosperity in this life. The religious goal of Taoism and Ch'an is not to experience another realm but to become aware of the true nature of this one; the miraculous function of Ch'an is "fetching water and chopping wood." In contrast to the Indian preoccupation with *karma* and rebirth, there was little concern about what happens after death (Confucius: "You do not yet know about life, so why do you concern yourself about death?") and little consciousness of sin or the need for salvation. "Indian Buddhism was generally a metaphysical teaching about the past and future worlds of man, but the Buddhism which spread among the common Chinese was often a Buddhism of spells and prayers."[5]

The phenomenalism of Japanese culture means that the sacred is not distinct from this world but suffused in all things. There are millions of gods, even trees and grass have *kami*. No profound reflections on the soul or death are found in Shinto, the only indigenous religion; death is simply impurity. In contrast with Indian asceticism and less extreme tendencies in Chinese Buddhism and Taoist yoga (in the latter case usually practiced to gain physical immortality), there was an acceptance of natural dispositions (e.g., sex, alcohol, meat-eating) even for priests. Zen Buddhism emphasized the spiritual significance of everyday life: tea-drinking, flower-arranging, killing others, and, should the occasion require, oneself. Not-killing is the first precept of Indian religions (wars were fought mainly by mercenaries), while Zen became popular because it taught the *samurai* how to kill and how to die—that is, how to play their role in what Nakamura calls the *social nexus*. He says there are "very few instances" in Japanese history of individuals sacrificing themselves for universal principles such as religion and truth, yet innumerable *samurai* (and other vassals) sacrificed themselves for their lord, not because he was any better than any other lord but simply because he was *their* lord. Indian renunciants abstained from work and begged for their food; Chinese Buddhists were more practical (Pai-chang: "A day without working is a day without eating"); Japanese Buddhism came to repudiate most traditional spiritual disciplines in favor of those that promote productive activities, exemplifying a general trait that Robert Bellah identifies as the most important characteristic of Japanese society: its goal-oriented behavior.[6] Indian preoccupation with metaphysics and abstract principles contrasts with Chinese pragmatism and even more strongly with Japanese lack of interest in theoretical principles in favor of acting. This helps to explain the rapid modernization of Japan after 1868 and its rapid recovery after 1945. However, Nakamura is concerned that such a religious view "may easily degenerate into the sheer utilitarianism of profit-seeking activities, should it lose sight of the significance of the absolute, which underlies the productive life of all vocations. It is especially true with a people like the Japanese, who are not too preoccupied with religious matters."[7]

Harmony. Indian emphasis on *duḥkha* correlates with pessimism about the possibilities of this world of *saṃsāra*. This implied a submissive attitude toward one's fate and conditions of life; *karma* was understood to mean that they are regulated by an invisible power beyond immediate control. The physical body tended to be belittled. Indian thought is not anthropocentric: The distinction between humans and other living beings is not emphasized, evidently because all phenomena become equivalent insofar as they are other than the Absolute. The emphasis in education was on religious philosophy, particularly metaphysics, which seeks to comprehend the whole.

Instead of understanding this world as a *saṃsāra* to be fled, "everyday mind" is enlightenment in Chinese Ch'an. Mahāyāna Buddhism, which claims that *saṃsāra* is not other than *nirvāṇa*, did not survive in India yet became the one Indian school of thought to thrive north of the Himalayas. With the notable exception of Hsun tzu, Chinese thinkers understood human nature to be basically good, as part of the larger natural law. Since nature is not opposed to man, it is not to be conquered but harmonized with; natural disasters were a sign that the ruler had lost his mandate to govern. For both the social system and the physical environment, harmony is the key concept. Bellah's *Tokugawa Religion* views Chinese and Japanese societies as similar in many ways, yet distinguishes the Chinese emphasis on integrative values from the Japanese stress on political or goal-attainment values.[8]

In the religious sphere, this implied syncretism among the three major Chinese religions, widely believed to be essentially the same. While Indian thinkers disputed over philosophical principles, ignoring the practical and social implications of their debates, Chinese scholars preferred the more practical problems of social relations. Hence Chinese thought is more humanistic and anthropocentric. The most notable exception to the Chinese lack of interest in metaphysics is the Hua-yen doctrine of all phenomena as mutually interpenetrating. As discussed in chapter 3, Hua-yen philosophy elaborated concrete metaphors such as Indra's Net, water and waves, and a golden lion, in order to demonstrate that the Absolute is not something transcending this world but is the totality of such interpenetrating relations. Chinese philosophy has little logic, dialectic, dialogue, or argument; being figurative and intuitive, it is weak in formulating abstract laws. Indian Buddhists accepted perception and reasoning as valid *pramanas* (modes of knowledge); Chinese Buddhism deferred more to the authority of the Buddhist canon and accepted strange new doctrines (e.g., *cittamatra*) solely on the authority of Śākyamuni Buddha rather than as a result of reasoning. The syncretic tendency may also be seen in the way that the Chinese organized different doctrines into a hierarchical system (e.g., T'ien-t'ai), rather than deriving such systems by developing their logical connections. This attitude toward the Buddhist teachings was part of a general conservative emphasis on the authority of antiquity and its precedents, which overruled abstract principles such as logical consistency. It was believed that all important truth could be found in the Five Classics; Confucius said that he merely imitated and revived past customs. Hence "China has never had a revolution in her world of thought."[9] (Maoism was not an exception to this but exemplifies it.) Later no independent school of thought was allowed to exist in opposition to Confucianism, and intellectual life became confined to the acceptance of traditional classics and commentary on them.

Since Shinto gods were suffused into almost everything, the Japanese have never viewed the natural world as cursed or *saṃsāra*. Japanese love of nature developed as a subtle appreciation of minute, delicate, transitory things (e.g., cherry blossoms). This phenomenalism included an acceptance of human dispositions, desires, and sentiments as natural, too, and therefore not to be struggled against. Buddhism in Japan became less ascetic; spiritual disciplines were repudiated as unnecessary (e.g., Shinran), and later alcohol, meat-eating, and marriage were allowed for priests—not to weaken the influence of Buddhism, as has been argued, but to ratify abuses which had become common.

Even more than in China, emphasis on the harmony of the social nexus meant a lack of interest in divisive argument and critique. Nakamura notices a deficiency in the spirit of criticism. In many cases rapprochements occur "for the sake of convenience and in the mood of opportunism . . . lacking in the radical spirit of confrontation and criticism." Buddhist priests "very reluctantly" reflect on the great differences between the doctrines they espouse and the actions they and others perform, preferring to follow the accepted social nexus.[10] The militant nationalism of almost all Japanese Zen masters during World War II remains an embarrassment for many Western Zen students.[11] Nakamura notes a lack of will to drive home a concept or an idea that could threaten social harmony; the sociologist Chie Nakane agrees that there is little social sanction in Japan for entertaining ideas and opinions that are different from the head of one's family or community.[12] Virtue is simple and unproblematic. The highest value is placed on honesty, understood as straightforward truthfulness and loyalty to one's superior, rather than commitment to some abstract moral code.

Nakamura emphasizes the non-rationalistic tendencies of Japanese ways of thinking. Shinto has no doctrine. In discourse, logical rules are neglected; the primary importance placed on one's limited social nexus means there is little inclination to make each person's understanding rational or universal. Hence logic developed slowly. Indian Buddhist logic was studied, yet in a dogmatic fashion, which revered the founder as highest authority and studied his teachings in a spirit that defended the faith. Such works tended to become an esoteric tradition. Writings (e.g., Dōgen's *Shōbogenzō*) were kept secret and privately transmitted in a catechistic way not intended for public dissemination as a teaching beneficial to all. While the Chinese classified Buddhist sects hierarchically, the Japanese simply distinguished their own from all other inferior ones. Nakamura notes that the Japanese people have been said to be adept at imitation and adaptation yet sterile in invention; foreign cultures are assimilated not through study of their general principles and structures but by precipitately importing only those parts suitable for immediate practical use. Japanese are weak in studying the objective basis of their action because, he writes, they are too eager to accomplish the action.[13] Phenomenalism in education makes learning a matter of collecting information. Even today, the notorious university entrance examinations require an extraordinary memory for facts, without much need to understand their relationship or significance. In his study of Japanese high schools, Thomas Rohlen notices that "schooling in logic is as old as Western civilization itself," something even more true for traditional Indian education, which emphasized philosophical debate. "By contrast, the Japanese tradition . . . has long emphasized memorization and imitation. One approach helps the internalization of a moral and intellectual frame of reference, the second aids adjustment to the environment."[14]

Early Shinto was hardly distinguishable from animism and shamanism; and, according to Nakamura, whenever ruling classes lost control over the peasantry, magical or shamanistic trends became important again. Imported doctrines were not immune from this tendency: "As a new religion, Buddhism was compelled to meet the popular requirement that it should be effective in exorcism. The Japanese type of Buddhism was largely one of prayer and exorcism. It mainly aimed at praying for benefits and wealth in this world and the next, in the interest of the state as well as of individuals. Even the reading of sutras was considered to have an exorcistic significance."[15] Shingon esotericism predominated in early Japanese Buddhism, whereas it was rare in India and China, where it developed. Japanese Confucianism (which in China denounced magic and exorcism) also had to become more tolerant of such tendencies.

Church and State. In traditional India, political leaders rarely intervened in religious matters or interfered with religious institutions. Kings tended to defer to sages and spiritual organizations, for the highest authority was the universal law or *dharma*, understood as the foundation of the universe on which all things are grounded. Faith (*śraddhā*) was invested not in particular persons but in this Truth transcending the transitory affairs of humans. Different world views were understood to be different parts of that one Truth, which encouraged a spiritual tolerance, with little conception of heresy, in the Western sense, as something dangerous that must be extirpated. The desire for a direct relationship with the Absolute led to emphasis on one's own efforts. The Buddha appointed no successor, whereas one's spiritual lineage became extremely important in China and Japan.

Indians had little racial or national consciousness, and even today they are more inclined to form religious than political organizations. Aśoka's edicts indicate that he wanted to be remembered not as King of India but as preserver and actualizer of the *dharma*. India's many legends and myths contain very few *national* heroes. It was a virtue to offer one's property and life for the happiness of others, yet self-sacrifice on behalf of a particular race or nation was never taught.[16] I emphasize this because it will be important to my argument later: Since Indian culture defined itself in relation to a transcendental realm, it did not become nationalistic or sacralize political authority.

In China and Japan, there was much greater esteem for the hierarchy that structured the social nexus, and corresponding emphasis on the formalism in behavior which usually accompanies such esteem. In both countries the high value placed on rank and social position subordinated religious values: that is, *religious institutions were dominated and controlled by secular authorities*, who thereby neutralized the threat that such sacred authority (*dharma*) offered to their power and appropriated that authority for their own political ends.

Sākyamuni had had to choose between becoming a world monarch (*cakravartin*) or a world savior (a Buddha); the two were never conflated in India, nor was there ever much doubt about which was the nobler accomplishment. Starting with the T'ang dynasty, the Chinese emperor gradually became deified, coming to be viewed as a Bodhisattva or the Tathagata himself. Under his rule, property rights existed but not freedom by law. The conception of human rights that developed in the West—that one can have the protection of law against one's own government—had some Indian equivalent in respect for the *dharma*, as another kind of law that can supersede the secular; devotees who renounced the world were usually beyond state jurisdiction. Both notions were (and for the most part still are) alien to Chinese and Japanese political institutions.

Japan perfected this tendency to identify religious and secular authority. Only in Japan did the mythology that accounts for creation of the world also found the imperial family. In China, dynasties were overthrown, in Japan the same family has reigned since the beginning of history. Chinese Confucianism allowed for revolution should the emperor lose "the mandate of heaven." Japan has no place for such a possibility; imperial authority is not derived from any abstract principle such as divine right but abides in his person. The fundamental importance of this for Japanese society may be appreciated from the stress Nakamura places on "the tendency to emphasize, and unconditioned belief in, a limited social nexus," which takes form in "absolute devotion to a specific individual symbolic of the social nexus": that is, emperor worship.[17] In contrast to the religious-like nationalism of Nazi Germany, which emphasized a future-oriented ideal (a "purified" Aryan world without any Jews, etc.), the religious-like nationalism of Japan emphasized the present real: the emperor as God.

Japanese this-worldliness meant that Buddhism too was changed, into a religion centered on this world. Shinto and Buddhism were perceived as compatible for the pragmatic reason that differences of religion were not important unless they damaged the social nexus—precisely the opposite reason for Indian tolerance, which was based on the preeminence of *dharma*. In other words, religion in Japan was not considered important in itself; as Nakamura says, its value was its utility in serving as the foundation of the state. He also points out the problem with this: "The inclination to regard as absolute a limited specific human nexus naturally brings about a tendency to disregard any allegedly universal law of humanity that every man ought to observe at any place at any time." When this way of thinking is pushed to an extreme, it ends up emphasizing "ethno-centrism or supernationalism, and with its emphasis upon the specificity of the time, in opportunism."[18]

When the social nexus is primary, hierarchical relationships and rules of propriety take precedence over the individual. Emphasis is on complete devotion to one's social collective. Good and evil become solely a matter of social morality: what profits the group or harms its welfare. This implies a type of moral self-reflection that, as Nakamura notices, is very different from that of Christian Europe. The pre-eminence of social cooperation prompts a deep concern about social esteem, what others think of me, rather than an internalized anxiety about my sinfulness before the all-seeing, transcendent eye of God. Although the family was the predominant social unit, as in China, the whole Japanese nation was regarded as the extended family of the father-emperor. The cult of *bushido* taught complete devotion to one's lord, who was also one's true parent. It is not difficult to see that same unconditioned loyalty in contemporary Japan, psychologically transferred to one's company. Association with religious temples and sects was not a matter of individual commitment but the social relationship of one's family clan. Today funerals and memorial services (in which priests are necessary as intermediaries) are almost the only social role of Buddhism in Japan, yet neither was a function of original Indian Buddhism. In order to win a place in Japanese society, Buddhism had to promote such civic virtues as loyalty to the emperor and devotion to one's parents, values alien to Indian Buddhism. The Mahāyāna goal of "the happiness of all sentient beings" became "the prosperity of the imperial family."

The result of this absolute devotion to a particular individual who symbolized the human nexus, as opposed to the Indian way of symbolizing the cosmos in an impersonal way, was loss of social freedom. Unlike the contracted and delimited responsibilities in European feudalism, the Japanese vassal devoted his whole existence to his lord. The problems of ultimate value and social relationships were solved by conflating them. At the end of *Tokugawa Religion* Robert Bellah concludes:

> Religion reinforced commitment to the central value system by making that value system meaningful in an ultimate sense. The family and the nation were not merely secular collectivities but were also religious entities. Parents and political superiors had something of the sacred about them, were merely the lower echelons of the divine. Fulfillment of one's obligations to these superordinates had an ultimate meaning.

Bellah sees a connection between this and militarism: "The great difference from China is that whereas the military aspect tended to atrophy and particularistic loyalty to one's lord, though important, was not primary, in Japan the militaristic aspect remained important even if it had to be only symbolic and the idea of loyalty to one's lord continued to override all other ethical concepts."[19] Herman Ooms, in his more recent study, *Tokugawa Ideology*, concludes with the same observation: "Military regimentation came to inform the model of the social order." And today? "That obsession with order has continued undiminished."[20]

The basic problem is that such an order allows for no "categorical imperative" which transcends the limitations of one's particular human nexus. Since all things were judged according to that nexus, ecclesiastical authorities in Japan were always subject to secular authorities, and up to this day they have tended to be subservient to the state. As Max Weber put it, the state was not a patron of religion, as in India, but a religious police. Religious institutions in Japan have never had much authority, nor have men of religion been as highly respected as in India or the West. "The Japanese accepted Buddhism without changing their own standpoint an iota. That was why Buddhism spread with such speed." Even though it became accepted as the national religion, Buddhism was always regarded as imported; and if Buddhism did not change Japan, neither did Japan change Buddhism, which was "when viewed from the larger standpoint of Buddhist history, a mere branch of Buddhism growing out of the Buddhism of China." Yet Japanese Buddhists believed that only in Japan was the highest message of Sakyamuni revealed.[21]

Nakamura emphasizes the weakness of the Japanese religious consciousness and concludes that "religion, in the true sense of the word, never deeply took root on Japanese soil."[22] But if denying the authority of the sacred amounts to sacralizing secular authority, there is another way to understand Nakamura's point: The religion of Japan was and is ... Japan.

Transcendence

One could continue to draw such contrasts indefinitely, yet enough has been said to notice the pattern. Nakamura summarizes his study as follows: In India ultimate value is placed on religion, in China on the family, and in Japan on the state. However, this may be further simplified. The main contrast is between India and the other two, for the difference between China and Japan tends to be a matter of emphasis. In China the extended family functioned as a small state; in Japan the state was one big family. Both are *this-worldly* in assigning primary value to those societal structures. To state that Indian culture emphasizes religion means that India is not this-worldly, because this world is understood (and devalued) by juxtaposing it with another possibility: There is constant reference to a transcendental realm or dimension. *From the east Asian perspective*, the distinction between this phenomenal world of *saṃsāra* and a "higher," sacred reality is a fundamental determinant of Indian ways of thinking. We can find some elements of such a distinction in Chinese and Japanese culture— most of them imported with Buddhism—yet those cultures were not affected to the same extent. Quite the opposite, *from an Indian perspective* it is the absence of a transcendental/secular distinction that explains many of the characteristics of Chinese and Japanese culture.

So much is fairly evident by now, yet some of its implications are not so obvious. The above claim is not that the Japanese and Chinese traditions lack a transcendental or sacred *dimension*. As the previous chapter has argued, such a religious dimension is unavoidable because our sense of *lack* is inescapable; when we consciously deny any spiritual reality, our worldly pursuits assume a religious-like importance. In east Asia we can readily detect that religious dimension in the sacred authority appropriated by secular rulers. The Chinese emperor became deified, and the authority of the Japanese emperor was even greater because irrevocable. Without a transcendental authority understood as separate from the secular, the sacred dimension manifests in east Asia as the social structure: in terms of *lack*, the problem of human groundlessness is addressed by embedding human beings more tightly within society. The social nexus is taken to be more important than the individuals that enter into it—or, if we adopt the east Asian perspective, more real than the persons that can be abstracted from it.

When the members of a society are not unified by their common commitment to a transcendental reality, or by their acceptance of a transcendental authority, what binds them together? Earlier it was noticed that Chinese and Japanese society share greater esteem not only for hierarchy but for the formalism which concretizes such esteem. Common submission to a transcendental and universal moral code tends to be a democratizing force, for, to cite an example, we all become "children of God." When one is subjected solely and wholly to secular authority, formalism takes on many of the functions of morality, as part of the process which sacralizes those power relations.

In east Asia hierarchical (and by democratic standards oppressive) social relations came to be accepted much like the weather because they too were perceived as natural. Describing the situation in Japan before the Meiji Restoration, van Wolferen notes that "the political arrangements of the Tokugawa period were presented as perfect in that they conformed to 'the order found in the manifold natural phenomena of heaven and earth.'"[23]

This attitude seems peculiar and unnecessary to us because we can view it from "outside," in this instance less from an Indian perspective than from a Western one, which did not accept hierarchical political and economic structures as natural and whose history has been punctuated by radical attempts at social improvement. The disastrous consequences of so many of those efforts (e.g., most political revolutions) should make us hesitate before denigrating the east Asian model of social relations. Such comparisons are a sword that cuts both ways. Although it is easy to ridicule Japanese groupism, it is becoming more difficult to offer the individualism of the contemporary United States as a better model. Viewed from a land where everyone seems to be looking out for Number One, the unconditioned loyalty of a *samurai* to his lord seems an admirable example of selflessness—until one looks for the principles which motivate that lord. Loyalty to people becomes attractive when we remember all the killing that has been done on behalf of abstractions such as God or the future socialist state; yet if that devotion plugs into a hierarchical social structure itself unaccountable to any "higher" dimension, we should not be surprised that a sacred ideology sometimes becomes indistinguishable from a militant nationalism.

These reflections suggest (and the evidence in the first section supports such a conclusion) that *transcendence* should be understood as referring not only to some sacred, otherworldly dimension but also to the authority of ethical universalism (which was usually derived from such a "higher world," like the Decalogue handed down by Yahweh). Today the authority of the sacred has been largely eclipsed in Western societies—American church-going notwithstanding—while the function of such universal values has expanded to fill much of the breach, ranging from legal inscriptions such as the U.S. Bill of Rights to our informal sense of fair play. In that sense the transcendental is still very much with us, and indeed it has been necessary to protect the newly evolved individual from the state and to regulate one's competition with other individuals. It is no coincidence that this form of transcendence has also been lacking in east Asia. In his perceptive study, *The Enigma of Japanese Power*, Karel van Wolferen concludes that "the crucial factor in the exercise of Japanese power" has been "the absence of a tradition of appealing to transcendental truth or universal values."

Yet expanding our understanding of transcendence to include universalist values is still not broad enough. The full implications of the term are suggested by its etymology: *Latin trans + scendere*, to climb over or rise above. Most generally, transcendence is that which abstracts (*Latin ab[s] + trahere*, to separate, draw out from) us from the given world by providing a theoretical (*Greek theorein*, to look at) perspective (*Latin per + specere*, to look through) on it. The etymologies suggest how much our English vocabulary for "higher" thought processes involves "rising above" the given, *which allows the possibility of leverage over*, of changing that given. This too is consistent with the contrast drawn in the first section between Indian preference for an abstract, theoretical (metaphysical) perspective on life, versus Chinese concreteness and Japanese phenomenalism. Archimedes said that if he had a fulcrum sufficiently far away he could move the entire earth. Historically, that fulcrum has been provided by the transcendental, whether we understand it as the realization of another dimension of reality or as a product of the human imagination. As Renan said about the supernatural, the transcendental is the way in which the ideal makes its appearance in human affairs.

With this trivalent understanding of transcendence—as higher realm, as ethical universal, and as critical perspective on the given—we are ready to address what is perhaps the most interesting question: Why did an explicitly transcendental dimension arise in certain places, such as India, and not in others, such as China and Japan?

"Transcendence," whether it takes the form of divine revelation or of theoretical cosmology, implies a search for authority outside the institutionalized offices and structures of the seeker's society. Even its most concrete form, the law code, implies a transfer of authority from the holders of office to the written rule. Transcendental impulses therefore constitute, by definition, an implicit challenge to traditional authority and indicate some dissatisfaction with it. . . . new transcendental visions are . . . likely to be presented by persons in a precariously independent, interstitial—or at least exposed and somewhat solitary—position in society; they are therefore particularly likely to occur in societies sufficiently differentiated to have specialized social roles with distinct bases of authority, but not complex enough to have integrated these roles into functionally differentiated structures. (Humphreys)[24]

Humphreys argues for this by referring to axial-age (first millennium B.C.) Greece. She finds the necessary precondition for a transcendental perspective on society in the privileged and relatively independent position of its intellectuals, such as the Sophists, whose special linguistic skills provided "the ability to recreate social relationships and manipulate them in thought."[25] However, her criterion may be applied more widely. She could also have cited the role of the "interstitial" Hebrew prophets—especially Amos, Isaiah and Jeremiah—who developed the ethical monotheism of Judaism that had been established by the Mosaic covenant. Inspired by Yahweh, they understood themselves as intermediaries to the children of Israel, charged to fulminate against the impious people and particularly their rulers. Max Weber drew attention to how their precarious and somewhat solitary position was supported by their ability to alternate between prophesizing in towns and withdrawing into the hills.

The case of India supports Humphreys' conclusion even better. According to Louis Dumont, a two-stage process created fertile conditions for the development of a transcendental perspective. The first occurred in the Vedas, whose "extreme development of specialized macro-religious action and representation" exalted the role of priests into a pre-eminence never thereafter lost. By the time of the Brahmanas (probably 800–500 B.C.) "the priest was supreme, though the king was his master." Soon thereafter, and about same time the caste system began, there appeared "a full-fledged and peculiar social role outside society proper: the renouncer, as an individual-outside-the-world, inventor or adept of a 'discipline of salvation' and of its social concomitant, best called the Indian sect."[26] Two of the most famous examples were contemporaries: Śākyamuni Buddha and Mahavira, the founder of Jainism.

Dumont wonders why political rulers assented to the loss of their pre-eminence. Everything falls into place, he says, once we start with the king as "priest-cum-ruler": then the Indian development becomes understandable as "a differentiation within this institution, whereby the king lost his (official) religious function in favor of the priest. In other words, kingship had been 'secularized,' as we say, at an early date."[27] The fragile distinction between secular authority and sacred authority acquired an institutional foundation. Our problem in perceiving this is that we usually take this distinction for granted, whereas it now begins to look more like the exception than the rule.

The meaning of that distinction becomes more apparent and more important when we consider what occurred in some other civilizations, such as Mesopotamia and Egypt, or rather what did not occur, since no such differentiation happened. In Mesopotamia, the scribes who composed the educated elite never challenged the authority of the priest-cum-king. The most important religious practices were not public, and in fact there seems to have been little religious role for the common people. Instead, the main rituals were performed by religious specialists, especially the king: "It is from the heart [i.e., the king] of the community, but almost unbeknownst to it, that the divine benediction radiated. None of them could break with the practices: the king because he was the only guarantor of an order that depended on them; the people because they believed they benefited from them, without participating directly; the priests because their entire education pushed them into preserving what they had acquired."[28]

In twelfth-century Egypt, the Pharaoh Akhenaten attempted to establish the sole worship of Aten, but soon after his death there was a return to the traditional polytheistic cultus. "One major reason for this was the divine status of the Pharaoh himself. It was through the Pharaoh that the divine order benefited society. A break in the continuity of kingly ritual could have had disastrous social consequences."[29] When the responsibility for our collective *lack* is believed to rest upon the king, the worst possible scenario is a rupture between him and the powers that he alone can communicate with in order to assuage our *lack*.

The parallels are remarkable. In Mesopotamia and Egypt, as in Japan, the sacral dimension was not suffused throughout society, for it functioned through rulers who were as much religious as political authorities. Unlike India, Greece, and Judea, no clear distinction between secular and sacred authority evolved successfully, and therefore no other transcendental perspective to challenge the inherent conservatism of such societies. To revolt politically against the powers-that-be would amount to questioning the socially maintained religious project that resolves society's collective *lack*.

In China the situation was more complex, although it still fits into this pattern. The *Shi ching* (*Book of Poetry*) and *Shu ching* (*Book of Documents*), the first extensive literary texts, envision an all-encompassing social, political, and cultural order in which people relate to each other according to a highly structured system of familial and political roles.

All of these roles and role relationships are governed by elaborate normative rules of behavior (*li*). The human order is not closed off from the cosmic order. Within the cosmos, the various gods of mountains, rivers, winds, stars, and localities, and the ancestral spirits also play their roles. Within the larger political order of the cosmos, the rulers of men must, in fact, relate themselves by proper ritual behavior (*li*) to the governing spirits of the universe as well as to each other. At the apex of the human order is the universal kingship, which is the central focus of communication, as it were, between the king, who is ultimately responsible for the maintenance of the normative human order, and the supreme God or Heaven (*shang ti, t'ien*), who maintains harmony and order in the world of the spirits presiding over the forces of nature as well as over the world of ancestral spirits.[30]

Again, we see a functional equivalence between the lack of a sacred/secular dualism and the role of religio-political authority as nodal point of communication between the human and the cosmic orders. As with Mesopotamia and Egypt, there is nonetheless a sacral dimension in society, but it manifests itself through the apex of the social pyramid and therefore serves to sacralize that hierarchy. This is in striking contrast to transcendence in Humphreys' sense: a challenge to traditional authority which allows for the possibility of everyone having his or her own personal relationship with that transcendental order, and which therefore allows for the possibility of my taking personal responsibility for my own *lack*.

Obvious counter-examples spring to mind for China, most notably Confucius himself and Taoist sages such as Chuang-tzu. Yet both support my thesis. Confucius, although a precariously independent and "interstitial" intellectual, did not challenge the transcendental function of the political order; he emphasized respect for it, he wanted to be employed by it, and his legacy became used as an apologetic for it. He allowed for the possibility of revolution, but only if the king failed in his divine duty to preserve the human order by maintaining communication with the divine order. Taoist sages such as Chuang-tzu had their own personal experience of the Tao, yet the critique of society which followed from that was employed not to reform social relations but to withdraw from them. For the Taoists of his time, the alternative was not political reform but being co-opted and corrupted by the powers-that-be. Thus neither Confucians nor Taoists offered any serious challenge to the secular-cum-sacred authority of the political rulers. By the time Buddhism arrived, it was evidently too late to challenge the pattern that had been established. This was even more true in Japan, where Buddhism was first imported as an aristocratic religion to support the prosperity of the imperial family.

Mesopotamia, Egypt, China, and Japan versus India, Judea, and Greece: All of these examples validate Humphreys' criterion of transcendence as involving a search for authority outside institutionalized offices and structures. Such an authority never became established in the first four civilizations, while it did in India, Judea, and Greece, thanks to "interstitial" world-renouncers, prophets, and intellectuals, respectively. In the first four cases, an effective transcendental/

secular bifurcation did not evolve, which does not mean they lacked a sacral dimension; rather, it means that political power and religious authority never became distinguished. The distinction between them is extremely important for the way people have understood their sense-of-*lack*. Without it, the responsibility for our collective *lack* is channelled into a pyramidal social system that makes the expiation of *lack* a function of the king's ritual behavior, and therefore binds us all the more tightly into that socio-religious system. When secular and religious authority become separated, other ways to understand and address *lack* become possible—and perhaps necessary.

The Transcendental Subject

Where does the modern West fit into this schema? One can point to the historical connection between Indian and Western transcendence. The Aryans who settled in India were ethnically and culturally related to those who peopled Europe. Greek, Latin, and the major European languages evolved from the same Indo-European root as the Sanskrit family of languages. On the other hand, Western civilization originates primarily from a cross-fertilization between Hebrew and Greek ways of thinking, and although Platonism and mystical sects such as Orphism might have been influenced by Indian religion—a controversy that may never be settled— there does not seem to have been any relationship between Hebrew monotheism and the Vedas. Rather than undertake a dubious argument for such an influence, I have already noticed how apparently indigenous transcendental perspectives developed with the Hebrew prophets and Greek intellectuals. The interaction of their somewhat different dualisms led to a determinative transcendental/secular distinction which throughout the history of the West has appeared in many different forms—religious, philosophical, and scientific.[31]

Today, of course, the nation-states of the West are secular societies very much preoccupied with the opportunities provided by this world. However, that does not bring us back to the situation in ancient Mesopotamia, Egypt, China, and Japan, in which there is no transcendental/secular dualism. Rather, and as Nietzsche predicted, the gradual attenuation of the "higher world" has left the West with the painful task of revaluing the devalued objectified world, ushering in an age of nihilism which seems far from over. We suspect there is something unique about our situation today that fails to fit into the pattern analyzed above. The first two sections concluded that the alternative to a transcendental/secular distinction is tighter embeddedness in a sacralized social nexus. Yet this was not true in England in 1649, France in 1789, Russia in 1917. As God abdicated from Western society, the desire to reform economic and political structures (whose authority was no longer supported by His authority) did not diminish but became more urgent, with mixed results. Understanding society as a human construction which should be reconstructed led to various types of democracy and individual rights, as well as horrible experiments in social engineering that caused incalculable suffering.

When we look at the religious roots of the Western tradition, we can see some other factors that influenced the Western penchant to "improve" the objectified world. In contrast to the Indian perspective, which did not emphasize the difference between humans and other living beings, the Pentateuch established a three-tiered universe by elevating man (who gave names to all the animals) over the rest of creation. This tended to give us free rein over the natural world, and later, when God disappeared, there was nothing to stop us from befouling our own nest.

Another factor was the more serious dualism between good and evil in the Semitic religions, which emphasized the importance of this world not for what it is but for what it could become. The Indian distinction between transcendental and secular valorized the former: This world is a manifestation or condensation of the Absolute, the physical body a sheath of the $\bar{a}tman$. That is why the goal is to transcend this world; as long as there is that better possibility, why bother to try to improve it? On the other side, we have noticed how Chinese and Japanese culture were inclined to accept the given world, including our natural desires and dispositions. The Zoroastrian struggle between Ahura Mazda and Angra Mainyu, which influenced the Hebrews during their "Babylonian captivity," provided a perspective radically different from both the above. Humans became understood as suspended between light and darkness, the battleground of a cosmic war which will end in an apocalyptic victory over the forces of evil; but until then, tempting demons and guardian angels whisper alternately in our ears. Throughout the history of Western Christendom, Satan has been a more palpable and fearsome power than the impersonal $avidy\bar{a}$ of Buddhism and Hinduism, the interminable fires of its hell more terrifying that the wheel of rebirth. India did not bother to improve the realm of $duhkha$, and east Asia saw little need to reform it, but once Satan became identified with this world a no-holds-barred war to transform it became inevitable.

These factors help us to understand some of the differences between Indian and Western transcendence. Yet they explain only half the story. They tell how the West came to objectify the world but not how it came to subjectify the self, and one does not happen without the other. One way to focus this issue is to ask again: What has happened to the transcendental dimension (which I have argued is inescapable) in the modern West? If "God" cannot die, where did He go?

When we remember that the transcendental is, most fundamentally, that which provides a "higher" perspective on the world and leverage for changing it, the answer becomes evident: The transcendental dimension was internalized to become the supposedly autonomous, self-directed individual, who began to develop at the end of the Middle Ages. The "rebirth" of Europe occurred when traditional Christian answers to questions of ultimate value and meaning no longer satisfied the cultural elites, who went on to find their own solutions to the problems of life and *lack*. Later Luther encouraged this by sanctifying a more private relationship with God. Instead of believing in a corporate church and relying on a collective salvation, now everyone must work it out for oneself. The importance of this can hardly be overemphasized. Personally having a direct line to transcendence provides the leverage to challenge all worldly authority, religious as well as secular institutions. Convinced he was following God's will, Luther refused to shut up: "Here I stand; I can do no other." This sanctioned a principle that we today take for granted: One's personal understanding and moral principles can provide an appropriate perspective to confront social structures. Luther was more than a prophet; after him everyone had to become his or her own prophet. Eventually God could abdicate because by then his causal role had been largely assumed by the self-sufficient self-consciousness that Descartes described. But his disappearance also left each of us alone with his or her own *lack* and the problem of what to do with it.

Contrary to our usual understanding, then, transcendence has not disappeared from the West; it just went inside and became the Cartesian self. The result was an increasingly anxious individual, increasingly inclined to rely on his own judgment, to measure the world according to his own standards, and to use his own resources to challenge the social environment as much as the physical one. As an increasingly ultimate commitment, the possibilities of the sense-of-self and the dangers of the sense-of-*lack* were unprecedented. As they say, the rest is history.

We end up with three different cultural paradigms for the relationship between sacred and secular, transcendental and worldly—which may also be understood as three different models for ways of addressing our *lack*. In terms of Yalom's psychotherapeutic paradigm of death-denial through individuation or fusion, the post-medieval West has favored the specialness of individuation, while East Asia has preferred the fusion of assimilation in the group; India developed the various possibilities of religious salvation. Comparing these three paradigms reveals what is problematical about each. In response to the quest for an ideal transcendental realm, we must live in this world and strive to improve it without ever expecting to perfect it. In response to the alienation that results from individualism and objectification of the world, we need to become one with the world, with less sense of separation from it. And in reaction to the problem with embeddedness in a "natural" social order, which sacralizes and fixates political and economic structures, there is also need for the transcendence that grants us perspective on and creative leverage over those structures.

A new cultural paradigm does not seem to be the sort of thing that can be consciously constructed, yet we may conclude by noticing that the metaphor of Indra's Net suggests a way to meet all three of these needs. The Hua-yen doctrine perceives transcendence in the mutual interpenetration of all phenomena, and therefore derives universalist values from our identification with that whole. Indra's Net locates the sacred dimension in this world not by privileging particular social structures or even *Homo sapiens* as a species, but by sacralizing the totality. The crisis of the biosphere testifies to our need for this type of universalist perspective, not for a "higher world" that is other than and therefore opposed to this world, but for the kind of overview that is able to evaluate and respond to the needs of the whole because it is not limited by the demands of a specific nexus (such as one's own social class or nation or species). Since rain forests and whales cannot vote or protest, we must realize that their needs are our needs. Perhaps that is what is unique about *Homo sapiens*: We are the species which can transcend itself by making that leap to identify with everything. The challenge for us today is whether we will actually be able to do so. If, rather than being "in" it, each of us is nondual with the entire universe, as Mahāyāna Buddhism claims, our needs for nonduality and for transcendence may be satisfied at the same time.

Notes

1 The Nonduality of Life and Death

1. Erich Fromm, *Greatness and Limitations of Freud's Thought* (London: Sphere Books, 1982), 1, 3.
2. Otto Rank, *Beyond Psychology* (New York: Dover, 1958), 278.
3. Ernest Jones, *Life and Writings of Sigmund Freud, Vol. III, The Last Phase 1919–1939* (New York: Basic Books, 1957), 279.
4. See, for example, Ernest Becker, *The Denial of Death* (New York: The Free Press, 1973), hereafter DD, Chap. 6, and Irvin D. Yalom, *Existential Psychotherapy* (New York: Basic Books, 1980), hereafter EP, 59–74.
5. EP 62; Yalom italicizes this sentence. *Studies in Hysteria* "illustrates strikingly a selective inattention to death, and it laid the foundation for the exclusion of death from the entire field of dynamic therapy which it spawned" (EP 59).
6. Sigmund Freud, *Inhibitions, Symptoms and Anxiety*, trans. A. Strachey (London: Hogarth Press, 1936), 130.
7. Quoted from the original German edition of Freud's *General Introduction to Psychoanalysis*, by Ludwig Binswanger in Rollo May *et al.*, eds., *Existence* (New York: Basic Books, 1958), 319.
8. Sigmund Freud, *The Ego and the Id*, trans. J. Riviere (London: Hogarth Press, 1927), 85.
9. Sigmund Freud, *Civilization and Its Discontents*, trans. J. Riviere (London: Hogarth Press, 1930), 99, 102.
10. Carl G. Jung, "The Soul and Death," in Herman Feifel, ed., *The Meaning of Death* (New York: McGraw-Hill, 1959), 10–11.
11. Sigmund Freud, "Our Attitude toward Death," reprinted in *Civilization, Society and Religion* (The Penguin Freud Library, Vol. 12), 89.
12. Sigmund Freud, *Beyond the Pleasure Principle*, trans. James Strachey (London: Hogarth Press, 1950), 70.
13. See, for example, Sigmund Freud, *An Autobiographical Study* (London: Hogarth Press, 1946), Chap. 3; "Repression" in *Collected Papers*, 5 vols., ed. J. Riviere and J. Strachey (New York, London: The International Psycho-Analytic Press, 1924–1950), Vol. 4, p. 86; Sigmund Freud, *New Introductory Lectures on Psycho-analysis*, trans. W. J. H. Sprott (London: Hogarth Press, 1933), Chap. 3.
14. Norman O. Brown, *Life against Death: The Psychoanalytic Meaning of History*, hereafter LAD (New York: Vintage, 1961), 271.
15. DD 96.
16. DD 1, 5. "We admire most the courage to face death; we give such valor our highest and most constant adoration; it moves us deeply in our hearts because we have doubts about how brave we ourselves would be" (DD 11–12).
17. EP 41.
18. DD 26.
19. DD 27, 66, 60, 29; Ernest Becker, *Escape From Evil*, hereafter EE (New York: The Free Press, 1975), 163. Becker's italics.
20. DD 54, 55.
21. EE 158. Such "ontological" guilt will be discussed in chapter 3.

173

22. Philippe Aries, *The Hour of Our Death* (Harmondsworth: Penguin, 1981), 606.
23. Johan Huizinga, *The Waning of the Middle Ages*, trans. F. Hopman (Harmondsworth: Penguin, 1987), 30, 134.
24. James Hillman, *Re-Visioning Psychology* (New York: Harper Colophon, 1975), 206.
25. Jacob Burckhardt, *The Civilization of the Renaissance in Italy* (New York: Macmillan, 1921), 65–66.
26. LAD 118. "Being both in-itself and for-itself" is a self-refuting contradiction in Sartre's ontology. His formulation of this hopeless human project will be considered in chapter 3.
27. This point is important not only in Buddhism but in the other enlightenment traditions of India. The dualistic Sāṁkhya and Yoga schools, for example, emphasize the basic difference between pure consciousness (*puruṣa*) and the material world (*prakṛti*), the latter including everything that can be objectified, including even the sense of "I" (*ahamkara*). Advaita Vedānta singles out this confusion as the primary ignorance that needs to be eliminated: "In particular, says Śaṁkara, we are prone to superimpose the properties of the object of awareness on its subject, and vice-versa. That is, we identify ourself *qua* seat of consciousness with ourself *qua* body, mind, memory, etc., all of which are objects, not subjects, and so have at least one property that the self *qua* subject cannot have. It is this primary superimposition that constitutes ignorance (*avidyā*), and it is this confusion in particular that needs to be eradicated through knowledge." (Karl Potter, ed., *Encyclopedia of Indian Philosophies: Advaita Vedānta up to Śaṁkara and His Pupils* New Delhi: Motilal Banarsidass, 1981], 69). The Buddhist deconstruction of the sense-of-self will be discussed in chapter 3.
28. LAD 270.
29. Freud's *An Autobiographical Study*, quoted in DD 147; DD 129, 146–152. Perhaps fetishism is a manifestation of the same aptitude for transference, more narrowed down by being focused on an inanimate thing. The beloved's shoe is secure, but that much more a diminished world.
30. EE 132, 166. Examples in recent American politics are not hard to think of.
31. LAD 252. Latin *praestigium*, "delusion, illusion, juggler's trick," from *praestingere*, "to bind tight, blindfold." The Buddhist and Vedantic equivalent is *māyā*.
32. DD 55.
33. EE 132, 95; Erich Neumann, *Depth Psychology and a New Ethic* (London: Hodder and Stoughton, 1969), 50.
34. Freud, *Civilization and its Discontents*, 61; EE 108 (quoting Rank's *Will Therapy*), 114, 112 (ref. Zilboorg). This also explains why we are often attracted by games of life and death: Russian roulette, automobile "chicken," etc. When we can make death-anxiety more conscious by objectifying it into a specific fear, we feel more alive because then we have some control over our fate; we are no longer paralyzed by something repressed and formless that we can get no grip on.
35. EE 109.
36. EE 115, 91, 136. "Man is neither angel nor brute, and the unfortunate thing is that he who would act the angel acts the brute," (Pascal, *Pensées*, trans. W. F. Trotter [New York: Dutton, 1958], 99, no. 358). Sufficient unto the day is the evil thereof.
37. Aries, *The Hour of Our Death*, 614; EE 123. Robert Darnton, in an article on the French Revolution in *The New York Review of Books* (19 January 1989), confesses himself "incapable of explaining the ultimate cause of revolutionary violence" (p. 6), yet on the previous page he writes: "Throughout the bloody business, the people

who committed the massacres talked about purging the earth of counter-revolution. They seemed to play parts in a secular version of the Last Judgement, as if the Revolution had released an undercurrent of popular millenarianism."

38. EE 116. Here modern gnostics like Jung and Hesse do not quite grasp the point. Jung urged the acceptance of sin and the shadow as necessary to escape the self-defeating dualism of good-versus-evil. What is needed is not accepting both poles but escaping them, by understanding how our morality represents our craving to qualify for immortality, for *being*. This will be discussed in chapter 4.

39. LAD 112–113.

40. EP 188.

41. DD 178ff; quotation in Robert Jay Lifton, *The Broken Connection: On Death and the Continuity of Life* (New York: Basic Books, 1983), 223. On p. 227, Lifton quotes Harold Searles, who was struck by the fact that the "very mundane, universal factor of human mortality" seems to be a major source of anxiety in "this overtly most exotic of psychopathological processes"; people "became . . . and long remained schizophrenic . . . in order to avoid facing . . . the fact that life is finite."

42. DD 181–182 (quoting Roy D. Waldman); 66, my italics.

43. Etty Hillesum, *Etty: A Diary 1941–1943*, trans. Arnold J. Pomerans (London: Jonathan Cape, 1983), 131–132.

44. Aries, *The Hour of Our Death*, 333.

45. DD 157, 55, quotation 275.

46. DD 158.

47. DD 157, 159 (ref. Paul Pruyser), 202.

48. DD 156, 279, 89, 55, 279.

49. Ortega y Gasset, *The Revolt of the Masses* (New York: Norton, 1937), 156–7.

50. Freud, *Studies in Hysteria*, in *Collected Works*, Vol. 2, 305.

51. EE 124.

52. Robert Jay Lifton, *The Life of the Self* (New York: Simon and Schuster, 1976), 50.

53. *Udana* 6; 7: 1–3.

54. *Majjhima Nikāya*, sutra 130; see Edward Conze, *Buddhist Thought in India* (London: Allen and Unwin, 1962), 72.

55. All quotations from Yung-chia are from an unpublished translation of his *Cheng-tao Kê* (*Song of Enlightenment*) by Robert Aitken.

56. Norman Waddell, ed. and trans., *The Unborn: The Life and Teachings of Zen Master Bankei* (San Francisco: North Point Press, 1984), 45. I have not been able to determine how large a soapberry is.

57. *The Unborn*, 47, 52, 55. Compare the following passage from the original "inner chapters" of the *Chuang Tzu*, where Nu Chü teaches the Tao to Pu Liang I:

> After he had managed to see his own aloneness, he could do away with past and present, and after he had done away with past and present, he was able to enter where there is no life and no death. That which kills life does not die; that which gives life to life does not live. This is the kind of being it is: there's nothing it doesn't send off, nothing it doesn't welcome, nothing it doesn't destroy, nothing it doesn't complete. (Trans. Burton Watson)

When the modern Advaitin Ramana Maharshi was asked if one's actions affect one in after-births, he too replied in Zen-like fashion: "Are you born now? Why do you think of other births? Let him who is born think of death and palliatives therefor" (*Talks with Ramana Maharshi* [Tiruvannamalai: Sri Ramanasramam, 1955], 13).

58. Lifton, *The Broken Connection*, 69.

59. *Vajracchedika-Prajñā-Pāramitā Sutra* (*Diamond Sutra*), trans. A. F. Price and Wong Mou-lam (Boston: Shambhala, 1990), 46.

60. From Dōgen's *Shōbōgenzō*, trans. Dan Welch and Kazuaki Tanahashi, in *Moon in a Dewdrop: Writings of Zen Master Dōgen*, ed. Kazuaki Tanahashi (San Francisco: North Point Press, 1985), 74–75, 93–94, 70–71.

61. In "Philosophy as Self-Transformation" (*Historical Reflections/Reflexions Historiques* 16, 2/3 [1989]: 171–198), Horst Hutter describes freedom and immortalization as the two aims of classical Western philosophy, and understands immortalization in a way congruent with Dōgen as I interpret him in this chapter: "Immortality here may be understood, not primarily as freedom from the universal necessity of dying, but as freedom from the universally experienced feelings of fear and dread that usually accompany the process of dying. Thus immortalization as an aim of philosophical self-cultivation need not be considered as a physical or spiritual survival after the death of the body. Indeed, most ancient philosophers, with few exceptions, do not seem to have believed in such immortality of the soul as the soul's persistence after death in some form or medium. Even the references to the immortality of the soul in some Platonic dialogues are ambiguous; they may all be understood elliptically and metaphorically. The important point to be kept in mind here is that even those philosophical schools, such as the Cynics, the Epicureans, and the followers of Aristotle, who categorically denied immortality, still spoke of immortalization as one of the goals of philosophical cultivation" (187–188).

62. James Hillman, *Suicide and the Soul* (New York: Harper Colophon, 1964), 63.

63. Nietzsche used the same argument in *Thus Spake Zarathustra* to refute Schopenhauer and introduce his will-to-power: "He who shot the doctrine of 'will to existence' at truth certainly did not hit the truth: this will—does not exist! For what does not exist cannot will; but that which is in existence, how could it still want to come into existence? Only where life is, there is also will: not will to life, but—so I teach you—will to power!" (*Thus Spake Zarathustra*, trans. R. J. Hollingdale [Harmondsworth: Penguin, 1961], 138).

64. Ludwig Wittgenstein, *Notebooks 1914–1916*, trans. and ed. G. E. M. Anscombe (Oxford: Blackwell, 1961), 75e, dated 8.7.16.

65. LAD 277.

66. Ludwig Binswanger, "The Case of Ellen West," *Existence*, 311 fn, 328–329.

2 The Moving Image of Eternity

1. LAD 284.

2. Later, after his *Kehre* "turning", Heidegger's attitude changed markedly, but his later approach will not be not addressed in this book. For a more positive evaluation of his later writings, see David Loy, *Nonduality: A Study in Comparative Philosophy* (New Haven: Yale University Press, 1988), chap. four.

3. Nietzsche, *Human, All Too Human*, trans. R. J. Hollingdale (Cambridge: Cambridge University Press, 1986), 12–13.

4. Translating *Sorge* as care is incomplete, for in the vernacular *Sorge* also means worry, which brings the meaning closer to anxiousness—about which more later.

5. Freud, "Our Attitude toward Death," reprinted in *Civilization, Society and Religion* (The Penguin Freud Library, Vol. 12), 77.

6. Martin Heidegger, *Being and Time*, hereafter B&T, trans. John Macquarrie and Edward Robinson (New York: Harper and Row, 1962), 308, 311; Heidegger's emphasis.

Cf. Michael E. Zimmerman's excellent *Eclipse of the Self: The Development of Heidegger's Concept of Authenticity* (Athens, Ohio: Ohio University Press, 1981), 71–73.

7. B&T 298, 310.
8. Cf. Walter Kaufmann, in Herman Feifel, ed., *The Meaning of Death* (New York: McGraw-Hill, 1959), 52–54.
9. Zimmerman, *Eclipse of the Self*, xxxiv.
10. EP 112ff.
11. The best of these biographies is probably Hugo Ott's *Martin Heidegger: Unterwegs zu seiner Biographie* (Frankfurt: Campus, 1988). "Marvelling at the extent of Heidegger's naivety, Ott shows that the relationship between his thought and his political actions was grounded in his own personality. Indisputably a great thinker, Heidegger also had delusions of grandeur. It was his unswerving conviction about his fated role as Germany's spiritual leader which led him to absolve himself of moral guilt for his actions in the 1930s and to make a scapegoat of others. . . . Ott concludes that he was guilty of 'monstrous hubris' not only in his political actions in the 1930s, but in his postwar belief that he alone knew what was required for the West to make a 'new beginning'" (from Michael Zimmerman's review in the *Times Literary Supplement*, May 5–11, 1989, p. 481). I quote this not to belittle Heidegger, but to show how his concepts of resoluteness and authenticity are colored by his own attempt to embody them.
12. LAD 105.
13. Rilke's 1899 essay "Ueber Kunst," as quoted in LAD 66–67.
14. B&T 320; Zimmerman, *Eclipse of the Self*, 75.
15. B&T 330–331, translating *Grund* as "ground" rather than "basis." Italics in original.
16. The existential psychoanalyst Binswanger found *Being and Time's* analysis of care insufficient and emphasized *love* as its ontological complement: On the ground of care there is the eerie, overwhelming nothing, but on the ground of love there is home-like security.
17. Martin Heidegger, *Kant and the Problem of Metaphysics*, trans. James S. Churchill (Bloomington: Indiana University Press, 1968), 200–201.
18. Cf. Zimmerman, *Eclipse of the Self*, 111.
19. B&T 474, 477.
20. B&T 351, italicized in original; 476, 479. Cf. J. L. Mehta, *The Philosophy of Martin Heidegger* (Varanasi: Banaras Hindu University Press, 1967), 281.
21. B&T 499, fn xiii.
22. Ken Wilber, *Up from Eden* (Boulder, Colo.: Shambhala, 1983), 60.
23. J. M. Keynes, *Essays in Persuasion* (New York: Harcourt Brace, 1932), 370. Pascal, *Pensées*, no. 172.
24. Michel Foucault, *Mental Illness and Psychology*, trans. Alan Sheridan (New York: Harper Colophon, 1976), 33.
25. The Japanese language contains only two primary tenses, the past and the present (the latter incorporates the future). According to John Mbiti, a contemporary African philosopher, traditional African consciousness also lacks the Western category of the future. Time is divided into those events which occurred in the past, those happening right now or in the immediate future, and those that recur in the rhythms of natural phenomena. Anything that does not fit into these three categories is not apprehended as time. "The most significant consequence of this is that, according to traditional concepts, time is a two-dimensional phenomenon, with a long *past*, a *present*, and virtually *no future*. The linear concept of time in Western thought, with an indefinite past, present, and infinite future, is practically foreign

to African thinking" (John Mbiti, *African Religions and Philosophy* [London: Heinemann, 1969], 21). So perhaps Heidegger's concepts of temporality and authenticity develop the implications only of the West's conception of time. What Mbiti says of Africa seems to be true for traditional cultures generally, which emphasize the patterns of the past, whereas we are driven by the future.

26. James P. Carse, *Death and Existence: A Conceptual History of Human Mortality* (New York: John Wiley and Sons, 1980), 30.

27. These examples are quoted in Ken Wilber, *The Spectrum of Consciousness* (Wheaton, Ill.: Theosophical Publishing House, 1977), 92–93.

28. This section expands on some arguments previously presented in my *Nonduality* 215–224.

29. Nāgārjuna, *Śunyatāsaptati*, verse 58.

30. Hannah Arendt, *The Life of the Mind* (New York: Harcourt Brace Jovanovich, 1978), Vol. I, 45. Compare also Plotinus (evidently alluding to Plato's *Timaeus*): "This is how 'Time'—as we read—'came into Being simultaneously with' this All: the Soul begot at once the Universe and Time; in that activity of the Soul this Universe sprang into being; the activity is Time, the Universe is a content of Time" (*Enneads* III.vii.12, trans. Stephen MacKenna [London: Faber and Faber, 1962). This Tractate ("Time and Eternity") is generally compatible with the understanding of Buddhism presented in this chapter. Nos. 11–12 argue that time is the life of the Soul in movement as it develops toward self-realization. As the Soul returns to rest, time is reabsorbed into eternity and the Cosmos realizes its ideal.

31. As quoted in Masunaga Reiho, *The Sōtō Approach to Zen* (Tokyo: Layman Buddhist Society Press, 1958), 68.

32. *Moon in a Dewdrop: Writings of Zen Master Dōgen*, 76–80. I have changed "the time-being" into the more usual translation "being-time."

33. Nāgārjuna, *Mūlamadhyamikakārikās*, hereafter MMK, XIII 5. Unless noted, all MMK quotations are from Candrakīrti's *Lucid Exposition of the Middle Way*, trans. Mervyn Sprung (Boulder, Colo.: Prajna Press, 1979).

34. Ludwig Wittgenstein, *Philosophical Remarks*, trans. R. Hargreaves and R. White (Oxford: Blackwell, 1975), 85.

35. Wittgenstein, *Notebooks* 75e, dated 8.7.16.

36. *Samyutta Nikāya* 1, 5.

37. EP 161.

38. Ken Wilber, *Spectrum of Consciousness*, 123.

39. In May's *Existence*, 133.

40. From Chang Chung-yuan's trans. of Chap. 48, in his *Tao: A New Way of Thinking* (New York: Harper and Row, 1977).

41. In *Tibetan Yoga and Secret Doctrines*, ed. and trans. W. Y. Evans-Wentz (Oxford: Oxford University Press, 1958), 134, 136; brackets interpolated by translator.

42. In Chang Chung-yuan, ed. and trans., *Original Teachings of Ch'an Buddhism* (New York: Vintage, 1971), 22.

43. *Bhagavad-gītā* IV.18, 20, trans. Radhakrishnan, in Radhakrishnan and Moore, eds., *Sourcebook in Indian Philosophy* (Princeton: Princeton University Press, 1957), 117.

44. Nicolas Berdyaev, *The Beginning and the End* (New York: Harper, 1952), 206.

45. *Timaeus* 37d, trans. Benjamin Jowett, in *Plato: The Collected Dialogues*, ed. Edith Hamilton and Huntington Cairns (Princeton: Princeton University Press, 1963), 1167.

46. *The Selected Poetry of Rainer Maria Rilke*, trans. Stephen Mitchell (New York: Random House), 171, 193, 195.

3 The Pain of Being Human

1. "The drugs that people take for non-medicinal reasons do more than numb pain or enhance pleasure or induce entertaining perceptual distortions. They are a weapon against the void. In his book on opium, Jean Cocteau wrote that every human activity 'takes place in an express train hurtling toward death.' To take drugs, he proposed, is to get off that train. The potent illusion that drugs provide is called upon when the more commonplace illusions fail, and especially when life appears as nothing more than the conduit between birth and death. Drugs populate the empty landscape, supply the missing heaven, extend the movie into the third dimension." Luc Sante, in *The New York Review of Books*, July 16, 1992, 16.
2. Otto Rank, *Beyond Psychology* (New York: Dover, 1958),194; LAD 270.
3. Erich Neumann, *The Origins and History of Consciousness* (Princeton: Princeton University Press, 1973), 179.
4. Soren Kierkegaard, *The Concept of Anxiety*, ed. and trans. Reidar Thomte (Princeton: Princeton University Press, 1980),107–109.
5. "'Sin'. . . constituted the greatest event in the entire history of the sick soul, the most dangerous sleight-of-hand of the religious interpretation" (Nietzsche, *The Birth of Tragedy and the Genealogy of Morals*, trans. F. Golffing [New York: Doubleday Anchor, 1956], 277).
6. LAD 270.
7. Melitta Schmideberg, "Multiple Origins and Functions of Guilt," *Psychiatric Quarterly* 30 (1956), 476.
8. Nietzsche, *Thus Spake Zarathustra*, 162. *The Will to Power*, trans. Walter Kaufmann and R. J. Hollingdale (New York: Vintage, 1968), no. 765, p. 401.
9. James Hillman, *Re-Visioning Psychology*, 98–99.
10. Abbot Justin McCann, ed. *The Cloud of Unknowing*, 6th rev. ed. (London: Burnes Oates, 1952) 60, 26.
11. Carl Jung, *Collected Works, Vol. XI: Psychology and Religion: West and East* (Princeton: Princeton University Press, 1958), 45.
12. *Inhibitions, Symptoms and Anxiety*, in Freud's *Collected Works*, Vol. 20, 148–149; Vol. 5, 581; Vol. 19, 15.
13. Karen Horney, *Neurosis and Human Growth* (New York: Norton, 1950), 18, 21–24.
14. H. S. Sullivan, quoted in Rollo May, *The Meaning of Anxiety* (New York: Norton, 1977), 145–146.
15. May, *The Meaning of Anxiety*, 198, 182.
16. Nietzsche, *Human, All Too Human*, 179–80, no. 491.
17. May, *The Meaning of Anxiety*, 183.
18. Vasubandhu's *Trimśikāvijñāptikārikā*, in Edward Conze, trans., *Buddhist Texts through the Ages* (New York: Harper, 1964), 210. Vasubandhu lived in Kashmir, probably in the fourth or fifth century A.D.
19. EP 221–222. Yalom nonetheless cites some evidence for it. For example, Adah Maurer and Max Stern have separately conducted research into the night terrors of very young children. Stern concluded that the child is terrified of nothingness. According to Maurer, the infant's first task is to differentiate between self (being) and environment (nonbeing), and during a night terror the infant may be experiencing "awareness of nonbeing" (EP 89).
20. Quoted in EP 141–142 and also in May, *The Meaning of Anxiety*, 115.
21. Peter Berger, Brigitte Berger, and Hansfried Kellner, *The Homeless Mind* (Harmondsworth: Penguin, 1973), 124; italicized in original.

22. May, *The Meaning of Anxiety*, 212.
23. Ibid., 351.
24. The quotations in this section are from Soren Kierkegaard, *The Concept of Anxiety*, trans. Walter Lowrie (Princeton: Princeton University Press, 1957), 155–162. For Heidegger too, of course, death as the never-outstripped possibility of my impossibility is what can transform our lives into authenticity, but Kierkegaard has a different idea about the consequences of this awareness of death.
25. Kierkegaard, *The Concept of Anxiety*, 61. Kierkegaard's emphasis.
26. Rollo May, ed., *Existential Psychology* (New York: Random House, 1969), 155.
27. Kierkegaard, *The Concept of Anxiety*, 108.
28. Norman O. Brown, *Love's Body* (New York: Random House, 1966), 260. "Satori, when the ego is broken, is not final victory but final defeat, the becoming like nothing" (Powell, quoted in ibid., 262).
29. Freud, *The Ego and the Id*, 12, 19ff.
30. EP 222; Yalom's italics. A similar realization—that the ego not only represses, but represses the fact that it represses—was a turning point in Freud's career, redirecting his investigations from the nature of the repressed to the nature of repressing.
31. In LAD 149.
32. Rollo May, *The Discovery of Being* (New York: Norton, 1983), 154.
33. Carl Jung, *Psyche and Symbol*, ed. Violet S. deLaszlo (New York: Anchor, 1958), 8.
34. The implication is stronger in the original Latin: emotion is *affectus* and passion is *passio*, "suffering," as in the passion of Christ.
35. Arthur Schopenhauer, *The World as Will and Idea*, trans. R. B. Haldane and J. Kemp (London: Routledge and Kegan Paul, 1883), book four, second aspect.
36. Ibid., book three, second aspect.
37. *Chāndogya Upaniṣad* VI.ix.4.
38. But what about neurotic pets? Do they take on *our* neuroses?
39. Jean-Paul Sartre, *Existentialism*, trans. Bernard Frechtman (New York: Philosophical Library, 1947), 15.
40. Jean-Paul Sartre, *The Words*, trans. Bernard Frechtman (Greenwich, Conn.: Fawcett Crest, 1964), 52, 101. See also pp. 69–70 and 159 for the metaphor of the traveller without a ticket. Ronald Hayman's *Writing Against: A Biography of Sartre* (London: Weidenfeld and Nicolson, 1986) gives ample evidence of Sartre's need (and his awareness of his need) to be a hero. "I had killed myself in advance because the dead are the only ones to enjoy immortality. Between the ages of nine and ten I became entirely posthumous" (p. 28).
41. Jean-Paul Sartre, *L'être et le néant* (Paris: Gallimard, 1943), 196. Sartre is sometimes accused of not understanding *Being and Time*, yet he grasped the main point quite well. Simone de Beauvoir: "What he really is, he believes, exists in the future, and in consequence he never feels any vanity about what he has done in the past... On the other hand, he displays immense pride when he talks about what he's expecting to do" (in Hayman, *Writing Against*, 6).
42. "*The Open Countryside*. We enjoy being in the open countryside so much because it has no opinion concerning us" (Nietzsche, *Human, All Too Human*, no. 508). How disturbing, then, are those occasions when we suddenly realize that someone is there who does.
43. Jean-Paul Sartre, *The Transcendence of the Ego*, trans. Forrest Williams and Robert Kirkpatrick (New York: Noonday, 1957), 48. Sartre's arguments about reflexivity may be compared with the argument John Levy uses against the sense-of-self in *The Nature of Man according to the Vedanta* (London: Routledge and Kegan Paul,

1956), 66–67 (even the example, reading a book, is the same), and my discussion of Levy in *Nonduality*, 139–140.
44. Cf. Robert Denoon Cumming's excellent introduction in *The Philosophy of Jean-Paul Sartre* (New York: Vintage, 1965), 43.
45. Sartre, *The Transcendence of the Ego*, Sartre's emphasis.
46. Quoted in P. Kapleau, ed., *The Three Pillars of Zen* (Tokyo: Weatherhill, 1966), 205, 153.
47. Jean-Paul Sartre, *Being and Nothingness*, trans. H. E. Barnes (New York: Citadel Press, 1956), lii.
48. *Majjhima Nikāya* I.135.
49. Pascal, *Pensées*, 41, no. 139, and 49, no. 171.
50. Berger, *The Homeless Mind*, 74, 77.
51. Antoine Vergot, *Guilt and Desire*, trans. M. W. Wood (New Haven: Yale University Press, 1988), 125.
52. *Anātta-Lakkhana Sūtra* (*On the No-Self Characteristic*), *Samyutta Nikāya* XXII, 54.
53. In Pali literature the major texts for the doctrine are as follows: in the sutras, the *Nidāna Samyutta* of the *Samyutta Nikāya* and the *Mahā Nidāna Sūtra* of the *Dīgha Nikāya*; in the Abhidharma, the *Paccayakara Vibhaṅga* and the *Paṭṭhāna*; in the early commentaries, the most detailed and systematic exposition is in the *Visuddhi-Magga* chap. XVII. For a scholarly examination of *pratītya-samutpāda* in early Buddhist literature, see Govind Chandra Pande, *Studies in the Origins of Buddhism*, 2nd ed. (Delhi: Motilal Banarsidas, 1983), 407–442. "Apart from the central idea . . . the formula has grown through accretions, fusions and analyses. In its full grown form, consequently, it has about it an aura of vagueness, and in the details, even of inconsistency" (441).
54. *Vigrahavyāvartanī*, verse 29.
55. The translation used in this book is Mervyn Sprung's, included in his edition of *Lucid Exposition of the Middle Way* (Boulder, Colo.: Prajna Press, 1979), Candrakīrti's classic commentary on the MMK. Sprung translates *śunyatā* as "the absence of being in things."
56. Francis H. Cook, *Hua-yen Buddhism: The Jewel Net of Indra* (University Park: The Pennsylvania State University Press, 1977), 2.
57. Ibid., 2.
58. Thich Nhat Hanh, *The Heart of Understanding* (Berkeley: Parallax Press, 1988), 3–5.
59. MMK X:19, 22. For more on this, see Loy, *Nonduality*, chap. six, section four.
60. In Paul Williams, *Mahāyāna Buddhism: The Doctrinal Foundations* (London: Routledge, 1989), 121. See also MMK VII.34.
61. Michel Haar, describing Nietzsche's philosophy in "Nietzsche and Metaphysical Language," in David B. Allison, ed., *The New Nietzsche: Contemporary Styles of Interpretation* (New York: Delta, 1977), 7.
62. This may be compared with one of Nietzsche's most brilliant passages, "How the 'Real World' at last Became a Myth" (subtitle: "History of an Error"), which mocks the difference we are inclined to make, in one way or another, between the "Real" or spiritual world and our "apparent" one. Over the centuries the Real world (Plato's Forms, the Christian heaven, Kant's *noumena*, etc.) gradually became more abstract, more remote, until now it has become so superfluous that we abolish it. "What world is left? the apparent world perhaps? . . . But no! *With the real world we have also abolished the apparent world!*" (*Twilight of the Idols*, 40–41).

182 NOTES 94–104

63. Sprung, *Lucid Exposition of the Middle Way*, 262.
64. This and all other quotes from the *Cheng-tao Kê* are from an unpublished translation by Robert Aitken.
65. *Saṁyutta Nikāya* XXXV, 23–26.
66. *Moon in a Dewdrop: Writings of Zen Master Dōgen*, 70.
67. *The Zen Teaching of Huang Po*, trans. John Blofeld (London: Buddhist Society, 1958), 41.
68. Ch'an master Po Shan, in "Discourses of Master Po Shan," in *The Practice of Zen*, trans. and ed. Garma C. C. Chang (New York: Harper and Row, 1959), pp. 94–102. The eighteenth century Japanese Zen master Hakuin's quotes are from D. T. Suzuki's *Zen Buddhism* (New York: Anchor, 1956), 148. For more on this process, see Yasutani-Roshi's "Commentary on the Koan Mu" in Kapleau, ed., *The Three Pillars of Zen*, 71–82.
69. *Bodhicaryāvatāra* 9: 35. Cf. MMK VII.16: "Any thing which exists by virtue of relational origination is quiescence in itself."
70. MMK XXV:24.
71. *The Perfection of Wisdom in Eight Thousand Lines and Its Verse Summary*, trans. and ed. Edward Conze (Bolinas: Four Seasons Foundation, 1973), 1: 5–7, 10; pp. 9–10. Compare Keats on "negative capability": "A Poet is the most unpoetical of any thing in existence; because he has no Identity—he is continually in for—and filling some other Body.... It is a wretched thing to confess; but is a very fact that not one word I ever utter can be taken for granted as an opinion growing out of my identical nature—how can it, when I have no nature? When I am in a room with People if I am ever free from speculating on creations of my own brain, then not myself goes home to myself: but the identity of every one in the room begins to press upon me that, I am in a very little time annihilated—not only among Men; it would be the same in a Nursery of children..." (letter to Richard Woodhouse, 27 October 1818).
72. *The Perfection of Wisdom in Eight Thousand Lines*, 22: 399–400, pp. 237–238.
73. *The Zen Teaching of Huang Po*, 29. Blofeld has "the One Mind" but the original Chinese has no such capitals.
74. *The Zen Teaching of Hui Hai*, trans. and ed. John Blofeld (London: Rider, 1969), 56. When Dōgen returned to Japan, he was asked what he had learned in China; he said he had learned his eyes are horizontal and his nose is vertical. "So I returned home with empty hands. Therefore, I have not even a strand of hair of Buddhism."
75. *The Sutra of Hui Neng*, 85.

4 The Meaning of It All

1. Friedrich Nietzsche, *The Will to Power*, no. 617, p. 330.
2. Some other comparative studies with different approaches are found in Freny Mistry's monograph *Nietzsche and Buddhism* (Berlin: De Gruyter, 1981); Nishitani's *Religion and Nothingness* (Berkeley: University of California Press, 1982); and Graham Parkes, ed., *Nietzsche and Asian Thought* (Honolulu: University of Hawaii Press, 1990).
3. Nietzsche, *Beyond Good and Evil*, no. 108, p. 78.
4. Friedrich Nietzsche, *Twilight of the Idols and The Anti-Christ*, trans. and ed. R. J. Hollingdale (Harmondsworth: Penguin, 1968), 54.
5. Nietzsche, *The Will to Power*, no. 55, p. 35.

6. Nietzsche, *Beyond Good and Evil*, 79, no. 116. See also, e.g., *The Will to Power*, no. 273.
7. *Beyond Good and Evil*, 175, no. 259.
8. Ibid., 93 no. 188.
9. Nietzsche, *Human, All Too Human*, 9.
10. Ibid., 30, no. 19.
11. R. J. Hollingdale, in an appendix to his ed. of Nietzsche's *Twilight of the Idols and The Anti-Christ*, 196.
12. Bernard Blackstone, in *English Blake* (Cambridge: Cambridge University Press, 1949), 426.
13. EE 81, 114.
14. DD 154.
15. EE 123.
16. EE 136; James P. Carse, *Finite and Infinite Games* (New York: Free Press, 1986), 33.
17. Nietzsche, *Twilight of the Idols and The Anti-Christ*, 129.
18. Nietzsche, *Beyond Good and Evil*, 2, also identifies the fundamental faith of metaphysicians as "faith in antithetical values," but the Buddhist solution is different than, e.g., *Will to Power*, 272, where Nietzsche is concerned to demonstrate "how everything praised as moral is identical in essence with everything immoral."
19. Hee-Jin Kim, *Dōgen Kigen—Mystical Realist* (Tucson: University of Arizona Press, 1975), 294; his italics.
20. "At bottom I am all the names in history" (Nietzsche, letter to Burckhardt, 6 January 1889). Michel Haar reflects on the significance of this loss of "proper" names: "Every identity, including that of the self and that of proper names, comes down to an interchangeable mask bound up with the universal Game, which is itself only an indefinite shifting of masks" ("Nietzsche and Metaphysical Language," in *The New Nietzsche*, 35).
21. Nietzsche, *Will to Power* no. 786, dreams of the antithesis between egoism and altruism disappearing in the future, when finally "one grasps that altruistic actions are only a species of egoistic actions—and that the degree to which one loves, spends oneself, proves the degree of individual power and personality." Buddhism implies the reverse, that egoistic actions are a subspecies of altruistic (i.e., nondual) ones, inverted by the delusion of a self/subject which believes itself to be other than the world.
22. Nietzsche, *The Gay Science*, trans. Walter Kaufmann (New York: Vintage, 1974), no. 347, p. 287.
23. Ibid., no. 355, pp. 300–301. "I am convinced that the desire to formulate truths is a virulent disease. It has contracted an alliance in me with a feverish personal ambition" (William James, letter, 1903). Because Nehamas, in *Nietzsche: Life as Literature* (Cambridge: Harvard University Press, 1985), does not perceive how this desire for security motivates our search for truth, his discussion of truth in Chap. 2 is somewhat vitiated.
24. Sigmund Freud, *Collected Papers*, ed. Riviere and Strachey (New York: The International Psycho-Analytic Press, 1924–50) Vol. II, 130–131. See LAD 235–236.
25. Nietzsche, *Will to Power*, no. 585, pp. 316–317.
26. Nietzsche, *Beyond Good and Evil*, no. 211, p. 123.
27. Nietzsche, *Twilight of the Idols*, 49. This is the second of "the Four Great Errors."
28. "On Truth and Lie in the Extramoral Sense," in *The Viking Portable Nietzsche*, trans. and ed. Walter Kaufmann (New York: Viking, 1964), 47. *The Will to Power*, no. 493 (see also no. 609).

29. The German Musarion Collected Works of Nietzsche, Vol. IX, 190.
30. Nietzsche, letter to Fuchs, 26 August 1888.
31. EE 124; DD 189.
32. DD 178, 6.
33. Trans. Arthur Waley, in J. M. Cohen, ed., *The Rider Book of Mystical Verse* (London: Rider, 1983), 160.
34. *The Sutra of Hui Neng*, 132.
35. Hee-jin Kim's trans. of a passage in the *Sansuikyo*, "The Mountains and Rivers Sutra" fascicle of Dōgen's *Shōbōgenzō*; Kim's emphasis. This quotation is included in Kim's paper "Method and Realization: Dōgen's Use of the Kōan Language," presented at a Dōgen Conference at Tassajara Zen Mountain Center, October 8–11, 1981.
36. Kim, *Dōgen Kīgen*, 110.
37. Ibid., 259.
38. Carse, *Finite and Infinite Games*, 145.
39. If philosophy too can be a way not to grasp reality but to deconstruct it, we may rethink a philosophical commonplace. The truth or falsity of a philosophical position cannot be determined by evaluating the person who claims it; *ad hominem* appeals to authority and prejudice are not acceptable reasoning. Yet can that truth be carried too far, if there is an organic relationship between the quality of a person's life and the quality of his/her thought? Insofar as philosophy can be a path of intellectual liberation, one of the things we want to know is how liberating thoughts were for their thinker. What kind of life did he/she lead? What values did that life embody? What kinds of freedom? These biographical factors are not the last word, but they are a consideration. I think our interest in "great lives," including philosophers', points to an intuition of this fact. From this perspective, it is important to inquire into the relation between, e.g., Heidegger's philosophical thought and his politics.
40. Martin Heidegger, *What Is Philosophy?* trans. W. Kuback and J. T. Wilde (New York: Twayne Publishers, 1958), 25.
41. "On Truth and Lie in the Extramoral Sense," in *The Viking Portable Nietzsche*, 46–47.
42. Carse, *Finite and Infinite Games*, 106.
43. Jacques Derrida, *Writing and Difference*, trans. Alan Bass (Chicago: University of Chicago Press, 1978), 111. MMK XXIV.8–10.
44. Arthur Kleinman, M.D., *Rethinking Psychiatry: From Cultural Category to Personal Experience* (New York: The Free Press, 1988), 136–137.
45. EP 343. Yalom's italics.
46. Canki-sutta, *Majjhima Nikāya*, no. 95.
47. Nietzsche, *The Gay Science*, 273–274, no. 341.
48. Paul Tillich, *The Courage to Be* (New Haven: Yale University Press, 1952), 57.
49. Friedrich Nietzsche, *Thus Spoke Zarathustra*, trans. R. J. Hollingdale (Harmondsworth: Penguin, 1961), pp. 333, 331–332. The passage from *The Gay Science* quoted above as an epigraph to this section says: "Or have you *once* experienced a tremendous moment. . . ." See also *Will to Power*, no. 1032.
50. Nietzsche, *Thus Spoke Zarathustra*, 331.
51. Haart, "Nietzsche and Metaphysical Language," 31.
52. Nietzsche, *The Will to Power*, no. 617, p. 330.
53. Ibid., no. 585a.
54. Jean-Paul Sartre, *Existentialism*, trans. Bernard Frechtman (New York: Philosophical Library, 1947), 58.
55. Nietzsche, *Beyond Good and Evil*, no. 78, p. 74; the last sentence of *The Genealogy of Morals*.

56. "Meeting is to be experienced in living action and suffering itself, in the unreduced immediacy of the moment" (Martin Buber, *The Eclipse of God*, trans. Maurice S. Friedman [New York: Harper Torchbook, 1957], 35).
57. EP 466; Yalom's italics.
58. In EP 469.
59. "Neither question can be answered in a general fashion, but only in relation to a particular situation and person." Viktor Frankl, *The Doctor and the Soul* (Harmondsworth: Penguin, 1973), 72.
60. EP 482. The Wittgenstein quotation is from *Tractatus Logico-Philosophicus*, trans. D. F. Pears and B. F. McGuinness (London: Routledge and Kegan Paul, 1961) no. 6.521, p. 149.
61. DD 171–172, 206.
62. DD 172–174.
63. Nietzsche, *Beyond Good and Evil*, 126, no. 213. Cf. Loy, *Nonduality*, 150–161, 236.
64. DD 172.
65. Nietzsche, *Beyond Good and Evil*, no. 94, p. 76.
66. Jacques Derrida, *The Archaeology of the Frivolous*, trans. J. P. Leavey (Pittsburgh: Duquesne University Press, 1980), 118.
67. Selected passages from Carse, *Finite and Infinite Games*, part one.
68. Nietzsche, *The Gay Science*, 346, no. 381.
69. James Hillman, *Re-Visioning Psychology*, 191.
70. Joseph Campbell, *The Masks of God*, Vol. 1 (New York: Viking, 1964), 122. Hillman, *Re-Visioning Psychology*, also speaks of "the love of an old man, the usual personal content of love voided by coming death, yet still intense, playful, and tenderly, carefully close." (p. 197).
71. Rufus M. Jones, *Spiritual Reformers in the Sixteenth and Seventeenth Centuries* (New York: Macmillan, 1914), 177. See, for example, Boehme's *Aurora* xiii 48–57.
72. DD 201, 202.
73. Carse, *Finite and Infinite Games*, 15.

5   Trying to Become Real

1. Lewis H. Lapham, *Money and Class in America* (New York: Ballantine, 1988), 230. "The fever of renown" is from Dr. Johnson's poem "The Vanity of Human Wishes."
2. Alan Harrington, *The Immortalist* (Millbrae, Calif.: Celestial Arts, 1977), 112. His italics.
3. Marcus Aurelius, *Meditations*, trans. George Long (Chicago: Encyclopaedia Britannica, 1952), Book VIII no. 44, p. 289.
4. Oswyn Murray in the *Times Literary Supplement*, June 16, 1989, p. 656; see also Leo Braudy, *The Frenzy of Renown: Fame and Its History* (New York: Oxford University Press, 1986), 28, 59–60.
5. Braudy, *The Frenzy of Renown*, 56, 160.
6. Jacob Burckhardt, *The Civilization of the Renaissance in Italy*, 139ff.
7. Braudy, *The Frenzy of Renown*, 378.
8. Ibid., 429. "We will have to wait till the eighteenth century—for even the Renaissance does not truly bring the idea of progress—before men resolutely enter the path of social optimism;—only then the perfectibility of man and society is raised to the rank of a central dogma, and the next century will only lose the naivete of this belief, but not the courage and optimism which it inspired" (Johan Huizinga,

The Waning of the Middle Ages, trans. F. Hopman (Harmondsworth: Penguin, 1987), 36–37.

9. Associated Press, 12 February 1978, in Braudys, *The Frenzy of Renown*, 3; 562.
10. Braudy, *The Frenzy of Renown*, 589, 592, 590.
11. Ibid., 6, 461–462.
12. Miguel de Unamuno, *Tragic Sense of Life*, trans. J. E. Crawford Flitch (London: Macmillan, 1921), 52, 54.
13. Carse, *Finite and Infinite Games*, 72–73; Carse's italics.
14. Braudy, *The Frenzy of Renown*, 589.
15. Denis de Rougemont, *Love in the Western World*, trans. Montgomery Belgion, rev. ed. (New York: Pantheon Books, 1956), 15–16. All italics are de Rougemont's.
16. In that fashion our notion of love "is linked with a theory of the *fruitfulness of suffering* which encourages or obscurely justifies in the recesses of the Western mind a liking for war" (de Rougemont, *Love in the Western World*, 257). All's fair in love and war because in both we think we have discovered the proper way to suffer to overcome *lack*.
17. De Rougemont, *Love in the Western World*, 43. "When in the twelfth century unsatisfied desire was placed by the troubadours of Provence in the center of the poetic conception of love, an important turn in the history of civilization was effected. Antiquity, too, had sung the sufferings of love, but it had never conceived them save as the expectation of happiness or as its pitiful frustration.... Courtly poetry ... makes desire itself the essential motif, and so creates a conception of love with a negative ground note" (Huizinga, *The Waning of the Middle Ages*, 104).
18. "There exists a condition which with me at least is not all that rare in which the presence and the absence of a beloved person are equally hard to endure; or at least in which the pleasure derived from their presence is not that which, to judge from the intolerableness of their absence, one would have expected it to be" Georg Christoph Lichtenberg, *Aphorisms*, trans. R. J. Hollingdale (Harmondsworth: Penguin, 1990).
19. De Rougemont, *Love in the Western World*, 55, 40–41, 15, 21–22.
20. Ibid., 145 (de Rougemont italicizes the entire passage).
21. Ibid. 35–36.
22. Ibid., 179. James Hillman generalizes this point into a critique of our preoccupation with "inter-personal relationships": "By our use of them to keep ourselves alive, other persons begin to assume the place of fetishes and totems, becoming keepers of our lives. Through this worship of the personal, personal relationships have become the place where the divine is to be found, so the new theology asserts. The very condition that modern rational consciousness would dissuade us from—personifying—returns in our relationships, creating an animistic world of personified idols. Of course these archetypally loaded relationships break down, of course they require constant proprietary attention, of course we must turn to priests of this cult (therapists and counselors) for instruction concerning the right ritual for relation to persons.... We seek salvation in personal encounters, personal relations, personal solutions. Human persons are the contemporary shrines and statues where personifying is lodged" (*Re-Visioning Psychology*, 47).
23. Huizinga, *The Waning of the Middle Ages*, 108.
24. De Rougemont, *Love in the Western World*, 300, 294.
25. Plato, *Symposium*, 211a–b.
26. Ernest Becker, *The Revolution in Psychiatry* (New York: The Free Press, 1964), 246.

27. Hillesum, *Etty: A Diary, 1941–43.*
28. LAD 240–241.
29. Quoted in Lapham, *Money and Class in America*, 8.
30. LAD 271.
31. Georg Simmel, *The Philosophy of Money* (London: Routledge and Kegan Paul, 1978), 431. The passage continues: "But since money itself is an omnipresent means, the various elements of our existence are thus placed in an all-embracing teleological nexus in which no element is either the first or the last."
32. LAD 246. "The magical properties, with which the Egyptian priestcraft anciently imbued the yellow metal, it has never altogether lost." (John Maynard Keynes, *Treatise on Money* [New York: Harcourt, Brace, 1930], Vol. 2, 290). "Money" derives from the Latin *moneta*, "aware of, forewarned," a name given to the goddess Juno in memory of her saving Rome from a surprise attack. The first Roman mints, in 269 B.C., were in her temple and the coins carried her effigy.
33. Simmel, *The Philosophy of Money*, 187.
34. EE 76, 79 (ref. Geza Roheim), 80–81.
35. Philippe Aries, *The Hour of Our Death*, 136–137. "We, at the present day, can hardly understand the keenness with which a fur coat, a good fire on the hearth, a soft bed, a glass of wine, were formerly enjoyed" (Huizinga, *The Waning of the Middle Ages*, 9).
36. EE 85 (ref. Rank). This lends psychological support to Weber's theory about the influence of the Protestant ethic on the rise of capitalism. You and I shall die, our children will die, but there is something else to invest in, which can take on a life of its own. "Death is overcome on condition that the real actuality of life pass into these immortal and dead things. Money is the man; the immortality of an estate or a corporation resides in the dead things which alone endure." Instead of erecting time-defying monuments like the pyramids, now we find solace in the numbers sent to us by banks. "By continually taking and piling and accumulating interest and leaving to one's heirs, man contrives the illusion that he is in complete control of his destiny. After all, accumulated things are a visible testimonial to power, to the fact that one is not limited or dependent. Man imagines that the *causa sui* project is firmly in his hands, that he is the heroic doer and maker who takes what he creates, what is rightfully his" (LAD 279, EE 89).
37. In LAD 262.
38. R. H. Tawney, *Religion and the Rise of Capitalism* (New York: Harcourt, Brace, 1926), 31.
39. Ibid., 86.
40. Sigmund Freud, *The Origins of Psycho-analysis*, ed. M. Bonaparte *et al.* (New York: Basic Books, 1964), 244; LAD 266.
41. LAD 265.
42. Otto Rank, *Beyond Psychology* (New York: Dover, 1958), 194.
43. Weston LaBarre, *The Human Animal* (Chicago: University of Chicago Press, 1954), 173.
44. LAD 270–271.
45. LAD 272.
46. LAD 261.
47. LAD 256, 258, 285.
48. Philip Slater, *The Pursuit of Loneliness: American Culture at the Breaking Point* (Boston: Beacon Press, 1970), 44.

49. Bertrand Russell was in his thirties when the Wright brothers flew the first time, and he lived to watch man land on the moon.
50. Aries, *The Hour of Our Death*, 595; Martin Heidegger, *Holzwege* (Frankfurt am Main: Vittorio Klostermann, 1972), 279, in *Poetry, Language, Thought*, trans. Albert Hofstadter (New York: Harper and Row, 1971),125.
51. Harrington, *The Immortalist*, 119.
52. Donald Phillip Verene, "Technological Desire," in *Research in Philosophy and Technology* (London: JAI Press, 1984) Vol. 7, 107.
53. Bill McKibben, *The End of Nature* (Harmondsworth: Penguin, 1990), 77. The Burroughs quote is on pp. 66–67.
54. Verene, "Technological Desire," 108–109; Verene's italics.
55. In *The Awakening of Europe*, Philippe Wolff describes the origins of European science in Moorish Spain: "It must also be admitted that the products of Arabic science were not always viewed in Europe in their loftiest and most fertile aspect. It was not only the pure, disinterested thirst for knowledge which drove so many savants to Spain and to work so hard when they got there, nor was this alone what made their writings so valuable. Much more important was a naive desire to acquire power over the hidden forces of nature by wresting her secrets from her" (Harmondsworth: Penguin, 1968, p. 283).

Conclusion: Transcendence East and West

1. Much of the data in the first section is from Hajime Nakamura's encyclopedic *Ways of Thinking of Eastern Peoples*, rev. trans. ed. Philip P. Wiener (Honolulu: University of Hawaii Press, 1964) hereafter WTEP; Nakamura's own italics in all quotations from him. It contrasts Indian, Chinese, Tibetan, and Japanese ways of thinking, mainly by comparing the structure of their different languages and the different ways each culture assimilated Buddhism.
2. WTEP 219, 143.
3. WTEP 350ff.
4. Both quotations from WTEP 166, 144. Early Buddhism did not accept a higher Self, but distinguished this world of *saṁsāra* from *nirvāṇa*, often understood as a transcendental goal. *Pratītya-samutpāda* (dependent origination) suggests a more dynamic understanding of reality, yet Mādhyamika conclusions from that doctrine were expressed in static terms: everything is *śūnya*, nothing arises or passes away. Even this was not enough to keep Buddhism alive in India, once the more orthodox Indian traditions had absorbed what they could learn from it.
5. WTEP 236.
6. Robert N. Bellah, *Tokugawa Religion: The Cultural Roots of Modern Japan* (New York: The Free Press, 1957), 188.
7. WTEP 513.
8. Bellah, *Tokugawa Religion*, 188.
9. WTEP 208.
10. WTEP 402.
11. Including me. My great-grandfather in the Dharma, Harada Sogaku (1870– 1961), abbot of Hosshin-ji, wrote: "Forgetting [the difference between] self and others in every situation, you should always become completely one with your work. [When ordered to] march—tramp, tramp; [when ordered to] fire—bang, bang; this is the clearest expression of the highest Bodhi-wisdom, the unity of Zen and war" (Quoted in Daizen Victoria, "Japanese Corporate Zen," *Bulletin of Concerned Asian Scholars* 12, no. 1, 1980, p. 65).

12. Chie Nakane, *Japanese Society* (Harmondsworth: Penguin, 1973).
13. WTEP 562, 575.
14. Thomas P. Rohlen, *Japan's High Schools* (Berkeley: University of California Press, 1983), 268.
15. WTEP 578.
16. WTEP 118, 121.
17. WTEP 407ff.
18. WTEP 579, 393, 399.
19. Bellah, *Tokugawa Religion*, 194, 196. In his introduction to the paperback edition of 1985, Bellah agrees with the criticism of the Japanese sociologist Maruyama Masao, who questions whether the particularism of Japan—which still "remains unchallenged" (181)—could really be an adequate substitute for ethical universalism, as Bellah originally thought (xiii). Twenty-eight years after the first edition of his book, Bellah seems more aware of the problems with that particularism.
20. Herman Ooms, *Tokugawa Ideology: Early Constructs, 1570–1680* (Princeton: Princeton University Press, 1986), 297.
21. WTEP 527, 529, 346, 349.
22. WTEP 530.
23. Karel van Wolferen, *The Enigma of Japanese Power: People and Politics in a Stateless Nation* (London: Macmillan, 1989), 337: "The proponents of formally tolerated Tokugawa thought all propagated the view that the order that had been imposed was immutable, being in tune with nature and in accordance with the will of a multitude of divinities." Bellah and Ooms make similar points.
24. S. C. Humphreys, "'Transcendence' and Intellectual Roles: The Ancient Greek Case," in *Daedalus* (Spring 1975), "Wisdom, Revelation, and Doubt: Perspectives on the First Millennium B.C.," 92, 112.
25. "'Transcendence' and Intellectual Roles," 111. Humphreys distinguishes four stages in the development of their conceptions of society and cosmos: "Hesiod's vision of Boeotian society as part of a theological order, the pre-Socratic vision of a natural order in the universe, the search for a new moral order carried on simultaneously in the fifth century by tragic poets and philosophers, and Plato's demand for a radical transformation of society in accordance with a transcendental standard. Criticism, detachment, internalization, alienation" (110).
26. Louis Dumont, "On the Comparative Understanding of Non-Modern Civilizations," in *Daedalus* (Spring 1975), 162, 163.
27. Ibid., 165.
28. Paul Garelli, "The Changing Facets of Conservative Mesopotamian Thought," in *Daedalus* (Spring 1975), 53.
29. Ninian Smart, *The Religious Experience of Mankind* (London: Collins, 1969), 289.
30. Benjamin I. Schwartz, "Transcendence in Ancient China," in *Daedalus* (Spring 1975), 58–59.
31. One of the less obvious but more important is science. When we remember the third meaning of transcendence—that which abstracts us from the given by providing a theoretical perspective on it—we can see how the scientific process also involves transcendence because it constructs general laws to account for the behavior of concrete particulars. As Pythagoras would have understood, physics is a kind of mathematical metaphysics.

Index